YACHT STYLE

YACHT STYLE

*Design and Decor Ideas
from the World's
Finest Yachts*

DANIEL

SPURR

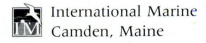

International Marine
Camden, Maine

International Marine/
Ragged Mountain Press

A Division of The McGraw·Hill Companies

First paperback edition published 1997

10 9 8 7 6 5 4 3 2 1

Library of Congress Cataloging-in-Publication Data
Spurr, Daniel, 1947
    Yacht style : design and decor of the world's finest yachts
/ Daniel Spurr
    p.   cm.
    Includes bibliographic references.
    ISBN 0-07-060563-7
    1. Yachts and yachting. 2. Ship decoration I. Title
VM331.S68   1990
623.8'223—dc20   90-4292
                                  CIP

Questions regarding the content of this book should be
addressed to:
International Marine
P.O. Box 220
Camden, ME 04843

Questions regarding the ordering of this book should be
addressed to:
The McGraw-Hill Companies
Customer Service Department
P.O. Box 547
Blacklick, OH 43004
Retail customers: 1-800-262-4729
Bookstores: 1-800-722-4726

Printed by Welpac Printing, Singapore
Design by Patrice M. Calkin
Edited by Jonathan Eaton

For my father

TABLE OF CONTENTS

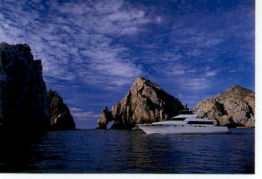

PART III

DETAILS

ACKNOWLEDGMENTS

The concept for this book was presented to me by Jon Eaton, editor of International Marine Publishing Company, and it is due largely to his vision that the project was undertaken. His ideas, support, and understanding make him a fine example of the editor's profession, the sort of editor every writer wants and needs but few are lucky enough to work with.

I enjoyed tremendously working with the many fine photographers who contributed their precious images to these pages. Having watched them get sharp, vivid photographs while bouncing along at 30 knots in a chase boat, crouching in small, dark cabins, and hanging out of helicopters, I have great admiration for their skill. Each, in his or her own way, taught me something about the photographer's art—composition, lighting, exposure, subject, and perspective. Above all, they helped me learn to *see*.

The photographers' names appear elsewhere in the book, but they deserve to appear here, too. In no particular order they are Rick Friese, Susan Thorpe Waterman, Robert Hagan, Billy Black, Neil Rabinowitz, Charley Freiberg, Onne Van Der Wal, Larry Dunmire, Joe Deveney, and in particular Sandy Brown. Sandy took a keen interest in the project, going out of her way to take many of the detail shots that didn't seem to exist anywhere else. Without her help I just don't know how we could have done it.

Thanks to the many designers, builders, surveyors, brokers, and decorators in the boating industry who talked with me about their areas of expertise. In more than one instance, technical readers Anne Brengle, an interior decorator, and Jeremy McGeary, a naval architect, saved me, I'm sure, from embarrassing myself.

Also deserving of mention are the many boat owners who mailed me photographs of their boats for consideration. It is too bad that more couldn't have been used, for in every instance their boats were beautiful.

PREFACE

A few days ago I was busy photographing the saloon of a lavishly finished pilothouse sloop at the Newport International Sailboat Show. Great expanses of teak were evident on deck and below, every inch varnished or hand-rubbed with oil to a mirrorlike gloss. In the cockpit a salesman was working hard on a middle-aged couple, feverishly trying to close the deal. From below I could see the sweat beading on his forehead, his hands wringing a brochure.

Another couple stepped aboard. The newly arrived man dropped into the cockpit, addressing the salesman loudly: "Your teak looks great but you can bet the next boat I buy won't have *any!* My present boat has a fraction of the teak on this boat and it seems all I ever do is varnish."

Obviously disgruntled, the salesman looked up and snapped, "Yeah, but take all the teak off and it's not a yacht anymore, it's just another boat."

The tirekicker shrugged and said, "Call it what you like; all I know is I work for a living, and I'd rather spend my spare time sailing than on my hands and knees."

Later, recalling the conversation, I thought about the distinction between a boat and a yacht. The former term is perhaps too generic, the latter a mite pretentious, at least in the United States. In England, "yacht" has fewer pejorative connotations; indeed, even the homeliest little craft is referred to as a yacht, though good taste dictates that the owner never call his own boat by that name.

Nautical dictionaries describe a yacht as any vessel used for pleasure, noting that Lloyds of London does not apply the term to craft under 30 feet. A boat, we are told, is a craft capable of being carried on board a ship.

Such distinctions lose all practical significance in Newport Harbor on a busy summer evening. The waterfront observer sees small yachts just as surely as he sees big boats, and he and his companions may argue the borderline cases to their hearts' content. They are all reading from roughly the same pages, even if they can't give shape to the words. I've asked others for their understanding, without any great revelation. One said a yacht is any boat that is cared for "as a yacht" by its owner—a tautological definition at best. Another attempted a muddled explanation involving brightwork and "class." But no one could give me a definition that satisfactorily embraces both a Rozinante canoe yawl and the *Trump Princess*, or a bare steel ketch and a custom cold-molded sportfisherman, or a frumpy lifeboat conversion and a classic 12-meter racing sloop, or a fiberglass replica of a tug and a skipjack with two pipe berths and oyster shells still sprinkled in the hold.

In my estimation, all are or at least *can* be yachts, though I'm not sure I can tell you why. I *am* certain, however, that every boat pictured in this book is also a yacht. If you ask me for a common thread I will say it is beauty. But beauty, as the saying goes, lies in the eye of the beholder. What may appear as Venus to one may be gauche, overstated, or sterile to another. Suffice it to say that I judged each of these boats to be a good example of what it is intended to be, whether a classic schooner or an ultramodern megayacht. It is not necessary that I lust for each and every one, and I would not want to offend the many beautiful ladies in these pages by revealing the object of my true passions. Each of these boats is beautiful to *someone*, and that is good enough for me.

This is not really a how-to book, nor is it purely for vicarious pleasure; it is, rather, an idea book, a resource for boat owners and would-be buyers interested in exploring the many ways a boat can be constructed and finished. Hopefully you'll discover features that can be incorporated in your own boat during construction or renovation. The text and photographs are intended to help guide you through different approaches to design, style, and materials.

There is no one "right way" of doing things. Engine or sail, ash or teak, cable or hydraulic steering: Any choice is valid if it is made within the context of the owner's purposes and satisfies those who live with it. Only when I discuss safety issues, such as lifelines and window size, does my advice become dogmatic; it is difficult to quarrel with the accumulated wisdom of designers, builders, and seamen, who have learned a thing or two about their professions, and the sea, the hard way.

The focus of this book is less on hull design than on comfort and aesthetic appreciation. It is more interested in color and texture than speed/fuel consumption curves and polar performance diagrams; it looks more closely at joinerwork than at the quarter wave. We may love speed and power, and our business on the water may be fishing, cruising, or racing, but there is an undeniable fascination with the minutest parts of the machine itself. This is true whether the boat is sleek or chunky, bold or sweet. Who does not feel good when he sees the silhouette of his boat at dusk? Take pride in a gleaming stainless tower or brass Dorade? Feel a tactile rush when he runs his fingertips over the grain of a sanded hardwood? Marvel at the resonant thrumming of the closely machined pistons and valves of a well-kept engine? Or find peace with a soft pillow behind his head and a warm afghan covering his feet?

No matter how you view your boat, time, money, and sentiment make it something more than the sum of its parts. Perhaps this is because a boat can become a self-contained, all-sustaining world unto itself, a means of escape from the harshness of life ashore. Whether you call it a boat or a yacht is of little consequence; it is your appreciation of her, and how she affects you, that distinguishes between the base life and the extraordinary.

D. S.

Part I

Principles of Design ■

Assessment and Planning

The purchase or major overhaul of a boat will likely represent a family's largest financial expenditure after the house. Because selling a boat may take months or even years, and because such transactions seldom result in a profit, a well-reasoned strategy should serve to increase the number of years of ownership and to minimize losses. Be honest about your emotional prejudices and real or imagined requirements, and be realistic about financial constraints before putting money on the table. The farther you progress along the branches of your decision-making tree—whether a formal plan on paper or a rough road map in your head—the more the swirl of facts and feelings will sort itself out and the better your chances will be of making the right decision the first time.

ASSESSMENT

Let's begin with the premise that you don't have what you want. Life is like that. Even the most self-confident, self-approbatory individual at least occasionally dreams of making more money, living in a larger house, having a prettier face, a stronger back. Alack, some things we can change, others we cannot. Perhaps that is why so many of us channel our creative energies and adventuring instincts into boats. If we can't be perfect or conduct our lives without fault, perhaps our boats can become what we cannot: the absolute, unerring realization of a perfect vision.

Well, it is at least a goal. Money and time are mitigating factors. So too are skills, or the lack thereof, and the constant degradation boats

This handy little boat is a 24-foot Culler Harbor Launch, designed by Pete Culler and built in 1986 by New Fogartyville Boatworks of strip-planked juniper over laminated Honduras mahogany. The plumb bow and fantail stern balance well, and the low wheelhouse, with its traditional vertical face and radiused forward corners, is a perfect complement to the hull's low freeboard.

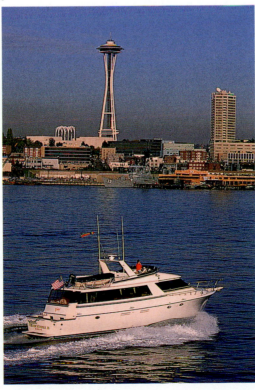

1 An Aires high-performance sportboat runs toward night. The tunnel between the hulls enables the boat to ride on a "monorail" of water.

2 Sportfishermen are the greyhounds of the ocean. They cut down big waves with their deep-V forward hull sections, and get to the fishing grounds fast with powerful turbocharged diesels. The topsides are flared to keep down spray.

3 There's a lot to account for in a motoryacht such as the Vantare *Knot Accountable II*, steaming toward Seattle's Space Needle.

suffer by exposure to weather. Still we push toward that vision, whether by refurbishing the boat we already own, or by purchasing another vessel closer to that impossible ideal.

This book is not intended to tell you how to buy a boat. All that really takes is a checkbook. Its focus is more on helping you create the boat that is right for you—especially in terms of space, layout, furnishings, and overall style— and one that is amenable to the ever-changing picture in your mind's eye. Let's face it: No boat, new or used, is going to be everything you want at first blush. In the pages that follow you'll find many ideas for transforming your boat from its existing state to a more perfect embodiment of your dream. With the inspired optimism of a seagoing Professor Henry Higgins, let us recognize and accept the challenge: to take *Betty and Bob* into the shop and have her emerge as *Lady Elizabeth.*

THE RIGHT BOAT FOR THE RIGHT PURPOSE

The fundamental choice is power or sail. By borrowing the biologist's taxonomic classifications (and liberally twisting them) we can begin sorting out the many kinds. Think of boats as the *kingdom* (as in animal or plant), powerboats and sailboats as the two principal

phyla, and the various types of each as *classes* (sportfishermen, motoryachts). More subtle differences can be classified as orders (sedans, convertibles). The farther you descend in the hierarchy, the more specialized the designs become (shoal-water cruising sailboat, fresh-water bass-fishing boat). The more precisely you know what you want, the more accurately you can match your needs.

A few generalizations: Sailboats are often cheaper to buy, operate, and maintain, but require more physical effort to make go. They are slower, sometimes painfully so, but their range under sail is limited only by the wind and the provisions that can be carried. Sailboats also are quieter and in many cases more seaworthy because of their ballasted keels and low profiles. For sailors the equation often reduces to this conclusion: It's not how fast you get there, but where you can get to and how much fun you have along the way.

Sailors, however, don't have a monopoly on fun, even if they do think they're on the right side of the Great Schism. Powerboats are often roomier and certainly faster. Activities such as fishing, swimming, diving, and water-skiing are more easily pursued from their spacious cockpits, which allow standing close to the side of the boat. If access to the water is

Francis Marion, a husky trawler with twin steadying sails, steams for open ocean at the mouth of Rhode Island's Narragansett Bay. She looks all business with covered dinghy on deck, stainless steel guards around the ever-ready anchor, and custom side curtains with zippered windows.

Checking the bottom line

It is instructive and sometimes surprising to compare the cost of upgrading a currently owned or used boat with that of a new boat. In the following example, the new boat will cost about $17,000 more to own for three years than the used boat, not counting any difference in installment loan interest charges or major breakdowns. What is certain is that the cost will always be more than you expect.

New 35-foot production sailboat sloop

Base price	$100,000
Accessories (electronics, canvas, anchors, etc.)	15,000
Commissioning	2,000
Shipping/Delivery	5,500
Insurance (× 3 years)	6,000
Annual maintenance and storage (× 3 years)	10,500
	$139,000
Less projected 3-year resale value	$90,000
Cost to own 3 years	$49,000

Used 35-foot production sailboat sloop (10 years old)

Purchase price	$50,000
Accessories (add-ons and replacements)	8,000
Delivery	3,000
Insurance (× 3 years)	2,250
Yard cost to repower, refinish hull, etc.	10,000
Your man-hours: 300 × $15 per hour to upgrade (curtains, varnish, trim, fix shower, etc.)	4,500
Annual maintenance and storage (× 3 years)	12,000
	$89,750
Less projected 3-year resale value	$57,750
Cost to own 3 years	$32,000

restricted to narrow rivers and bays, a powerboat may be the more viable craft. It is an ideal after-work escape vehicle for windless evenings when a sailboat may not be able to escape at all.

Any boat, power or sail, can shelter you, restore you, show you beautiful sunsets and starry nights, and cultivate the romance in your life. Any boat can be your dream yacht if it is right for you.

Sail. Unlike the automobile industry, there are many small companies in the boatbuilding business. Some build just a few boats a year, relying on custom products as opposed to mass-produced lookalikes. With boats, status derives from the unique rather than the recognizable.

In the world of sail there are both. Pearson, Catalina, Tillotson-Pearson (J Boats, Freedom, and Alden), and Hunter are the major American production builders, accounting for about 80 percent of the new boats sold each year. The French company Beneteau is the world's largest and is making significant inroads into the United States market. Each of these companies builds good boats, though every boat is limited in its abilities by design and construction decisions. A mass-production boat intended to do most things well for a reasonable price can't compete with a single-purpose racer or an offshore cruiser.

Murray Davis, founder of *Cruising World* magazine, is fond of saying that there is no such thing as a bad boat, just one used for the wrong purpose. With intelligent modification, almost any boat can be sailed across the ocean. For example, Tony Lush sailed a J/35 in the 1984 Observer Singlehanded Transatlantic Race from Plymouth, England, to Newport, Rhode Island. In 1978 Patrick Childress circumnavigated the globe in a Catalina 27. The J/35 is essentially a round-the-buoys racer, and the Catalina 27 an economical family boat. Both are light, with fin keels and spade rudders. It would have been foolish for either of these men to have attempted their voyages in the stock versions, but by strengthening critical structures they succeeded in relative comfort and safety. Why aren't all boats built to cross

Brigadoon, a Lord Nelson Victory tug designed by Jim Backus and built in Taiwan, is very nearly a "replica yacht." Its appeal lies in the careful blending of workboat lines with yacht-quality trim. The design succeeds because it avoids (barely) the temptation of degenerating into a cutesy caricature; a beard on the bow would cross that fine line.

oceans? Because most owners never undertake such arduous passages, and the cost to engineer the boats to ocean voyaging standards would be prohibitive.

At the other end of the design spectrum is the large custom cruiser. Here is a hypothetical vessel: Commissioned by wealthy New York investment banker Levi Greenspan, the 76-foot ketch *Water Lily* was designed by the famous naval architect Ron Holland and built in the prestigious Dutch yard of Royal Huisman. The owner has no intention of racing his exquisite vessel, though she certainly possesses thoroughbred lines. Rather, he wants to cruise the Mediterranean and Caribbean in style and luxury, entertaining guests and cooling his heels until a legal investigation of his business dealings is completed. A professional crew performs routine maintenance—varnishing the teak, cleaning the chrome, changing engine filters—and when he is at last cleared of charges that he violated insider trading regulations, the boat returns to the United States and is hauled for a major refit at a reputable yard, Ted Hood's Little Harbor Marine in Rhode Island. The annual bill might equal the purchase price of a new 30-footer, which of course is no problem for Mr. Greenspan.

Between the stock family sloop and the custom world cruiser lies a world of boats: wood, fiberglass, aluminum, and steel; sloop, ketch, cutter, and yawl; fin keel, full keel; racer and cruiser; custom and production. Most boat owners begin with a standard production model and—if means and inclination permit—

progress upward to more expensive and more personal expressions of their taste in yachting. Experience is the best guide, and the wise owner makes sure that his expenditures do not outpace his knowledge.

Power. Much of the description of the sailboat industry applies to powerboats. Again, there are dozens of small builders as well as large ones. Power sales outnumber sail more than twelve to one; inboard power sales outnumber auxiliary-powered sailboats almost five to one. And the variety is seemingly infinite.

Because this book focuses on boats with sleeping accommodations, the overwhelming abundance of ski boats, runabouts, small fishing boats, and all manner of strange mutations are not mentioned. But a look at the variety of powerboats could begin with something as small as a Bayliner 21, powered by a Mercury outdrive (inboard/outboard, or I/O), or a Wellcraft Scarab 30 with twin outboard motors. Both have berths for two or more persons, portable toilets, and compact galleys. The Bayliner is an all-around family fun boat, intended for picnicking, overnight cruising, and fishing. The Wellcraft is a "muscle boat," reminding one of the Chrysler "hemi" cars of the 1960s, which had a four-barrel carburetor, Hurst four-speed transmission, and positraction differential gear. Speed and looks are paramount, resulting in obvious sacrifices in belowdecks space. Yet like many other muscle boat builders, Wellcraft takes great pains in making its interiors sexy and sumptuous, sometimes installing mirrors above the V-berth!

In the midsize range there are slow, economical, diesel-powered trawlers with husky "take-any-sea" looks, powerful sportfishermen with enormous power plants and steering/lookout towers erected high above the superstructure, and elegant though perhaps boxy-looking motoryachts with padded sofas and color-coordinated wall coverings. Each has its purpose—long-range cruising, billfish tournament competition, luxury-class entertainment of friends and business associates. The man who needs a sportfisherman but buys a trawler has made just as grave an error as if he had bought a 12-meter America's Cup yacht.

A number of noted builders supply the top end of the power market—Palmer Johnson, Burger, Diaship, Denison, Azimut, and Baglietto, to name but a few. Today these multimillion-dollar ships are almost always built of steel, aluminum, or a combination of the two. Custom megayacht builders seldom work in wood or fiberglass, though there are exceptions. A naval architect such as Holland's H.W. Frits DeVoogt is paid a handsome retainer to interpret the owner's needs and tastes and translate them into the design of a 130-foot megayacht. Interior design may be subcontracted to someone such as Britain's Jon Bannenberg, who will not only help lay out the accommodation plan and formulate a decor centered on valuable works of art, but will also see to the painstaking details of specifying lighting, furniture, fabric, and fixtures.

In a production boat, design details are decided for you, often by the builder alone. In a semiproduction boat, the owner has a large say in alterations from the norm. And in the lavish custom megayacht, where there are more details than any one man or woman can attend to, a team of designers makes the choices for the owner and calls it "a personal statement."

ASSESSING A USED BOAT OR THE BOAT YOU CURRENTLY OWN

Rare is the woman or man who buys a boat and keeps it for a lifetime, handing the revered craft down to children like a family heirloom. Most that do are admirable, and a few are a little strange. Some people just have simple needs and small dreams, and the relationship with their boat is symbiotic. As with a couple who marries once and builds on their love, compromise, self-sacrifice, and hard work are necessary expenditures, reinforced by the Judeo-Christian belief in suffering for a greater, later reward. Yet the paybacks in the here and now—intimacy, cost savings, the opportunity to craft something really fine—are considerable. For others—the zealots—a one-boat affair grows surly and obsessive as the owner struggles against the impossible to make his boat perfect. Over time he also begins to dread change itself, rationalizing his obstinacy with horror stories about the high cost of "moving up."

Fortunately, there is less social stigma and dislocation attached to changing boats than to switching spouses, and few people have a problem with it. Boats are not people.

The owner who decides a change is in order should first look at the boat he already owns. Is it really too small? Too slow? Too old? Or have you simply lost your infatuation with it? Could it regain its original luster if you were to replace old and worn gear, modify the interior plan, or redecorate?

If the basic design is satisfactory, answer the following questions:

- What is the current market value of the boat?

1

2

1 *Puck*, a fiberglass Dyer 29 built by the Anchorage, is a product of the resurgent interest in Down East-style workboats. Also referred to as "lobster yachts," these boats combine a high bow, V hull sections forward, and low freeboard aft for seakeeping ability and a pleasing profile. A small keel assists in directional stability.

2 *Namaste* is a 48-foot passagemaking motoryacht designed by Steve Seaton and Chuck Neville. The roller-furling jib and downwind head-sails set on poles improve performance and reduce fuel consumption under the right conditions. The aft poles mounted outboard of the rail are rigged for flopper stoppers to minimize rolling.

- What is the cost of the new boat you desire?

- What is the estimated cost of refurbishing the old boat?

- Is there sufficient quality in the old boat to serve as a foundation for major refitting?

- Is it in fact possible to remodel to your specifications?

A bit of work is required to answer these questions. Knowledgeable yacht brokers can provide valuable information on the market values of various boats. Consult classified listings and nationwide computerized brokerage services as well. To estimate remodeling costs, make a list of jobs to be done. Can you do any of these yourself? Itemize materials and obtain prices. Boatyards and custom builders will give quotes on work you do not want to do yourself. Subcontracting the work yourself to specialists such as carpenters, mechanics, and electricians may save money but also may take longer than a well-organized yard.

Retaining a professional yacht surveyor to identify problems and estimate costs is money well spent. Most insurance companies require surveys before issuing policies. You might even consult with a surveyor before deciding to sell or upgrade.

If structural alterations are warranted, it may be necessary to retain a naval architect for advice. For example, changing the rig of a sailboat from cutter to ketch may require strengthening the deck and hull in certain places to carry the new loads imposed. Moving interior bulkheads may dangerously weaken the hull or deck structure. Altering the keel and rudder could have significant effects on performance and stability. Adding a flybridge may dangerously reduce your boat's stability. Only a professional with a design and engineering background can give you the confidence necessary to proceed with wholesale modifications.

1 Representative of a new generation of high-performance megayachts, *Octopussy*, built by Diaship of aluminum alloy, is the world's fastest megayacht. She has been clocked at 53.17 knots, powered by three MTU diesels that generate 10,500 horsepower.

2 *Philela II*, a traditional 34-foot Gandy-built cruiser with plumb bow and varnished mahogany cabin structure, cruises the Pacific Northwest.

Effect of Modifications on Resale Value

	Modification	Effect—ROI*	Notes
Cosmetic	Oil/varnish wood	Excellent—100%	Keep off decks and hull
	Paint	Good—100%	Use two-part paint on hull and deck; must be neat—no brush strokes
	Install carpet	Fair—0%	Never fasten permanently
Electronics	Add electronics	Excellent—10%	Basic instruments expected
	Add solar/wind/water generator	Fair—5%	Most people don't need
	Add steering vane/autopilot	Excellent—10%	Autopilot more popular with most people
Deck	Add wood trim to deck	Poor—0%	Don't gild the lily on a production boat
	New canvaswork	Excellent—5%	Expected
	Lay teak decks	Fair—5%	Depends on model and workmanship
	Add bow platform/anchor rollers	Good—5%	Depends on workmanship
	Add dinghy davits	Fair—5%	Avoid on small boats
	Add windlass	Excellent—5%	Electric/manual best
	Add deck prisms	Fair—0%	
	Add vents	Poor—0%	Select site carefully
	Add storm shutters	Poor—0%	Most people don't need
	Add boom gallows	Good—0%	Cruising boats only
	Add bulwarks	Poor—0%	Traditional boats only
Interior	Reupholster cushions	Excellent—50%	Good taste counts
	Sew new curtains	Excellent—0%	
	Add new appliances	Excellent—10%	Stove fuel preference varies; LPG best, diesel and kerosene worst
	Add shower	Excellent—0%	
	Modify berths	Poor—0%	Avoid shortening settees
	Add counter space	Fair—0%	Depends on workmanship
	Install new lights	Excellent—0%	Expected
	New hull covering	Excellent—0%	Expected, good taste counts
	Replace windows	Excellent—0%	Expected—crazed Plexiglas looks bad
Major Changes	Move bulkheads	Bad—0%	Could affect structural integrity
	Strengthen hull/rudder keel	Bad—0%	Betrays weakness
	Repower	Excellent—25%	Diesel best
	Change rig	Fair—0%	Adding inner forestay OK; from sloop to ketch, ketch to schooner, etc., requires professional advice

*ROI = return on investment

Glory, a 54-foot racing sloop designed by Britton Chance, nearly broaches during the Clipper Cup series in Hawaii.

	Job	Materials	Tasks
Cosmetic	Varnish or oil bare wood	Sandpaper, brushes, varnish, rags, solvent	Sand and wipe clean. Apply varnish: 2 coats inside, 8 coats outside.
	Fill deck cracks	Gelcoat or epoxy resin and coloring agent	File edges, clean with solvent. Apply compound. Dry-sand the wood, wet-sand the fiberglass.
	Paint hull and/or deck	Orbital sander, sandpaper, paint, thinner, brushes, rollers, mask and gloves	Fill nicks, sand, clean, tape, prime, paint.
	Polish fiberglass	Buffing wheel, rubbing compound, polish	Clean, buff with rubbing compound, buff with polish.
	Restore metal hardware	Rags, metal polish	Clean and polish. Option to rechrome.
Structural	Move furniture	Plywood, veneers, glue and/or fiberglass, fasteners	Take measurements and make drawings. Remove old furniture, clean hull, etc. Bond structural pieces to hull; screw/glue other pieces in place. Finish with veneers, paint, varnish, etc.
	Strengthen hull (fiberglass)	Epoxy or polyester resin, mat and woven roving, foam or balsa coring, rubber gloves, mask, scissors, mixing pot	Clean hull area with acetone. Remove paint, etc. Cut materials to size. Apply mat, apply coring, apply mat, apply woven roving, apply mat, apply optional layer of cloth. Sand and paint.

Common Upgrade Projects

INTERVIEW: On Choosing a Yacht Broker

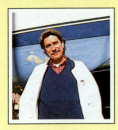

with Joel Potter

*W*hen I started selling boats, I sold both power and sail. I then began to specialize in cruising sailboats because that's what I like. It seems that the more successful brokers tend to focus on a specific segment of the market, either because of a desire to do so, or so as not to overlap areas of expertise with their associates. I've found I can service my clients better, both buyers and sellers, by specializing, as all my energies are directed toward knowing all I can about cruising sailboats.

My advice to buyers is to do some homework; preparation and knowledge are key. When selecting a broker, ask around the waterfront. Chances are that the same names will keep popping up. Try and match your requirements with a broker who has knowledge and a good reputation dealing in the specific types of boats you are interested in.

Pedigree is just as important with a broker as it is with a yacht designer or a yacht builder. Ask the following questions: How long has the broker been in business? Is he licensed or a member of any professional organizations or associations? Does he maintain a separate escrow account? Your comfort level with your broker should be paramount. You've got to feel that he or she is truly listening and working on your needs and requirements and not just trying to sell you what he has at the moment.

—*Joel Potter*
Yacht Broker
Fort Lauderdale, Florida

	Job	Materials	Tasks
Mechanical	Pressurize water system	Auto pump with pressure switch, reinforced hose, SS hose clamps, accumulator tank	Mount pump and accumulator tank. Connect hoses between tank, pump, accumulator tank, and faucets. Check for leaks.
	Hot-water system	Heater; either (a) holding tank for recirculated engine water or (b) instantaneous LPG or CNG unit); gas hose; water hose; clamps; Teflon tape	(a) Mount tank near engine. Install takeoff on manifold. Hose from manifold to tank to exhaust. (b) Mount unit on bulkhead. Special hose from LPG or CNG tank to unit. Hose from tank to pump to accumulator to unit. Hose from unit to shower and faucet.
	Install generator	Generator, wire, terminals, cable, terminals, AC outlets	Mount generator. Attach wire to starter panel, cable to batteries, hose to fuel tank, AC wire to outlets.
	Wheel steering (sailboat)	Pedestal steering system, plywood, fiberglass	Mount pedestal. Mount wire sheaves under cockpit. Remove rudder and post—cut keyway; reinstall. Mount quadrant on rudder post, install wire and adjust tension.
	Repower engine	New engine (other items depend on type, i.e., gas to diesel, diesel to diesel, brand to brand, etc.)	Remove old engine, clean area. Fabricate new beds. Put new engine in place, reconnect wires, hoses, etc. Align with propeller shaft. Test.

*A*sk the following questions of your-self or your surveyor, and let the answers help guide your decision to buy or remodel a boat.

Fiberglass hull and deck

- Is the hull basically sound?

- Are there indications that the hull has changed shape (such as doors that won't close)?

- Are there signs of osmotic blistering in the fiberglass?

- Has the hull been tested with a mois-ture meter?

- Most fiberglass decks are cored with wood. Are there signs of delamina-tion or sponginess?

- How is the hull-deck joint fastened? Does it leak?

- Does the deck "oilcan"?

- Are "spider cracks" in the gelcoat extensive?

- Has the gelcoat thinned such that regelcoating or painting is indicated?

- Are there stress cracks near bulk-heads, chainplates, mast steps, motor mounts, or "hard spots," such as where bulkheads join the hull?

- Are there cracks in the keel from groundings?

- Has external lead ballast separated from the hull?

- Are the keelbolts sound?

- Are the rudder(s) and stock sound? How much play?

- Have through hull fittings corroded?

- Do deck fittings need rebedding?

Wooden hull and deck

- Is the hull fair?

- Has the structure sagged?

- Is there buckling at the plank seams?

- Are the fasteners loose or corroded?

- How much checking in the wood? Has it dried too long?

- Is there extensive leaking?

- Is recaulking indicated?

- Is there dry rot in the keel, frames, transom, or other hard-to-replace members?

- Is there dry rot in the deck beams, deck planking, or house?

- What is the condition of the canvas-covered deck?

- Has the keel been damaged by groundings?

- Has external lead or iron ballast sep-arated from the hull?

- Are the keelbolts sound?

- Are the rudder(s) and stock sound? How much play?

- Have through hulls or other underwa-ter metal pieces corroded?

- Do deck fittings need rebedding?

Metal hull and deck

- Is the hull fair?

- Has fairing compound fallen away?

- Where and how extensive is the rust-ing of the steel (i.e., brown streaks or pools)?

- Where and how extensive is the cor-rosion of aluminum (i.e., piles of white powder)?

- Have you measured plate thickness with a sonic tester?

- Is repainting or application of other barrier coats indicated?

- Are welds sound?

- Are there other signs of electrolysis, galvanic, or crevice corrosion?

- Are dissimilar metals (e.g., stainless steel stanchions on aluminum decks) separated by suitable gaskets?

- Are the rudder(s) and stock sound?

- Are through hulls and other underwa-ter parts—metal or plastic—sound?

- Do deck fittings need rebedding?

Engines and drive system

- Is cylinder compression lower than specified?

- Are there signs of ring and piston wear?

- Can you hear valve chatter?

- Are the head and head gasket sound?

- How many hours of running time does the engine have?

- What color is the exhaust smoke? (Black smoke indicates inadequate fuel combustion; blue smoke is a sign of burning oil; white smoke that persists after engine warms up signi-fies water or air in the fuel, water in the cylinders, or misfiring.)

- Is there a maintenance log? (A well-kept engine log usually indicates a properly maintained engine.)

- Have you checked all engine and drive system components, including water pump, oil pump, fuel pump, oil cooler, alternator(s), starter, belts and pulleys, transmission and link-age, propeller shaft and couplings, propeller(s), Cutless bearing, stuff-ing box, V-drive, I/O and outboard lower unit, motor mounts, fuel tanks, filters, and hoses or tubing?

Electrical

- Is the electrical panel up to date? Does it use fuses or circuit breakers? (The latter are preferable.)

- Is there a sufficient number of cir-cuits for accessories?

- What is the condition of the wiring? Is it adequately sized?

- Is the wiring accessible? Is it color coded?

- Are wiring runs neatly bundled and adequately protected (as with PVC conduit)?

- Are there signs of corrosion (i.e., green powder)?

- Is there a voltmeter in the panel? Is there an ammeter?

- Is the lighting adequate? Fluorescent or incandescent?

- Is there a battery charger?

- Is there a shore power hookup?

- Are the AC outlets adequate? How much current?

- Is there any indication of stray cur-rents (i.e., corrosion or "hot" metal parts, low voltmeter reading)?

- What is the lightning ground system?

- Is there a bonding system with all major metal objects tied in per regu-latory agency standards?

Plumbing

- Are the through hulls in working order? Corroded?
- Are through hulls of the gate-valve type (worst), the barrel type (okay), or the ball-valve type (best)?
- What is the condition of hoses and clamps?
- What is the condition of pumps and float switches?
- What is the condition of the water tanks? Are they stainless steel, Monel, black iron, fiberglass? Are there vents? Baffles? Inspection ports? Gauges? Deck fills?
- Are the cockpit scuppers adequate?
- Does the deck drain adequately?
- Is there sufficient bilge pump capacity? Is there manual backup? Are there strum boxes on intakes?
- Is the pressure water system functional? Is there manual backup?
- What is the condition of the hot-water heater element and tank?
- Is there a seawater system for dish rinsing or deck cleaning?
- What is the condition of the toilet? The holding tank? The diverter valve?

Steering systems

- What type of system is it: hydraulic, cable/quadrant (pedestal), push-pull, pull-pull, tiller, worm gear, rack and pinion?
- How much play in the system is there? How much sensitivity?
- What is the condition of all wheels, fittings, linkages, and rudderheads?
- What is the condition of the rudder stops?
- Is there emergency backup (e.g., tiller)?
- How many stations are there? Is there one out of the weather?
- Is there comfortable seating?

Accommodations

- Is the number of berths adequate? Are they wide enough and long enough? Are they permanent or convertible?

- Are the cushions comfortable?
- What is the condition of the upholstery and curtains?
- Are table and seat heights satisfactory? Back rest angles OK?
- Is there adequate stowage space for clothes, gear, and provisions?
- Is there navigation space?
- How is the headroom? The leg room?
- Is the galley functional? How are the stove and oven? The sink(s)? The refrigerator or icebox? The cookware, dish, and utensil stowage? The food stowage?
- What type of stove fuel is used: alcohol, kerosene, diesel, wood, electric, liquefied petroleum gas (LPG), compressed natural gas (CNG)? What is the condition of tanks and safety gear (i.e., gas sniffers, solenoids, auto shutoffs)?
- Is privacy adequate?
- Are ventilation and natural lighting adequate? Are there hatches, portlights fans, vents, prisms, and artificial lighting?
- Are handholds adequate?

Other

Have you inspected and considered the following:

- Electronics
- Ground tackle, windlass, bow rollers, chain locker
- Mast and rigging, sails
- Auxiliary generator
- Lifelines and stanchions
- Autopilot or steering vane
- Shower
- Lazarette and cockpit locker space
- Alternative energy devices such as solar panels and wind generators
- Heating and air-conditioning systems
- Cosmetics: varnish, oil, paint, and decorative trim
- Safety gear: life raft, EPIRB (emergency position indicating radio beacon), fire extinguishers, life jackets, strobe, man-overboard pole, etc.

A chartered cruising trimaran rushes toward its anchorage on a hazy day in the Virgin Islands.

The Spectrum 42, designed in Great Britain by John Shuttleworth, is a fast cruising catamaran built of foam-cored fiberglass.

The trimaran *Curtana* lifts an ama as she participates in the 1987 Newport Unlimited Regatta, which allows monohulls and multihulls to compete for honors on corrected time.

NEW BOAT OPTIONS

Numerous choices confront the prospective buyer of a new boat. There are essentially three categories of boatbuilders, though of course numerous permutations exist. The buyer's decision should be a function of cost, expected date of delivery, matching of needs versus "what's available," and the degree of customization desired.

Production. The vast majority of boats sold are known as production boats. This means that all boats within the model series, especially fiberglass, have identical hulls. Occasionally the builder may offer different deck configurations, such as aft or center cockpit, sedan or flybridge. There may be a choice of two or three interior accommodation plans. For example, one layout may have a dinette in the main cabin; another, settees or chairs. Variations in berthing arrangements may also be possible, and of course there may be some choice in upholstery fabric, finishes, appliances, engine, and accessories.

Some builders are more flexible than others. Usually this is a direct function of price. An inexpensive boat is possible only when the builder doesn't have to set up for too many variables. One accommodation plan means just one set of patterns and jigs for cutting out plywood bulkheads, furniture, and hardwood trim. Two plans means two sets. Henry Ford proved the economies of the assembly line more than 80 years ago, and that hasn't changed since in the automobile or boat business.

Production builders achieve savings in other ways, too. The fabrication of fiberglass components such as inner liners, furniture foundations, and head compartments eliminates costly hardwoods and reduces the man-hours required to fit pieces together. Using the same upholstery material in all units, perhaps throughout the company line, permits the builder to buy in larger quantities and thereby obtain a lower price. The same is true of hardware and accessories.

When the day comes to sell, the market value of a standard production boat is more easily determined, since there are probably others for sale at the same time to serve as benchmarks. Popular models retain value better than others, though this is somewhat subject to regional preferences, cost-of-living differences, and availability.

Semiproduction. An increasingly popular approach offers the buyer a stock hull with optional variances from the standard model in such elements as rig, engine, and interior layout. Such builders tend to be smaller, finding their niche by specializing in customer contact and satisfaction. The main restriction is the space and shape of the hull, and the builder's willingness to customize. The buyer may specify an unorthodox accommodation plan, the types of wood he wants, finish materials, lighting, galley appliances, fixtures, and whatever else he fancies. A good yard will assist the buyer in making these important decisions, showing him samples of new products and letting him study other examples of the yard's work.

Some cost savings are achieved in fiberglass by having only one set of molds to tool, but because the cost of a hull is only about 10 percent of total purchase price, well-heeled buyers might get more for their money with a custom design. Expect to pay anywhere between 25 and 50 percent more for a semiproduction boat.

A variation on the semiproduction theme is to purchase a stock hull from a production builder and transport it to a custom yard or yacht carpenter for completion.

In the 1970s "kit" boats were popular; one could buy a bare hull and complete the rest himself, with or without company assistance and the purchase of additional components. This practice has since fallen into disfavor.

with Joel Potter

Boats are toys. All boats depreciate, some more than others. The only things that can make a boat appreciate in value are inflation and currency exchange fluctuation. I tell my clients that a SatNav is worth half what you pay for it when you open the box. Install it and it's worth a third. Turn it on, just once, and it's worth a quarter of the purchase price. People don't want to believe it, but a good analogy is to go to Sears and buy a blender. Take it home and make a milkshake. Then try to sell the blender to someone. If you can get five bucks for it at a yard sale, you're doing well.

Boats are similar. The minute you throw off the dock lines for the first time, you generally lose 20% of your investment. I'm not saying you can't turn a profit, as I've made money for people by buying a boat abroad and taking advantage of currency exchange fluctuations and maximizing any tax advantages that exist. Sometimes you can grab something at an introductory price (beware of hull number one!), and if the model becomes popular, you'll do alright.

The best way maximize both your value and enjoyment of a boat is to buy all the quality you can afford. When you buy a quality product you'll only cry once! You won't have to perform "triage" on it as you use it, and it will return a greater percentage of its value when returned to the market.

—Joel Potter
Yacht Broker
Fort Lauderdale, Florida

There is less profit in selling a bare hull, and companies are afraid that shoddy home workmanship will reflect badly on their reputations.

While production wood sailboats haven't been built since the 1950s (the 39-foot Concordia and 34-foot Hinckley Sou'Wester were two of the last), there are a number of companies building semiproduction wood powerboats. Rybovich and Merritt, of south Florida, for example, build cold-molded sportfishermen, in part because such boats are lighter and emit sounds purportedly more favorable to the catching of fish. Though the hulls of each model are basically the same, individual boats are completed to owner specifications.

Most metal boatbuilding in the United States is confined to commercial craft and megayachts. Several companies have tried to market production and semiproduction steel sailboats in the 40-foot range, but have found their acceptance lackluster. A few still sell bare hulls. In Europe, however, and particularly in the Netherlands, steel boatbuilding flourishes.

Custom. Without a doubt the most assured method of getting precisely what you want is to commission a custom, one-off design. While some builders may offer stock designs in wood, fiberglass, or steel, or employ an in-house design team, many buyers prefer to deal directly with a "name" naval architect in private practice. Through a number of lengthy meetings, the architect develops an understanding of your needs and preferences. Ultimately a complete design emerges. The architect often helps locate the right yard to build the boat, and will oversee its construction much in the manner of a Lloyd's inspector. The buyer of a custom yacht should be prepared to spend considerable time going over details with the architect and builder. Hence this approach is best suited to the knowledgeable yachtsman who knows what he wants, can articulate his thoughts, and has deep pockets to keep the project rolling. Too often an inexperienced person with a wad of cash is the victim of cost overruns because he keeps changing his mind; his learning curve, it seems, is fated to parallel the construction process. Frustration and dissatisfaction are likely on the part of all parties, and the frequent result is the selling of the boat at a substantial loss soon after completion.

Yet for the right person, directing the construction of a custom boat is a rewarding, once-in-a-lifetime experience. Like a custom house, the custom boat can be the clearest possible expression of individual style, taste, purpose, and accumulated knowledge. Expect to pay anywhere between 50 and 100 percent more for a custom, one-off boat than for a production boat of equivalent size.

with Joel White

Look for someone who's familiar with the type of boat and material you want—with good results. Go look at other boats built by that yard, and if necessary, have a surveyor inspect them.

We get a lot of our work based on our reputation and from referrals from surveyors and yacht brokers. And often it's the naval architect.

Communications are very important—between the builder and client, and between the builder and naval architect. You can't do it over the phone; meeting face to face is the only way to see if you're going to like and trust each other.

If a customer can't visit the yard regularly to check progress, and there isn't a naval architect to do it, consider hiring an agent. Most people won't spend money on expert advice, but if you're spend-

ing half a million dollars, what's $25,000 to be sure you get what you want?

We specialize in wooden boats, and wooden-boat customers seem to be pretty good people. Still, there's always room for problems. Some customers are overly optimistic about what they can get for their money. Tell the builder up front what you can afford. When a customer starts adding a lot of things, that's okay, but it can play hell with your schedule of other jobs. Likewise, when a customer starts paring his list, he should tell the builder before the work is done. If there's good communication, there are usually no problems.

—Joel White
Brooklin Boatyard
Brooklin, Maine

PLANNING

Custom building and major remodeling require careful planning to ensure satisfactory results. Because you are the one footing the bill, it is important to maintain control of the project. Make periodic inspections of even the smallest details—now is the time to correct problems, not when the job is done. Then it may be impossible, and the cost certainly greater. Like the clerk of the works in a large building construction firm, someone should keep a list of critical jobs, the order in which they should be completed, and check them off only after personal inspection. If you don't do this, who will?

COMMISSIONING A NEW CUSTOM BOAT

Let's envision a typical scenario. The German painter Friederich Wurmbrand decides to commission the building of a new 45-foot cruising motoryacht. Now living in Seattle, "Fred," as his American friends call him, and his wife, Gerlinda, are planning for their retirement and want a larger boat to live aboard for long periods. They plan to cruise the coastal waters of British Columbia and Alaska to the north and Baja California to the south. Room for occasional guests, including their children and grandchildren, is required, but because Fred and Gerlinda will be alone most of the time,

they don't want a clutter of extra berths occupying valuable space that could better be utilized for daily living.

Fred obtains the names of several naval architects from a yacht broker with whom he has done business in the past. By letter he solicits some basic information: Do they have experience designing boats of this type? What are some examples of their work, and could these boats be inspected before he signs a retainer? How long have they been in business? Do they work alone or does the office include other staff? If so, who will do the actual design work? Are they personally able to supervise the construction process? What is their fee structure?

Based on responses to these questions, the Wurmbrands select David B. Cooper and schedule a preliminary meeting. Gerlinda has a keen interest in what will be her part-time retirement home, and plans to attend all of the meetings with the architect. Fred makes some sketches that depict a semidisplacement hull of fairly low profile, comparatively narrow beam, flat sheer, forward and aft cabins, wheelhouse, and mast with steadying sail. He believes that a single diesel engine with auxiliary generator and emergency clutch/drive system to turn the propeller in case the main engine fails will be economical. A cruising speed of 12 knots is desired and a fuel consumption rate of about 18 gallons per hour expected. Fred also draws

1 Motorsailers are sometimes viewed as compromises, but the 100-foot *Fei Seen* challenges such convictions. Designed by Phillip Rhodes and built by Abeking and Rasmussen, *Fei Seen* sails at 11 knots (here enjoying the Virgin Island trade winds) and makes 10 knots under power, with NIAD stabilizers to smooth the ride.

2 The Oriana 26, a traditional family cruising cutter, has a fiberglass hull and wood cabin for what the builders feel is the best of both worlds. The bowsprit is a good home for the main anchor, and the deck box just forward of the cabin is a convenient stowage area for lines, winch handles, and other small gear.

3 *Adriana* is a 33-foot 1968 Pearson Vanguard sloop, designed by Philip Rhodes. Equipped with a steering vane, autopilot, canvas dodger, storm sails, and a host of other gear, she heads out of Narragansett Bay for an 18-month cruise of the East Coast and Bahamas.

1

2

3

up a list of basic design features and equipment that he would like.

Mr. Cooper studies the sketches and lists, then asks some pertinent questions: Does Fred prefer a specific hull material—fiberglass for instance—or is he open to wood? How many people will be aboard most of the time? What is the maximum number? What is the desired cruising range? Five hundred miles? One thousand? Do Fred and Gerlinda require a boat with open-ocean capability, or do they plan to spend most of their time in relatively protected waters? Mr. Cooper doubts that Fred's fuel consumption rate is realistic and for the moment plays the devil's advocate, making a case for twin engines. He also tries to get a handle on Fred's level of experience, not only to help him determine what is best for the Wurmbrands but also to decide if he wants to accept the project should Fred offer it to him.

Fred and Mr. Cooper reach a tentative agreement. Mr. Cooper's secretary draws up a standard contract, specifying obligations of both parties, work to be performed, and a schedule of fee payment. Before any drawings are begun, Fred must pay $2,500. This will cover Mr. Cooper's costs of preliminary drawings. There is an escape clause at this point if

neither wishes to proceed. If they do proceed, an additional payment of $3,000 is due. Mr. Cooper's ultimate fee is $35,000, plus an hourly rate of $70 should his work exceed 1,000 hours; the initial $5,500 is deductible from that amount, and the balance is due in payments tied to various project stages such as final drawings, completion of the hull and deck, delivery, and sea trials. Fred has his attorney review the proposed contract before signing.

During the next few months, Fred and Gerlinda meet with Mr. Cooper six times to discuss increasingly detailed features of their wooden retirement cruiser. Gerlinda wants a gas stove and oven, easy-to-clean counters and bulkhead surfaces, and a double berth that can be entered from both sides. Fred favors a simple, light decor with small amounts of ash trim. Besides the two principal staterooms, one of which has a generous desk for sketching and writing, the saloon must have a sleeper couch or other type of convertible berth for two children. Fred is concerned about visibility in the wheelhouse, emergency backup steering, and access to the engine for maintenance.

Mr. Cooper recommends a yard on Bainbridge Island to build the boat, and both he and Fred make visits to discuss the project with the yard owner. The Wurmbrands sign another contract with Paul Chen; an initial payment of $20,000 is stipulated, with additional sums due at the end of each month. Although Fred has received a written estimate, the total price will be a function of the actual cost of materials, plus labor at an agreed rate, plus a fixed fee to cover the yard's overhead and other expenses.

Mr. Chen's business is small and consequently he needs the Wurmbrand's downpayment to purchase materials before he can start. Also, Mr. Chen employs only carpenters and a few general shop helpers, including a mechanic. The electrical system and some other work will be subcontracted to others. Fred is concerned because he feels he must rely on Mr. Chen's judgment as to the subcontractors' work quality. Mr. Cooper however, vouches for the electrician, and Mr. Chen agrees to warranty the subcontractors' work.

As construction progresses, Fred and Gerlinda decide to make a few changes. They wish

The Fales Navigator 32/33 could be classified as a 50/50 motorsailer, that is, deriving equal motive power from sail and engine. The 360 square feet of sail, while not really enough to drive her alone, will make a difference in her overall performance. The engine is a 50-horsepower Perkins 4-107 diesel.

with David Pedrick

The requirements of a good working relationship with a designer are threefold: The client should have a good idea of the kind of boat he or she wants—that will narrow the field of designers. Second, for the best job, the client should be prepared to give the designer the financial freedom to do what he thinks is right. Third, the client and designer need to match in terms of design, engineering, and budget.

A good designer should have basic knowledge and creative talent; the ability to execute the design in terms of manpower and operating revenues; and the willingness to follow up with the builder to make sure the client gets the boat he wished for, plus the embellishments that the designer created.

Our firm is willing to commit more of our time without initial charge for a project such as an America's Cup boat that has a large potential payoff. But at the most basic level, a client should make an introductory phone call, followed by a personal meeting. We do preliminary design work for a fee. At that point, the client must decide whether to go ahead with the project, go to another designer, or kill it altogether. We end up wasting a lot of time

with people whose dreams aren't consistent with their pocketbooks. It's not fair to the professional designer to pick his brain and then go elsewhere.

I don't know of any designers who charge a percentage of construction costs as their fee. Some work on time and materials. But we settle on a mutually satisfactory fixed fee for a complete design. We are very careful to define the number of drawings and number of revisions allowed. Some builders have in-house design teams that can produce shop drawings; others need more detailed drawings.

It's important for us to assess early on the amount of handholding the client needs. We try to anticipate the depth of detail the client is going to want to pursue, and deal with it happily. Some designers don't like spending a lot of time with the client. But building a custom boat is a very special experience, often a once-in-a-lifetime experience, and we believe in helping the owner all the way. It's essential to getting repeat business.

—David Pedrick
Pedrick Yacht Designs
Newport, Rhode Island

---

to add reverse-cycle air-conditioning and heating, which requires routing ductwork throughout the boat and mounting the main unit in an already crowded engine room. Mr. Chen is a bit annoyed but doesn't show it. The change means removing some framing in the forward cabin and saloon, and will put him behind schedule. However, there is some additional profit for the yard. Because air-conditioning wasn't specified in the original contract, Mr. Chen quotes a price and Fred agrees to pay it up front.

After 14 months the boat is completed. The Wurmbrands retain a marine surveyor to inspect the boat and note any work that seems unsafe, sloppy, or not done to American Boat and Yacht Council (ABYC) and American Bureau of Shipping (ABS) standards. The surveyor also estimates the value of the boat at $490,000 for insurance purposes. Mr. Cooper and Mr. Chen accompany Fred and Gerlinda during sea trials, and after some minor adjustments are made, the new owners take their boat home.

During the next few months there are a few minor problems to work out, such as replacing a faulty motor mount, installing an antisiphon device in the toilet plumbing, and trimming a cabinet door that doesn't open and shut freely. On the whole, however, the Wurmbrands are quite pleased with their boat, which they christen *Valkyrie* after a favorite piece of music. They know that they wouldn't be able to recoup their investment should they be forced to sell the boat because of poor health or a change of plans; in fact, Fred figures they'd lose about 30 percent. But they aren't worried: They consider *Valkyrie* their last boat and plan to keep her for many years.

Oddly, during a summer cruise to Anchorage, Gerlinda falls in love with a commercial fisherman and leaves Fred after nearly 30 years of marriage. In the midst of his despair, Fred receives news from his agent that an exhibit of his work in New York has resulted in the sale of several nudes (for which Gerlinda modeled in her younger years). One in fact brings a whopping $1.2 million. Fred leaves the boat in

Anchorage and flies to New York, where he is adored by his new fans. Meanwhile, Gerlinda and her boyfriend, Skip, steal *Valkyrie* and head for South America. Fred is unmoved by this news. Thinking now of his native country, he plans a trip to his home town of Diepholz. Traveling with the attractive assistant curator of the gallery, he returns to a hero's welcome. And one night following an invigorating reception at the mayor's home, he places a transatlantic phone call to David B. Cooper to commission a new 60-foot high-performance motoryacht. He says to his companion, "All's well that ends well, darling."

UPGRADING A USED BOAT

Mary Ellen Brankowski is a 34-year-old single woman who teaches skiing in the White Mountains of New Hampshire in the winter and drives a yacht club launch in Provincetown, Massachusetts, during the summer. She loves sailing, and by choice often singlehands. In a few years she hopes to take off cruising.

Because she has limited funds, Mary Ellen has bought a secondhand fiberglass 30-foot sloop and plans to do some of the remodeling herself. She realizes, however, that some of the work is beyond her level of skill, so she plans to hire others to help rewire the electrical system and install a new diesel engine. Jimmy Delveccio, an electrician she met at the Yellow Kittens Club on Block Island a few years ago, quotes her an hourly rate plus materials; a new electrical panel with circuit breakers, voltmeter, and ammeter is the most expensive item. An engine dealer offers her a 10-percent discount on a new 18-horsepower diesel and agrees to install it for a flat rate of $600. The sales agreement stipulates that it is her responsibility to remove the old engine.

Mary Ellen has had her boat trucked to a yard near her rented apartment, where it will be convenient to put in short work periods. This boatyard, unlike some others, has no rules prohibiting her from performing her own work. The excessive use of imitation teak Formica bothers her. It has turned milky and looks passé; all of it must go, she decides. She intends to tear out most of the furniture in the saloon anyway, and build a new interior to her own design, thus killing two birds with one stone. This means moving the sideboard galley

Summary Work Chart

Of Fred and Gerlinda Wurmbrand's custom motor cruiser

1. Decided to take retirement cruise.
2. Agreed on areas to cruise and type of boat required.
3. Reviewed new and used boat market.
4. Decided to custom design and build.
5. Arrived at preliminary specifications: size, type, building material, equipment, etc.
6. Obtained list of naval architects.
7. Wrote naval architects soliciting information.
8. Selected naval architect.
9. Held preliminary discussion with architect. Agreed in general terms on how to proceed.
10. Signed contract. Paid initial fee for drawings.
11. Held six more meetings to fine-tune the design.
12. Visited yards and selected boatbuilder.
13. Signed contract with builder. Made downpayment.
14. Visited construction site and made adjustments in specifications and equipment.
15. Held sea trials.
16. Retained surveyor to ensure work was to specification and to satisfy insurance requirements.
17. Accepted delivery.
18. Made final payments to naval architect and builder.
19. Had warranty work done.
20. Departed on retirement cruise.

Summary of expenses	
Initial payment to naval architect	$ 5,500
Downpayment to builder	20,000
Electrician services	15,000
Electronics technician services and instruments	40,000
Balance to builder in monthly installments	330,000
Balance to naval architect, including surcharges	35,500
Total	$446,000

INTERVIEW: On Choosing a Surveyor

with Bruce Livingston

Look for one that's sober. Reputation means a lot. Check with your boatyard, insurance company, and yacht broker. Ask to see sample copies of his other reports. You need more than a checklist.

Most of us tend to be generalists. I do commercial fishing boats and recreational boats in wood, steel, aluminum, and fiberglass. Don't settle for an in-the-water survey; it's got to be hauled. A lot of people gripe when they read the safety recommendations. Come on! It's for their own damn good.

Ted Hood once asked me how I got started. I told him by building and repairing boats. He said, "Good. Because that's the only way you learn to do it right." It's a good point. A surveyor should tell you more than what's wrong with your boat; he should be able to tell you how to repair it.

—Bruce Livingston
Livingston Marine Associates
Jamestown, Rhode Island

from starboard and dividing it on either side of the passageway against the main bulkhead—stove and utensil stowage to starboard, sink and icebox to port. The portside dinette will be removed and settees installed port and starboard. In place of the Formica facings she'll use a birch veneer that comes in rolls, cuts with a utility knife, and is glued over the plywood furniture foundations with contact cement.

Mary Ellen begins by tearing out the old interior with a crowbar and chisels and framing in the new one with the plywood furniture foundations fiberglassed to the hull. She does this by carefully measuring the space inside the hull to determine the size and shape of each piece, such as the galley and settee facings and tops. Once drawn on the large sheets of plywood, the patterns are cut with a saber saw. The installation of the resulting pieces is the hard part. Some ingenuity is required to hold them in place while she fillets the joints between the plywood and hull with epoxy putty; this forms a temporary bond until she can wet out thin strips of fiberglass mat and

The classic schooner *Voyager* participates in the Opera House Cup at Nantucket, Massachusetts. The low-profile house barely clears the bulwarks.

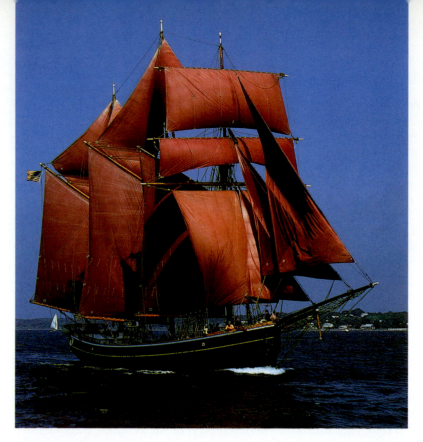

Lindo, a 125-foot Baltic Trader, is a "small" Tall Ship built in 1927 by Albert Svansson in Blekinge, Sweden, of pitch-pine planking on oak frames. Featured in the movie adaptation of Peter Benchley's book *The Island*, she has also appeared in numerous Tall Ship rendezvous around the world.

cloth with epoxy resin and cover the joints.

At the same time, she consults with the electrician, Jimmy Delveccio, who advises her to run PVC (polyvinyl chloride) conduit under the settees to carry service to the various accessories. He also instructs her not to remove old wiring.

When she has removed the galley and dinette framing near the engine box, Mary Ellen calls the engine dealer's mechanic. He instructs her to label and remove all wiring and hoses from the old gasoline engine. She also removes the starter and alternator and attempts to disconnect the propeller shaft coupling. It is badly corroded, however, and the yard manager advises her to cut the propeller shaft with a hacksaw. This requires her to lie on top of the engine and work in an extremely awkward position, but after breaking several blades and skinning her knuckles, she finishes this thankless task. The yard has been contracted to remove the old engine and uses its crane for this purpose. The mechanic installs the new engine, and afterwards Jimmy tears out the old wiring and panel and completely rewires the boat. Mary Ellen then finishes building her new interior. She makes her own cushions by buying blocks of foam, cutting

them with an electric knife, and sewing her own covers.

The boat is at last launched, and during sea trials Mary Ellen notices an annoying vibration in the engine drive train. Also, the masthead anchor light doesn't work. Later she calls the engine dealer's mechanic and asks him to realign the engine and propeller shaft. She assumes this will be covered by the $600 installation fee she has already paid, but he tells her that the shaft was properly aligned when the boat was sitting in its cradle; in the water the hull has apparently changed shape slightly and he considers it her responsibility to correct. Not feeling sure of her ability to jimmy a several-hundred-pound engine with crowbars and chain fall or to achieve an accuracy of three hundredths of an inch in mating the engine and propeller shaft couplings, she reluctantly concedes to paying him an additional $70 to realign the engine for her.

Jimmy stops by the marina dock a week later to check the masthead light. His tests confirm that the wiring is good as far as the connectors at the mast step; the problem, he tells her, must be inside the mast or at the light itself and cannot be repaired until the boat is again hauled and the mast unstepped. Even though his work was limited to wiring inside the hull and he considers the problem her responsibility, he has taken a shine to Mary Ellen and offers to repair the light free the next time the mast is unstepped. Mary Ellen resigns herself to waiting until fall to proceed further. In the meantime, she will use a battery-powered anchor light hung in the rigging.

Mary Ellen was not able to use her boat the entire first summer in the water, but she is well on the way to finishing a major refit. She is a bit worried, however, that the hull seemed to change shape in the cradle, and though factory engineers tell her this is not unusual, she decides to research the possibility of reinforcing the hull. It is a pity she didn't realize this before remodeling the interior, since the logical time to glass in stringers and add extra laminations inside the hull was at the time she had removed the old furniture. She has the winter to ponder her next move.

Beyond this matter, next spring she will concentrate on the exterior teak trim, polishing the topsides, bottom paint, and strengthening the rudder with extra laminations of fiberglass cloth. By performing much of the work herself, she has saved a lot of money. And by hiring others to do critical work she was unable to do, she has confidence in the seaworthiness of her new boat.

A few months later Jimmy calls Mary Ellen in New Hampshire. First he asks her for advice on skiing lessons, then summons his courage to ask her to dinner. Soon they are dating regularly and making plans to quit their jobs and go cruising. Sitting by the lodge fireplace with his arm around Mary Ellen, Jimmy says, "We've really got it wired!"

SUMMARY

The above scenarios are in some ways typical, but they certainly do not represent all the possible situations one might encounter when building or remodeling a boat. Some of the more important considerations in any project include the following:

- Thorough research of the boat type you think you want
- Thorough research of market values
- Consideration of other ways of getting what you want
- Credential checks of those persons hired to perform work
- Special attention to contracts—consult an attorney if large sums of money are involved

Involve yourself in every step of the project; the marine industry is largely unregulated, and in many cases *you* are the inspector/watchdog/ quality control. After all, it's your money!

Summary work chart

of Mary Ellen Brankowski's upgrade project

1. Decided to buy a sailboat.
2. Reviewed used boat market.
3. Retained surveyor to appraise chosen boat.
4. Considered necessary repairs and upgrades. Identified what could be done by owner, what had to be subcontracted out.
5. Made purchase.
6. Selected boatyard in which owner work was permitted. Moved boat.
7. Selected electrician. Shopped for engines and made purchase.
8. Removed old interior woodwork.
9. Missed opportunity to strengthen hull with stringers and extra fiberglass laminations.
10. Ran PVC conduit for new wiring to be installed later.
11. Unhooked old engine wiring and accessories, and cut propeller shaft.
12. Had yard remove old engine.
13. Had mechanic install new engine.
14. Had electrician rewire boat and install new panel.
15. Built new interior. Sewed new cushion covers.
16. Launched boat and conducted sea trials.
17. Noticed vibration in drive train. Noticed masthead light didn't work.
18. Had mechanic realign engine and propeller shaft for extra fee.
19. Had electrician check masthead light problem; since problem was in mast, postponed solution until haulout and unstepping of the mast.
20. Planned work for next haulout, concentrating on rudder and cosmetics. Put makeshift masthead light in place.
21. Launched.

Summary of expenses	
Purchase price of used 30-foot sloop	$22,000
Yacht surveyor's report	400
Yard fee for storage, stepping mast, and launching	1,000
Electrician's services (30 hours × $30)	900
Mechanic's services, including realignment of propeller shaft	670
Materials including fiberglass, resin, fabrics, PVC pipe, fasteners, foam, etc.	1,200
Yard crane fee for removing old engine	150
New diesel engine (less 10-percent discount)	3,500
Total	$29,820

Congere is a German Frers–designed Class A racing yacht, better known as a "maxi" on the grand prix circuit. Surfing through the blue waters of the Virgin Islands, she competes in the 1988 St. Thomas Maxi Regatta.

Principal boat types

Type	Characteristics	Strengths	Weaknesses
Sail			
Conservative Family Sloop	Moderate displacement. Single mast. Moderate proportions.	Simple to operate. Good accommodations. Safe.	Mass-production model, lacking distinctive features. May be slow. May have minor but annoying design or construction flaws.
Racer	Lightweight. Fin keel. Flat underbody. Long waterline.	Fast. Maneuverable.	Quick motion. Keel, rudder, and propeller vulnerable.
Offshore Cruiser	Moderate to heavy displacement. May have full keel and attached rudder. Protected propeller. Easy-to-handle downwind rig.	Seaworthy. Comfortable.	May be slow, lack maneuverability.
Catamaran	Two hulls. May have open or enclosed bridge.	Fast. Stable (5-degree heel). Light. Shallow draft.	Hulls easily punctured. Quick motion. May lack headroom.
Trimaran	Three hulls. May have open or closed wings.	Fast. Stable (15-degree heel). Light. Shallow draft.	Accommodations often confined to center hull. Quick motion. Hulls easily punctured. May lack headroom.
80/20 Motorsailer	Displacement hull. Large auxiliary.	Good power under sail or engine. Good accommodations. Seaworthy.	May be slow under sail.
50/50 Motorsailer	Displacement hull. Flat buttocks. Large engine. Motoryacht lines.	Speed under power. Off-the-wind sail-assist. Beamy.	Poor sail performance.
Classic	Long and narrow. Low freeboard. Long overhangs.	Unique style. May be fast.	Age. More Spartan accommodations than modern boat. Wet.
Tall Ship	Ship over 90 feet. Two or more masts.	Maximum accommodations. Unique style.	Intricate rigging. Poor windward ability. Expensive.
Maxi	Over 75 feet. Modern racer. Often flush-decked.	Maximum performance. Great accommodations.	Large crew required. Ultradeep draft. Expensive.

Type	Characteristics	Strengths	Weaknesses
Power			
Trailerable Family Runabout	Lightweight. Modified V-hull. Outboard or I/O engine.	Multipurpose. Economical. Easy to sell.	Limited seaworthiness. Light construction.
High-performance Sport Boat	Long, narrow, low, sleek. Powerful engine.	Very fast. Exciting to drive. Stylish.	Limited resale market. Minimal accommodations.
Sportfisherman	Deep V-hull. Flybridge and tower. Large aft cockpit. Power engines.	Fast. Smooth ride.	Fuel hungry. Cockpit and glass doors vulnerable.
Motoryacht	Big. Multilevel. Twin engines.	Maximum accommodations. Comfortable.	May roll. Fuel hungry. Boxy-looking.
Trawler	Commercial fishing boat lines. High bow. Sweeping sheerline. Displacement hull.	Economical. Generally seaworthy.	Slow. Single engine lacks maneuverability and backup.
Tug Yacht	Working tugboat lines. High bow. Plumb stem. Low freeboard aft. Vertical wheelhouse face. Displacement hull.	Economical. Generally seaworthy.	Limited accommodations. Slow. Single engine lacks maneuverability and backup.
Lobster Yacht	Maine lobsterboat style. High bow. Low freeboard. Long cockpit.	Economical. Seaworthy.	Open cockpit vulnerable. Limited accommodations.
20/80 Motorsailer	Keel. Comparatively low profile. Sloop or ketch rig for sail-assist off the wind. Displacement hull.	Seaworthy. Emergency sail backup.	Slow. Moderate roll.
Classic	Long and narrow. Low profile. Displacement hull.	Unique style. More economical than motoryacht.	Age. Fewer accommodations.
Megayacht	Ship over 90 feet. Metal construction. Multilevel. Twin engines.	Maximum luxury and accommodations. Long range.	Expensive. Poor resale value.

CHAPTER TWO

Attention to Style

here are numerous adjectives to describe a good-looking boat: Handsome, pretty, and beautiful are common, but no word connotes the delicate integration of line and body as well as style. Like the professional fashion model, the stylish yacht carries herself with grace, purpose, and self-confidence. She knows she is beautiful, yet betrays no sign of conceit or haughtiness. She appears to sit lightly on the water, belying the tons of water she displaces. Her parts are in exact proportion to one another, yet work together so well as to seem indistinguishable from the whole, whether underway or at rest. She has a presence that

the craftsmen of earlier generations called "yare"—nimble and lively, her lines fair and true, derived from the designer's meticulous pencil and the carpenter's fine-toothed saw and sharpened chisel.

Like novice students of art appreciation, many boat owners find themselves saying, "I don't pretend to understand yacht design, but I know what I like." With further study, however, the underlying reasons for beauty and ugliness begin to emerge. This is not to say that the aesthetics of beauty are immutable, for certainly new standards are continually evolving. For an example one need look no further than the female figure. The large-busted, hourglass figure of Jayne Mansfield, considered so desirable in the 1940s and 1950s, gave way to the slim, puckish shape of women like model Twiggy, with flat chests and boyish buttocks. Tastes in colors change, too. The pinks and turquoises so popular in the 1950s were considered garish during the 1960s and early 1970s' Earth movement, when pumpkin, goldenrod, and avocado were more in tune with the mood of the times. That pink (rose) and turquoise (teal) returned in the 1980s in the postmodernist movement, including the revival of Miami Beach's art deco district, only proves the subjectiveness of beauty. Beauty indeed lies in the eye of the beholder, or at least in the eye of a people's collective consciousness at a given point in time.

Ancient Greek philosophers such as Socrates and Aristotle thought quite the opposite was true. Beauty, they said, is governed by laws as steadfast and universal as Nature itself; the difficulty lies in their identification and definition. Similarly, there are yacht designers who believe that certain shapes retain their beauty regardless of age. The "classic" lines of Nathanael Herreshoff's *Reliance,* for instance, are said to be enduring. Fads such as center cockpits and aberrations such as International Offshore Rule (IOR) waterline bulges come and go, and while each may be thought to pos-

1

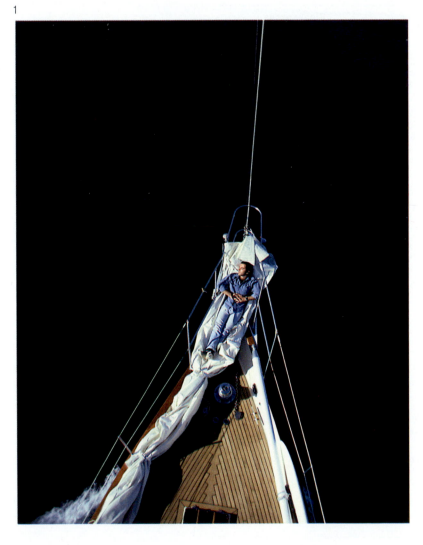

INTERVIEW: In Search of the Perfect Line

with Robert Perry

You never get it right. What makes a drawing right or finished is that you have to turn it over to the client. There's always that nagging, underlying feeling every time you look at something that you could do better. That's one of the beauties of computer fairing—you can quickly change a line before the client comes in at nine-thirty.

My advice is to let it sit overnight. If it still looks good in the morning, then maybe you have it.

The other way to look at it is this: It's right if the client thinks it is. We all pay attention to the guy who pays the bills.

—Robert Perry
Robert H. Perry Yacht Designers
Seattle, Washington

---

sess a degree of good looks in its context, there is some violation of art here that spells a short-lived appreciation.

These same designers, however, would never admit that the best lines have already been drawn. Such an assertion would put them out of business in no time! Just as Robert Perry has said that performance is a "moving target," timeless beauty is an ever-changing goal toward which they all must strive. Even though long-deceased designers may have drawn a perfect line or two in their careers, yachts are such complex structures that there is always room for improvement. Beauty is elusive, but always possible.

EXTERIOR STYLING

THE LINES DRAWINGS

We can think of the shape of a yacht as a three-dimensional sculpture with length, breadth, and depth. (Indeed, not so many years ago the carving of a wooden half-model was deemed a necessary prerequisite of construction.) The naval architect depicts these essential views in a series of drawings, each with a different name. The basic drawings include *sail plan* or *outboard profile* (side view), *general arrangement* or *floor plan* (bird's-eye view of interior accommodations), and the *lines drawing*, which in addition to profile, deck line, and waterline includes hull sections, waterlines, buttocks, and diagonals.

Nowadays there are computer programs that "draw" these lines on a CRT screen based on numbers entered by the designer; the hull skeleton can be rotated to show any cross section desired, including the all-important midsection with the lines of other stations superimposed. A computer drawing is not necessarily a thing of beauty, and its critics claim that while technology provides obvious time-saving advantages in producing, say, a table of offsets, it also eliminates the designer's artistic touch. The growing group of "computer nerds" no doubt disagree, and time probably will produce a new aesthetic that embraces electronic images. Nevertheless, while paper and pencils still exist, there remain a few naval architects who are admired within their profession not only for the beauty of their designs, but also for their drawing ability. Al Mason's pencilwork, as an example, is worthy of framing and would never disgrace an office wall.

Unfortunately, naval architects' drawings will soon become collectors' items, as strange and rare as hieroglyphics and pictograms.

What are we in fact looking at when we see a good-looking boat? Let's break it down to specific elements.

Sheer. Francis S. Kinney, in his well-read book *Skene's Elements of Yacht Design,* says, "Perhaps the one single line that crowns or damns the whole creation is the sheerline." This is the line of the top of the hull from bow to stern; often it traces the point where the deck meets the hull topsides. In the 1980s, sailboat sheerlines were flattened considerably to increase belowdeck accommodations, and thus disguise a high freeboard (the distance between waterline and deck). However, high freeboard does not necessarily result in a dryer

1 Anytime can be naptime on an ocean cruise, and there is no finer place to get horizontal than a furled sail on the bow.

The naval architect's basic drawings include a sail plan or outboard profile, general arrangement or floor plan, and lines drawings including the hull sections, waterlines, buttocks, and diagonals. Chuck Paine's handsome drawings of the Morris 36 show that there is more to producing quality blueprints than just drafting ability.

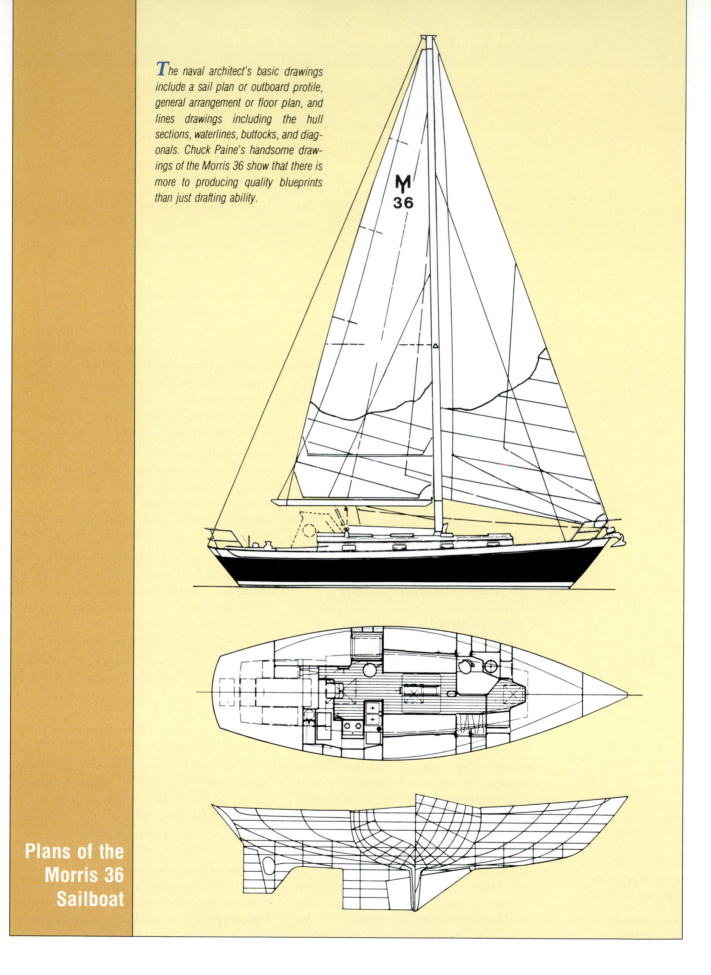

Plans of the Morris 36 Sailboat

1

2

3

1 *Magic Dragon* was designed and built by Michel de Ridder for long-range cruising; reverse sheer in a small boat adds interior volume and may enable standing headroom without a trunk cabin.

2 The lovely sweeping sheer of the 120-foot *Harbinger* is a classic interpretation that starts high at the bow, reaches its low point at about two-thirds of the distance aft, then "springs" up a bit at the stern.

3 Sheerlines, while seldom straight, can generally be described as flat, reverse, or sweeping (i.e., springy). *Rangga* is a modern 73-foot French schooner engaged in the Caribbean charter trade. Her nearly flat sheer increases space below and gives the boat a clean, fast look.

boat, since there is a hollow in the water amidships between the bow and stern waves.

Sheerlines tend to reflect the thinking surrounding major boat types—displacement power cruiser, sailboat racer, and so forth. Planing powerboats, for example, whose speeds are not restricted by known formulas of wavemaking resistance, may depart from convention with steps in the sheer, or reverse sheer, and dipped bows so that they almost look like cats ready to pounce. Designer Tom Fexas popularized this latter styling element with the S-sheer of his Midnight Lace series (even though he says the design doesn't really have S-sheer), and it has been much copied since. The "droop snoot" works because he integrates other lines with it—a sloping cabin face and a pronounced concave stem that reaches out over the water nearly like a breaking wave. Plus, he lifts the sheer at the stern slightly to help balance the ends, hence the S-shape. On high-performance sportboat designs with reverse sheer, the chines rise up to balance the drooping bow, and the strakes and accent stripes on the chine combine to produce a very pleasing convergence of lines.

In other types, such as small cruisers where space must be maximized, the sheer is manipulated for function rather than pure looks. Reverse, "banana," or "hogged" sheer, for example, is not an uncommon solution to the demand for increased accommodation in a hull of short waterline. It is a familiar sight on many small and midsize powerboats, though still rare on sailboats, where to many eyes it looks bizarre and has no basis in seakeeping ability.

Naval architect Ted Brewer is critical of sheerlines drawn from the arc of a circle. Maximum curvature amidships or forward of amidships may seem more symmetrical, but the line just doesn't look good. "In any case," Brewer says, "the circle is a monotonous and unimaginative line best restricted to life rings and portlights."

The sheerline is complemented by toerails, bulwarks, cove stripes, and bootstripes. Toerails should be deeper and taller at the bow than at the stern to be compatible with the typical proportions of high bows and low sterns, and boots normally echo the sheer, perhaps tapering as they move aft. Cove stripes

often appear better if they are flatter than the sheer.

Cabins and windows. After the sheerline, the look of the house, cabin, or superstructure grabs the eye. Foremost, it should be in harmony with the sheer. Often the line of the cabintop or coach roof is nearly straight, only faintly mimicking the sheer. Or the roofline may be drawn more parallel to the waterline, so that the two give a frame of reference for the sheer and set it off. Brewer says that sailboat rooflines should point toward the bow. This works with many modern yachts, both power and sail, in which a low-profile house slants dramatically forward into the bow, creating a sleek look and suggesting subliminally that the boat is so fast that wind resistance must be reduced.

If you think of the house or cabin as a rectangular box laid on top of the deck, the sides and ends of the house play key roles in the overall appearance of the boat. The trick is to keep it from looking boxy and incongruous, squatting on the visual center of the hull so that the ends of the boat seem to be bending up from the sheer weight of it. Should the ends be straight or slanted? How much? The answer of course depends on the style with which the designer is working. Vertical cabin faces look slow, stately, traditional. A swept-back cabin face looks fast, aerodynamically tested in a wind tunnel, modern.

As a rule, the house sides should never be absolutely perpendicular to the waterline, but slant slightly inward at the top—"tumblehome" it is called. Kinney says, "It is a subtlety of design that takes the curse off a boxlike house." (Painting the house a light, contrasting color also helps lower the apparent height of high sides.) Angles up to 15 degrees and sometimes more are acceptable, despite the vulnerability to rainwater. The higher the superstructure the more it should taper; Fexas has described the pilothouse on one of his powerboat designs as "a segment of a tapered cone." Perhaps no other error betrays the poor amateur effort so decisively as a house built with sides that appear to lean outboard.

Windows and portlight shapes are critical and must be selected with the proportions of

*T*he S-sheer has aesthetic as well as practical value. I've had it in my head since I was a kid. Remember the Lockheed Electra? It had a fuselage like that. The S-sheer, to me, is more interesting than a sweeping, hogged, or banana sheer.

It works especially well on boats with low freeboard, because it increases visibility and reduces windage. And it's a way to make a graceful transition from high freeboard forward to low freeboard aft without the use of a step. There should be a little spring at the stern . . . for purely aesthetic reasons. The spring finishes the line, whereas a line parallel to the waterline at the transom seems chopped off, incomplete.

People think the Midnight Lace has an S-sheer, but it really doesn't. The sheer never reverses; actually it's parallel to the waterline. On some of my boats the sheer does reverse, on others it doesn't. Whether it drops or flattens out is just a matter of degree, and what works with that particular design.

with Tom Fexas

—*Tom Fexas*
Tom Fexas Yacht Design
Stuart, Florida

Powerboat designer Tom Fexas popularized the S-sheer with his Midnight Lace series. In *The Yacht,* he said, "I set out to create the fastest, meanest, sexiest, most elegant boat possible. There'd be a touch of the 1947 Elco in her, some of the 1930 vintage commuter, and she'd be skinny and efficient with relatively low power. She'd run level and clean at a top speed of thirty-one miles per hour with a pair of one-hundred-and-seventy-five-horsepower diesels in her stern."

The canted cabin sides of *Night Runner* illustrate how tumblehome can be used to minimize the apparent height of superstructures. The custom 42-footer was designed by Robert Perry. Despite her traditional appearance, lightweight cedar and mahogany construction and a fin keel give thoroughly modern performance.

The design of the 120-foot *Antipodean*, styled by Jon Bannenberg and built in Australia by Oceanfast PTY Ltd., forges new territory in yacht styling. The winglike structures, huge round windows, and swept-back bridge make her look like a starship.

must think of the proportions of space one is working with; a large window in a topside with low freeboard will seem odd. Styling aside, the size of glass panes is dictated as much or more by safety considerations.

Custom powerboat side window shapes are a function of cabin design—hardly ever round and seldom entirely square—as well as sources of light. They may be trapezoidal, with hard or radiused corners, and may follow the adjacent lines of the cabin roofline and ends. On sport-fishermen and motoryachts you frequently see the effective use of slants and elliptical shapes, updated from the windows of early power-boats such as a Whiticar or Huckins, but more conservatively proportioned. A well-handled curve in the windows can effectively balance and harmonize with similar curves in the cabin coamings.

the house and hull in mind. What works on one boat won't necessarily work on another. Small, round, bronze opening portlights on a sailboat have a traditional, no-nonsense look, whereas the enormous, fixed circular windows on Jon Bannenberg's Oceanfast series of Australian-built megayachts seem bold, daring, up-to-the-minute, helped in part by a narrow, vertical bar that divides each "globe" into two "hemispheres." In the world of design, old concepts are continually being revived with a new twist, and suddenly an old-fashioned shape or color is chic, *au courant*.

For sailboats, Ted Brewer likes oval or rectangular portlights with a three-to-one length-to-height ratio. This is of course traditional thinking, but nevertheless the right treatment for traditional boats. But remember that "traditional" is merely a preconceived assemblage of characteristics with arbitrary boundaries. Designers are continually updating old notions, and if the change is subtle we are still apt to call it "traditional." But vary from it too far and it won't be traditional anymore—pretty perhaps, but something other than traditional. Even if a lot of people think it still is.

Windows or portlights placed in the topsides should be kept small and can sometimes be hidden by a connecting paint stripe. One

Ends. To complete the picture of the yacht in profile view, we lastly consider the ends. Our eyes are led fore and aft to the bow and stern lines where the sheer and waterlines terminate. Numerous styles have evolved over the years, some for what was thought at the time to be safest in big seas, some for beauty, others for speed.

Sailboat sterns range from flat and radiused transoms to canoe, counter, reverse, and wine-glass-shaped transoms. There are advantages and disadvantages to each, obviously; however, a few generalizations can be made. Canoe and double-ended sterns are typically slower because the buttock lines are elevated, thus causing increased water resistance. But they excite the eye weary of conventional counter sterns and the increasingly faddish reverse counter, which plays on the racing theme of reducing weight in the stern of the boat to minimize pitching motion. An unintentional bonus of the reverse counter, however, has been the integration of molded boarding steps, ladders, swim platforms, and under-the-cockpit sailboard and dinghy stowage compartments. Not only are these utilitarian, but they also represent a quantum leap in safety, as retrieving a man overboard is much easier at water level than anywhere along the beam of a boat with high freeboard.

Raked and long counter sterns have fallen into disfavor simply because they reduce waterline length, to the direct detriment of speed and interior accommodation space. Yet generous overhangs, which produce what some designers call a feminine style, provide reserve buoyancy and increase waterline length when heeled. Just wait: In another 20 years someone will reintroduce the long counter and call it a remarkable innovation!

Unless there is an inviolable design imperative such as maximum speed or interior volume, each transom style has its rightful place in yacht design; the key is selecting one that fits the rest of the boat. And this is usually part of the designer's mental picture before he draws even the first line.

Planing and semidisplacement powerboat bows and sterns are another matter altogether. Because these powerboats normally travel at higher speeds (20 knots plus), their bows tend to be fine at the stem, and higher and flared at the decks to deflect water.

It is no secret that broad transoms with flat hull sections aft tend to suppress and lengthen the quarter wave, thereby making them faster than double-enders. By pulling the transom out of the water, fuel savings are achieved as well. This is why round transom shapes are seldom seen on anything except slow, displacement-type hulls, although there are some exceptions, such as the semidisplacement torpedo-shaped transoms of some 1920s power cruisers, which were relatively fast. Interestingly, some designers are beginning to pare away the stern quarters and are elevating the buttocks of sportfishermen to help them back down more quickly—a vital quality when a big fish is running with the line.

1

2

3

1 The concave bow of *P'zzaz* essentially follows the curve of the flare in the topsides. Besides helping to keep the decks dry, a concave bow gives a bold, eager look. The 126-foot yacht was built of fiberglass by Delta Marine.

2 Power and motoryacht bows may be roughly classified in three types: plumb bow, raked, and concave. The plumb stem of this classic motorboat cuts a fine bow wave.

3 The lapstraked planks of this wooden powerboat rise to meet the stem, which is only slightly raked.

Style is as much the balance of the whole boat as it is any one line. And the balance is in the art of doing it. Don't try to mystify it, because there's very little mystery to most boat design. If there is any it's probably in the profile styling.

Profiles are crazy. You could make up a list of ten items and give them to five different designers and come out with boats that didn't look even remotely the same. Sheer and styling is more a function of whom you go to than it is any single element of the boat. If I do a dinner cruise boat I might copy a 1920s-looking steamer; I do research like anybody else and do something that makes strong references to that design. But there is no definitive anything when it comes to styling. Things evolve from boats you've done before, things that work and funnel back in, things that don't work and get thrown out. The marketplace perceives what fast boats should look like and what slow boats should look like. It wouldn't make any sense to make a trawler type of boat that looks like For Your Eyes Only. It's the old form-and-function argument.

There are all kinds of ways of coming up with magic numbers but I don't see many of them as working very successfully. Still, there are a few basic rules of thumb. For example, as you stack decks, the forward cabin or windshield angle should rake farther aft as you go up. If you make things dead parallel they tend to look like they're not. And so as each successive angle goes up, you might change it just half a degree, but it needs that half a degree to keep it from looking cattywampus. The principle is the same as positioning sailboat masts: If you take spars and put them up parallel to each other they'll always look like they're falling together or falling apart. You normally increase the rake of each spar moving aft.

Powerboats tend to be so full forward that they need, by my eye, a lot more spring at the bow than they're sometimes given. Because what will happen is they'll look great in the drawing, but when you see them in three dimensions they'll look like they're diving. And that's one mistake—the diving of the bow—because the deck is so broad, wrapping in so tight. I suppose if you got right down to the angle that the drawing was drawn from—right at the waterline or two feet off the waterline—and squinted your eye it might look fine. But from any other angle the thing is disturbing.

Designers of high-speed, high-flash boats seem to be saying, "I don't know how to do it better, but I sure as hell know how to make it different." There's nothing necessarily wrong with that, but I don't think it represents anything other than what it is. You drive downtown and see some office buildings you like and some that are just weird. You have to get attention and that's probably what they're intended to do. When a Donald Trump buys a boat, he damn well wants attention with it. To try to analyze those into some statement of design I think is kind of like analyzing poetry for the novice; in one sense you trivialize something that's important and in another sense you make something important out of trivia.

—Charles Neville
Charles Neville Associates
Palm Harbor, Florida

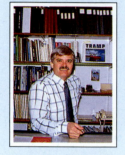

with Charles Neville

1 The bows of the fleet docked at a Lake Travis, Texas marina— each just a little different from the next—illustrate the free hands of their designers searching for the perfect line.

2

3

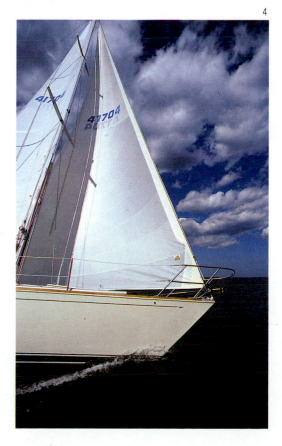

4

2 The charter schooner *Bill of Rights* has a traditional clipper bow with decorative trailboards.

3 Sailboat bow styles have nearly infinite variety. Three common ones are the spoon bow, raked bow, and clipper bow. This spoon bow has a high "chin," meaning that the fullest point of the curve is above the midpoint.

4 The Sabre 36's raked bow is a contemporary interpretation— no nonsense, no unnecessary lines.

1 *Kokkola* is a Baltic 51 designed by Cuthbertson & Cassian with a reverse counter to reduce hobbyhorsing by removing weight from the end of the boat.

2 *Aardvark*'s canoe stern evolved from a North Sea workboat design that favors a narrow, V-shaped transom to offer as small a target as possible to breaking following seas.

3 The reverse counters of IOR racers docked in Nassau, Grand Bahama after the 1986 Nassau Race of the annual Southern Ocean Racing Circuit, illustrate the variety possible within a given form.

4 The Hinckley Bermuda 40 *Diola* has a small vertical counter that wears well with time; indeed, this particular model has been built for more than 25 years, longer than any other production auxiliary.

5 *Alycone*'s heart-shaped transom is crowned by a substantial bulwark that doubles as the cockpit coaming at the stern. Without the varnished caprail and rubbing strake, this one might look rather plain. The schooner's builder is Prothero.

TRADITIONAL HULL STYLING

Despite the dwindling number of wooden boats built during the so-called Golden Age of yachting—about 1890 to 1930—some wonderful examples survive. There were also many good boats built during the Depression, when, as some students of yachting history believe, apprentices were let go and most yards retained only their journeyman carpenters. Plentiful supplies of seasoned wood also disappeared during the dark days of World War II, which essentially spelled the end of what we shall arbitrarily call the traditional style. For it was not long after the war that the postmodernism of the 1950s dramatically changed the way things looked: Buildings were plainly constructed of steel and glass, furniture was lean and sculpted, cars and runabouts grew fins.

In the world of yacht design, especially sail, the wheels of progress sometimes turn slowly, so that even in the 1980s there is what industry gadfly Garry Hoyt calls "an absurd devotion to the past." Though in decline, many elements of traditional yacht style persist. Of course more than one style is embodied in the term "traditional", but we shall examine only the most obvious and influential.

One interpretation of the classic sailboat sheerline begins high at the bow, to keep water off the deck, and initially runs aft in an almost straight line. Its curvature increases as it moves farther aft, reaching a low point about two-thirds of the deck length aft of the bow. There it turns up more dramatically before terminating at the stern. Francis Kinney says its theoretical projection beyond the stern should result in a ram's horn. Philip Rhodes drew this sort of sheerline well, as evidenced by his Bounty and Vanguard designs.

Classic sailboat bow styles include plumb, spoon, and clipper, and there are variations on each. Again, the arc of a circle never seems to look as good as when the maximum radius is placed above or below the center of the line. Clipper bows are best reserved for yachts in which the traditional aesthetic has been observed throughout the design. Bowsprits and trailboards are usually part of the package. Fine ends, sometimes tapering nearly to a point, are still admired for their delicacy and grace.

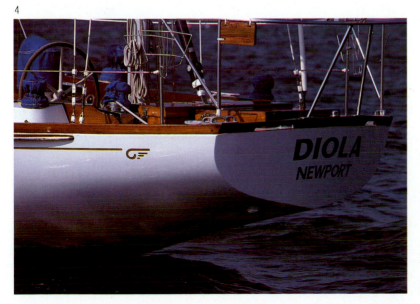

5

4

1 The square transom of *Felicidad*, a 94-foot Broward yacht fisherman with baitwell, fighting chair, and rod holders, delivers maximum space and performance.

2 Powerboat and motoryacht transoms vary mostly according to whether they belong to displacement, semidisplacement, or planing hulls. *Red Witch*, whose home port is near the birthplace of Chris-Craft, shows a fair amount of tumblehome in her topsides at the flat transom.

3 *Aphrodite*'s elegant torpedo transom doesn't provide much lift; hence light weight and narrow beam are necessary to get her moving fast—and she does.

4 *Adler*'s transom design is partly a function of her KaMeWa waterjet drives, though the top sections curve inboard and the quarters are radiused for a softer, molded appearance.

5 The fantail transom of *Kiyi*, a 1926 50-foot Leigh Coolidge cruiser built of Port Orford cedar, is a gracious style statement of the Roaring Twenties.

1

2

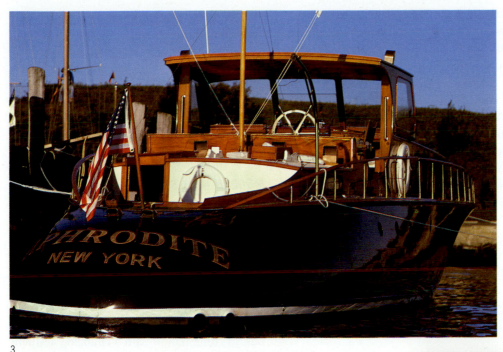

3

5

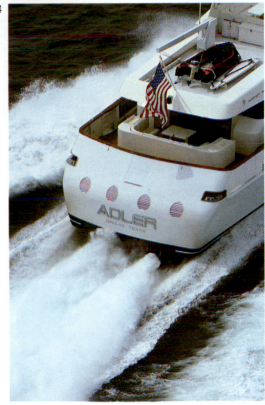

4

Traditional styling of both powerboats and sailboats often incorporates vertical house ends. On sailboats, these were generally limited to low-profile houses. But on early power cruisers such as Elcos, Consolidateds, and Dawns, both the cabin and wheelhouse ends were often not only vertical but quite tall. Plumb bows made for consistency if nothing else. Of course there was no pretense of breaking the sound barrier in 1924, and the design was practical. Ninety-degree vertical wheelhouse windows kept rain off—especially with the roof extended like a cap bill or visor—and meant that the designer didn't have to juggle awkward space inside. There wasn't a lot of reserve buoyancy in the plumb bows, nor was there as much flare at the deck, but then most of these commuter types were designed to operate in well-behaved coastal waters.

Arro, berthed at the Lake Union Wooden Boat Festival in Washington, has a traditional plumb bow and vertically faced wheelhouse—stately and sedate. This style works well for displacement cruisers.

A good deal of what we consider traditional styling owes its character to the chosen material of the day—wood. Maine boatbuilder Peter Chase complains that "fiberglass has eliminated the hard line." This is an interesting point indeed. Corners molded of fiberglass are necessarily rounded and cannot achieve the fine, crisp edge of two planks joined and planed. Hardwood does not like to be bent much, as it invariably loses strength, which explains why naturally shaped tree trunks were preferred to steam-bent frames. Beyond the shaping required of hull planking, the house and deck structures show a lot of hard, clean lines with only minimal shaping. And there was much opportunity for the skilled craftsman to sharpen his chisels and planes, taking extreme pride in a flawless cove or a tight scarf.

MODERN HULL STYLING

Despite the statements above, "modern" need not exclude wood. Indeed, cold-molded construction techniques using thin wood veneers bent over molds and stabilized with glue or epoxy can produce some lovely compound shapes. Even with fiberglass, laminated construction is the rule today. Nevertheless, the requirements of modern materials and methods, in combination with a changing aesthetic rapidly evolving from the scientific study of hydrodynamics and aerodynamics, has resulted in the more fluid styling of boats, airplanes, and automobiles. Again, we'll look at the essential elements.

The modern trend in sailboat design is toward flatter sheers, but because the ends are farther away from the eye of the observer and have a tendency to appear dipped (like railroad tracks disappearing in the distance, parallel lines seem to converge), some curvature in the sheer must be retained even if the intention is to make it look straight.

The contemporary sailboat bow is straight with a short overhang and a slight rake. It is the most practical when one is forced to accept a long waterline, and it is comparatively easy for the designer to "get right."

Cabintop heights have shrunk, often becoming camouflaged in nearly flush decks; Nautor, of Finland, was instrumental in developing this type through its Swan line of performance sailboats. On smaller boats this means raising freeboard to provide adequate headroom. This is because contemporary, flat-bottomed boats with fin keels don't have as much interior space below the waterline as earlier full-keel designs.

Keeping pace with lower cabintops has been the trend to eliminate windows and portlights, which are all too often small and

**with
Robert
Perry**

In the early 1970s there was Southern California Gothic, which I attribute to Hank McCormick, the marketing director of Islander Yachts. It was typified by crushed-velvet cushion covers, rattan locker fronts, paneled settee faces, and fluting on the fiddles. It sent yacht interiors on the way to becoming condos.

The Taiwan style was perfected by Bob Berg: drawers inside drawers inside drawers, corner moldings on corner moldings, odd-shaped shelves for macraméed whiskey bottles, teak-paneled bulkheads and butcher-block countertops. Wood everywhere ad nauseum. A lot of people thought that was the way a traditional interior was supposed to look, never knowing there never was an interior like that! The Taiwan style was a caricature of implied tradition.

You could call the minimalist approach of the Express, Olson, and Bill Lee boats Santa Cruz Clean. I like varnished Bruynzeel ply. They're

doing the most with the least, the idea of less is more, mostly because of the pressure to reduce weight.

The traditional painted-ply, varnished mahogany trim interior I call the Stalwart Capsule style because, like the "boy's cabin in the woods," it's a self-contained, self-sufficient pod in the universe. The ax and snowshoes are stacked by the door, the fire flickers, and there are special little bins for your binoculars and Chap Stick.

The East Coast production boats have no style. To borrow a line from Bob Dylan, "I don't call it anything." Other designers call it IMS [Ed: International Measurement System]! Everything is IMS today. I wish I could think of something funny that IMS stands for, but I'm not Neil Diamond and I can't just decide to be profound on Thursdays.

—*Robert Perry*
Robert H. Perry Yacht Designers
Seattle, Washington

fixed. "Eurostyle," which France began exporting to American sailors in the early 1980s, is typified by smoked Plexiglas or Lexan windows that wrap around the sides and forward end of the cabin. Eliminating conventional frames achieves a cost saving and rids the superstructure of small, boxy shapes that disturb the new, flat, flowing lines of the deck and cabin. Designers can hide window cutouts of just about any shape behind the dark glass. Beneteau has gone a step further with tall, narrow, fixed windows aft. Ultimately, window shape is limited only by geometry.

Considerable experimentation in recent years has produced ultramodern motoryachts with styling unthought of a decade ago. Large, high-speed "runabouts," such as Bannenberg's Oceanfast series, are prime examples. These feature winglike fins and huge, round windows, flush decks forward, stacked and semi-stacked cabins, and semidisplacement-cum-planing hull forms for 30- to 50-knot speeds. One outgrowth of this movement that seems unbound by any obvious tradition is the use of reverse transoms, perhaps with steps leading down from the fantail to a swimming platform.

Powerboat stems today are generally raked forward, either straight or more often with a concave curve. Not only does this give some pleasing shape to the profile, but (as in clipper-bowed sailboats) it provides for a more practical anchoring platform, including bow roller.

Powerboat cabin faces are typically swept back, which is in keeping with the trend toward starship shapes fostered by sci-fi comics, television and, to a lesser degree, the actual lines of rockets and space shuttles. They *do* look cool. Unfortunately, when transferred to boats, such radically raked lines create large, relatively useless spaces forward of the inside steering station (which has all but disappeared from the modern sportfisherman, along with forward-facing windows)—not a very efficient or practical use of space, but it seems a necessary consequence of aerodynamic styling.

On some commercial fishing boats and North Sea–type trawlers such as the Fisher line of motorsailers, the opposite treatment results in cabin faces that slant aft as they move down. This keeps the windshield out of the helmsman's face and provides needed space for mounting overhead instruments. The offshore fisherman naturally cares more about function and less about visual effect than most other boat owners.

TRIM AND ACCESSORIES

The exterior appearance of a yacht is more than black-and-white profile, for it is seldom viewed in just that perspective. Just as the designer may rotate the hull lines with a computer to gauge its fairness and attractiveness in three dimensions, the casual observer of a yacht sees it from many angles—from bow and stern as he cruises past in admiration, and from above when walking down a dock. He sees not only the principal lines drawn by the architect, but myriad other details—canvaswork, colored graphics, window tints, handrails, flagstaffs, antenna arches, outriggers, tuna towers, horns, windlasses, cleats, lifelines, and various bits of wood whose strategic placement about the cabin and deck may be either functional or purely artistic. While the designer cannot be held responsible for what an owner adds to his boat after delivery, the designer *is* responsible for basic decoration.

Wood. It seems that no boat, whether constructed of steel or fiberglass, is complete without at least a certain amount of wood trim. These accents are typically found in the form of handholds, coaming tops, and winch pads, where wood is as practical a material as any and as a bonus enhances the overall appearance. It does require maintenance, however, and the trend today is toward less wood and more metal and plastic.

While functional wooden parts such as handrails can serve double duty as accents, contrasting the rather austere look of fiberglass, aluminum, and steel, occasionally it is nice to use wood for purely decorative purposes. Good examples are eyebrows (half-round moldings fixed to the top of the cabin sides), wood-trimmed hatches, toerails, and hardware pads. Other materials could be substituted or the accent eliminated altogether, but few people would disagree that a little wood on deck looks good.

Metal. The modern theme in yacht design has supplanted wood with metal in many instances. Handholds fashioned from stainless steel pipe lend luster and a chromatic feel that is more compatible with sleek, high-performance styling. The same is true of stainless steel flybridge ladders, steering wheels, and rubrail guards. Toerails may be anodized aluminum, and cleats, chromed bronze castings. Few production sailboats are delivered today with wooden spars (a few Taiwan cruisers may be the exception); aluminum is the universal choice. Even trawler and motoryacht masts are made of aluminum, despite minimal load requirements.

A few boatbuilders still fabricate original metal fittings for the boats they build. The best-known American builder of small sailboats is perhaps the Henry R. Hinckley Company, which prides itself in the custom casting and welding of stemhead fittings, stanchions, cleats, and other deck hardware. A custom bow roller that has been distinctively designed and executed from quality metals and workmanship can set off the bow in a way that rough-cast, off-the-shelf rollers rarely can.

Metal deck parts are not maintenance free. They won't rot but they do corrode, especially if fastened with bolts or screws of dissimilar metal. Polishing is demanded of exposed metals to the same extent that wood demands oiling or varnishing. Aside from structural considerations, the selection of metal fittings on the hull and deck should be made with a view toward overall appearance—stainless steel handrails would look silly on a vintage Concordia yawl and wooden handrails just as out of place on a brand-new Hatteras sportfisherman.

Plastic and paint. A contemporary trend is the use of molded fiberglass, paint, or tinted Lexan "glazing" wrapped around the cabins or superstructure, partly as accent stripes, partly to break up the space, and partly to hide ordinary windows that would destroy the futuristic look of the yacht. The large forward-facing windows of sportfishermen, now admitted as being vulnerable to breaking seas, have been replaced with painted fiberglass or tinted

Lexan so that they retain the appearance of windows without the potential liabilities.

Miscellaneous gear. Various optional deck gear can alter the look of a yacht dramatically. For instance, carrying a small Boston Whaler on the flush foredeck of a large sport-fisherman may be practical, but it certainly disturbs its clean and powerful lines. Similarly, it is easy to "junk" up a deck with mast pulpits, vents, ground tackle, sailboard hangers, life rafts, and fender holders. An uncluttered deck looks best and poses fewer hazards to the working crewman. Clever designers are finding ways to stow even large objects such as dinghies, sailboards, and propane tanks in specially designed lockers under the cockpit, the coaming backrests, and the deck. Cockpit arches provide handy, out-of-the-way platforms to consolidate antennas, wind generators, and other items that otherwise are strewn about the cockpit and superstructure, making them bristle like a military base. The payoff is a clean, uncluttered-looking boat that draws the observer's eye to its essential lines.

INTERIOR STYLING

There was a time when brocade, bas-relief, and captain's lace were de rigueur in a yacht's interior. In the 1950s there was a trend away from these ornate trappings and toward the simple decoration in residential and commercial architecture and interior design, as well as in yachts. Rosewood inlays were out, one-wood surfaces were in; heavy weaves and highly patterned fabrics were less fashionable than light open patterns and solid-colored fabrics; dull colors were less exciting than bright primary and pastel colors; and easy-to-clean vinyl and plastic surfaces were preferred to less practical materials such as leather and shag carpeting. Baroque was broke. Easy maintenance, easy on the eye, easy on the pocketbook—those were the operative phrases of the 1950s.

Ludwig Mies van der Rohe summarized the style of this period with his line, "Less is more."

But a few decades later, designer Robert Venturi announced a new direction with the words, "Less is a bore." Decorative detail was back, but with new colors, new materials, and a new sense of purpose.

MAJOR DECORATIVE THEMES

Thankfully, there is more than one way to decorate a yacht's interior, though you might be hard-pressed to distinguish them at a boat show. The more space, the more options—which explains why Donald Trump can spend millions of dollars refurbishing a 235-foot megayacht. When working on such a grand scale, it is possible to incorporate a number of different schemes—perhaps changing them by deck levels, or between living areas and sleeping areas, guest quarters and crew quarters, indoor activity areas and outdoor pools and lounges—without having one clash with another. On the smaller yacht, say under 60 feet, it is generally wise to stick with one scheme throughout, presenting it with as much variety and personal taste as possible, using solid design principles in selecting the materials available.

Non-style. Decorative schemes are somewhat restricted on modern fiberglass production boats because of the extensive use of fiberglass inner liners and foundations. Builders, often working without professional design assistance, attempt to establish a certain look by manipulating a few basic elements: seat-cushion materials, cabinet doors and drawer facings, hull and overhead liners, cabin sole finishes, fixtures such as lights, and accessories such as handles and drawer pulls. One builder may choose a heavy textured woven upholstery, teak cabinet doors, vinyl hull liners, and carpeting over a fiberglass sole. The effect is warm, but the juggling of many textiles may tip the balance of texture and color out of control. To play it safe, the scheme is very monochromatic or neutral. Another builder might elect to use lightweight, cotton-duck cushion fabric in a dark primary color such as blue, caning in cabinet doors, ash ceiling on hull sides, and teak and holly veneer over plywood on the floorboards. Here the result is a light and cool feeling, more suitable to warm-weather climates. The effects of the two schemes are quite different, and neither is the height of fashion. While they won't be featured in glossy magazine centerfolds, they won't offend very many "average" buyers either. Whatever works, whatever is on hand: Call it safe or sterile, but any style it may possess is probably accidental.

Accommodation plans are pretty much those that have proven successful in the marketplace. Big head compartments, tiny or no navigation stations, V-berths forward, convertible dinette tables, under-the-cockpit berths. The more the better. Call it the "rabbit warren" syndrome.

Modern. Production French builders have pioneered the use of tinted Lexan wraparound portlights to filter sunlight, soft clothing stowage pockets in the V-berths to save weight and space, and vinyl-coated wire baskets in the galley to save weight and assembly time as well as to provide ventilation. These are representa-

tive of the minimalist approach—light, spare, and modern.

In modern styling, wood is out and synthetics are in. Dark is old, light is new. Dull surfaces are drab, shiny polished surfaces are alive. There are mirrors to create the illusion of more space. Padded wraparound Formula-type seats covered in synthetic suede or leather. Padded dashboards. Padded overheads. Color-coordinated staterooms. Plastic tables. Levolor mini-blinds. Seating "islands." Molded laminations of wood veneers to shape doorways and companionway stairs. Berths are few though large. Engineering and sea sense often play second fiddle to design.

The Italian designers understand this trend better than anyone else, it seems. Where the French sensibility is stunted by an impoverished socialist economic system, the Italians embrace their reputation as romantics by manifesting it in sexy sportscars and sleek yachts. Even if they cannot themselves afford such luxury, at least they have helped create such elegant objects for the gratification of others. Who

1

44

2

3

1 The black-and-white color scheme of *Miss Marty*'s saloon is accented by a blue glass etching of the Statue of Liberty and the yacht's profile. Custom contemporary artworks are a fancy of megayacht interior stylists.

2 Modern racing sailboats such as O. H. Rodger's winged Kiwi 35 favor spartan, lightweight interiors.

3 Wellcraft Marine, a leader in powerboat design, usually changes its interior designs with each model year. The 1988 Portofino galley has black-and-white cupboard facings, turquoise padding at the counter, and Lucite fiddles. The 43-foot Portofino might be called a cruising sportboat. She's capable of fast planing speeds with twin 375-horse-power diesel engines.

cares if the damn thing doesn't run! At least it has violated some silly old rules, smashed a few icons. Look at a Ferrari sportscar or Berlinetti motoryacht and you see new territory being explored.

Traditional. Traditional means old, conventional, and accepted. In boats it may mean different styles to different people, but above all it means wood. Mahogany, teak, oak, spruce, cherry, and holly. Preferably hand-rubbed with oil or satin varnish. The early Chris-Crafts are excellent examples of the popularity of red-stained mahogany that is clear varnished for maximum luster.

The British have long had an affinity for oak, a durable hardwood that is perhaps better suited to the heavy structural members of a wooden boat than to interior or exterior trim. But this is not surprising when you consider that much of that country's engineering excellence ceased to develop after World War II. Consider the MG sportscar, the Triumph motorcycle, the British Seagull outboard, and the bilge keel Vivacity sailboat: old designs, slow and small, and parts fitted with sloppy tolerance. Austerity and stodginess is, sadly, a part of their national psyche, and they are too

accepting of it. "Mad dogs and Englishmen go out in the midday sun."

Maine traditional is one of the most pleasing. Light wood ceilings, white-painted bulkheads, and varnished mahogany trim. A cabin so constructed and finished is bright yet strong-looking and balanced. It is practical in terms of ventilation and maintenance, and easy to take apart and modify.

Some of the schlockiest interiors are the all-teak jobs perpetrated by the eager-though-naive Taiwanese boatbuilders of the 1960s and 1970s. Cheap Burmese and Thai teak was plentiful, and it was hacked and hammered into every corner, with and without off-color fillers to hide sloppy joinerwork. Everything was made of teak: soles, tables, cabinets, ceilings, doors, hatches—you name it. And the pièce de résistance was the ubiquitous Chinese dragon bas-relief carved into the toilet room door. Sometimes it was a pagoda or poppy flower, but it was nevertheless held in high esteem by foreign owners. Americans couldn't buy these pirated designs of bow-down trawlers and "leaky-teaky" ketches fast enough. As P.T. Barnum said, "No one ever went broke underestimating the taste of the American public."

Traditional is conservative: Four berths in any boat between 20 and 40 feet, workable galley, quiet colors, strong, practical materials, polished hardware. Arrangements are straightforward: V-berths forward, settees in the main cabin, narrow passageways to provide frequent handholds when rolling, sinks on centerline. They are tried-and-true features but rarely exciting.

Custom. To fully appreciate the thought and work behind a custom yacht interior, it is useful to examine the extreme end of the scale. In today's jargon it's called a megayacht. Megayachts are giant and extraordinarily lavish, and cost millions of dollars, pounds, francs, rubles, yen—whatever currency you're counting. It is astonishing to read the brokerage pages of an international yachting publication and discover that there are a lot of these incredible vessels, many of which are only occasionally used by their owners. But that is changing,

Everything about *Dorade*'s interior seems traditional, from her pilot berths to the varnished mahogany bulkheads and cork sole. She is one of Sparkman & Stephens's most famous designs.

and satellite communications have helped by allowing businesspeople to keep in constant touch with shoreside associates. It is the royal oilman, the real estate tycoon, and the Greek shipping magnate we are talking about; after all, you don't pay for a megayacht with a job laying bricks or teaching comparative literature.

The interior of a megayacht must be considered on the same scale as a mansion on land, but with one obvious difference: The yacht's principal dimensions are by necessity long and narrow to facilitate movement through the water. On such a linear structure the tendency, designer Jon Bannenberg complains, is to run a corridor down the center, thereby halving all the space. To gain more freedom he likes to offset the corridors to one side or the other, as on Malcolm Forbes's *Highlander*. Traffic patterns are then dictated by furniture and cabins rather than straight hallways with a lot of boring doors.

Another well-known interior designer, Frenchman Pierre Tanter, lists these important guidelines: proportion, color, lighting, details, and comfort. Thought must be given to the size and height of each cabin; heavy colors must be avoided, lighting balanced, the owner's personal effects incorporated naturally, and comfort achieved without spoiling other elements.

Other designers speak to the whimsy of their clients when they refer to "quality of life," "joy of entertainment," and "earned lifestyle." With some commissions the designer is given a blank check and a free hand (hence his patronizing flattery); other times he must work around given parameters on a fixed budget. In either case, there is no doubt that such a designer considers him or herself an artist, if not in the strict sense of creating a single imaginative work, at least in the sense of selecting and arranging a wide array of furniture, fixtures, fabrics, and objets d'art that work together. Harmony is the operative word.

Thus the styling of a megayacht is highly individualistic, and is telling not only of the designer's talent and predelictions but of the owner's as well. In a world where furniture disappears at the touch of a button, fountains burble forth with champagne, special lights focus on priceless paintings, and king-size beds revolve to follow the stars, any fantasy is possible. Woe to the owner and designer whose yacht is too easily labeled by its critics.

Double-O-Seven's contemporary saloon is a good example of placing strategic focal points around a large area. Note the coral formation on the cocktail table and the red dining table chairs.

with Anne Brengle

Most design decisions come down to three basic elements: the use of proven design principles, choices in personal taste, and definition of personal style. Design principles can be researched. Taste is easy—either you like it or you don't. But how do you define personal style? And why would you want to do anything so contrived when, after all, we are talking boats here?

Throughout the process of buying or building a boat you are constantly making choices. These choices are driven largely by current trends and up-to-date information filtered through your previous experience, anticipated cruising range, and your intended use for your boat. The business of determining cabin layout, choosing fixtures and finishes, as well as selecting fabric and materials on board need not be based on anything more complicated.

People get into trouble when they buy a "look" without thinking about how it will suit their individual needs and lifestyle afloat. Just as you wouldn't build a breezy tile and stucco tropical interior in a log cabin mountain retreat, you also wouldn't put open bulkheads, acres of white Ultra-Suede, and pastel pillows on a boat you were outfitting for a one-year liveaboard sabbatical with three children, two dogs, and a parakeet. Often we are attached to a look regardless of whether or not it suits us, because it works visually. And, how could

we possibly put what we really want together and have it look great?

Start with the obvious. How are you going to use this boat and where? Make decisions that enhance the boat's purpose. Based on that, choose a decorative theme. If you are at a loss for a decorative theme, don't be afraid to resort to things that are meaningful to you, and build from there.

What about the ceramic tiles you bought because they have a geometric pattern that looks like waves, and a color you like? They would make a nice surrounding for your Shipmate stove. This becomes a focal point, and you build a color scheme from there. In the absence of an existing theme, choose a patterned material with a design and colors you like. Select one or two colors to repeat throughout the interior. Brush up on composition, pattern, and color theory; then you're off to the races.

Oftentimes boats are the product of a partnership with a variety of intended uses. Prudent interior design is the result of negotiation and compromise. However, before you buy a yellow-and-green chintz velour and shag interior for the boat in which you plan to bag a record catch at the Offshore Tuna Tournament, a word to the wise: Get another opinion!

—Anne Brengle
Design & Conservation
New Bedford, Massachusetts

DEVELOPING A THEME

When ordering a custom or semicustom boat, or renovating an old one, it is important to develop a plan before work commences. Materials must be purchased and the various tasks scheduled in the correct sequence. If you are working with a professional interior designer, he or she will no doubt ask you questions about your tastes, how you intend to use your boat, and of course how much you wish to spend. If you are dealing directly with the builder, you have in effect assumed the role of designer. Some builders will fabricate a mockup interior in the shop to test ideas. Not only does this give you a chance to check such critical dimensions as leg room under tables and whether you can reach the dishes while standing at the sink, it also presents an opportunity to check the compatibility of materials and colors next to one another.

If you are doing the work yourself, you have assumed the roles of both designer and builder. Let the two sides talk to each other! You may favor hardwood drawers with dovetailed joints, but how difficult will they be to build? Do you have a router with the right bits and jigs to make clean, tight-fitting joints? Do you have the skill? Do you have the time?

Begin in the saloon or main cabin. After all, this is where you spend most of your time. It is probably the largest space inside the boat and is the center of entertaining, reading, relaxing, and often eating and cooking as well. Do you favor a modern or a traditional look? Or do you prefer to experiment with your own original ideas? How much wood should be visible? What kind?

The art deco saloon of *P'zazz* includes coverings of ostrich hide, pony hair, Italian leather, and faux leopard skin— enough to make you bristle!

Think about textures. Wood grain has a very definite, pleasant tactile quality. Vinyl, Naugahyde, and woven textiles have very different textures. Do you enjoy touching them? Do they stick to your skin in hot weather? Do they feel cold when the thermometer drops? Formica and other laminated plastics, fiberglass, and stainless steel are much harder finishes. Though they are extremely functional in the proper application, such as head compartments and galley counters, they are not as comfortable or interesting to touch. And if you are considering nonmarine materials, such as silk wallpaper, be sure to determine its resistance to fading, mildew, delamination, and cleaning detergents before going ahead. Textured surfaces can make a significant impact on an interior's styling, but they can also hide dirt and make cleaning difficult. Soft materials can be vacuumed, hard materials must be scrubbed. Too much texture can make a cabin feel like a padded cell; too little can make you feel as though you're living inside a refrigerator.

Choose colors carefully. Bright primary colors work well in many materials, but it is important that the color of the wood grains be factored into the overall scheme when those materials are used near unpainted wood surfaces. Some colors may look great on your front door at home, but can you live with a burgundy door to the head? Boat cabins are smaller than the rooms in houses, and a little bit of strong color goes a long way. Quiet, neutral colors are best for large surface areas such as bulkheads and doors, but you can add zest with brightly colored light fixtures, drawer handles, and other small, carefully selected accessories. As a general rule, the more neutral paint or laminate surfaces in a cabin, the more bright color it will take. Woods, because of their organic earthiness, beg for a compatible palette. Develop a scheme that works for you. You might use dark colors in low areas, switching to lighter colors as the eye works upward toward the overhead. Or you might pick one color for all levels and use accents of another color at focal points.

Colors should not only coordinate with the materials and styling inside, but also agree with the overall look of the exterior. A high-performance powerboat would look silly with a varnished wood interior. On a small muscleboat you might opt instead for rolled and pleated seats in a gray neutral color with red or blue as the accent. Roy Sklarin, an interior designer of large, high-speed motoryachts, is known for his stylish and compatible art deco interiors with black and cream as the principal colors. By the same token, a classic wooden yacht would be compromised by a plastic interior with pastel cushions and molded fiberglass sinks. In other words, the concept of a yacht integrates interior styling with the external appearance to produce a harmonious whole.

Similarly, hardware must be selected with the rest of the decor in mind. Stainless steel is unique in that it is neutral and reflective and works well in a variety of styles.

Bronze and brass, because of their color, are not so versatile and should be restricted to interiors where perhaps wood is prominent and the colors are compatible. Steel and aluminum are important structural materials but are seldom used in decoration, as they do not hold paint well without difficult chemical baths, and if left unpainted, appear unfinished and unattractive.

The handsome yacht interior, regardless of size, is the result of successfully integrating a variety of materials, shapes, textures, and colors. Seldom do haphazard choices result in an attractive interior; too often "eclectic" is a lame excuse for poor planning or simply a bad eye.

At the very least, good design requires a sense of style, intelligent thinking, and careful planning.

SUMMARY

Beauty may lie in the eye of the beholder, but the observance of certain rules will surely result in a prettier design. A yacht is in essence a three-dimensional sculpture that must look right from any view, inside and out. The key elements to consider in achieving consistency and harmony are the following:

- sheerline
- house or cabin lines
- windows and portlights
- bow and stern shapes
- design and placement of accessories
- hardware
- materials
- color
- texture
- consistency and harmony of styling elements

Decked Out

ife aboard a boat centers on deck. After all, being outdoors near the water is the reason people take to the lakes and seas of the world. The difference between riding on deck and sitting inside a cabin is comparable with that between riding on a motorcycle and lounging inside a limousine; Robert Pirsig described it in *Zen and the Art of Motorcycle Maintenance* as a wholly different experience:

> *In a car you're always in a compartment, and because you're used to it you don't realize that through that car window everything you see is just more TV. You're a passive observer and it is all moving by you boringly in a frame. On a cycle the frame is gone. You're completely in contact with it all. You're* in *the scene, not just watching it anymore, and the sense of presence is overwhelming.*

As on a motorcycle, you sit on deck and the wind rushes past the yacht cockpit, whistling in your ears and slapping your face like a thousand tiny hands. Looking over the side, you find that the water seems very close, and as the boat leaps and crashes spray flies over the deck. You are aware of certain risks—of falling or getting wet. You are vulnerable. It is exciting. That's why you're in the middle of the Gulf Stream at midnight, en route to Bimini. The stars are out, a pale moon is rising, and the waves break in a phosphorescent clash. To go below now would be unthinkable.

Even if you never go out on the water at night, being out there anytime is a special kind of experience. Perhaps a major outing is simply running across the bay to picnic at a favorite island. Range and conditions don't really matter as long as you're having fun. That is the great thing about boats, about being on deck, for whether your vessel is large or small, slow or fast, you may still feel, as Pirsig calls it, the *overwhelming* sensation of being in full contact with the world you live in.

Positive experiences like these would be much less likely to happen without the knowledge that you are comfortable and safe on deck. The seating is designed to hold and support with every lurch and at any angle of heel. There are good handholds and footholds should it become necessary to leave your seat and move about the deck. And if a thunderstorm breaks loose, there is protection under a canvas dodger or inside a partially or fully enclosed wheelhouse.

The design of the deck and cockpit is critical to enjoyment afloat. Experience counts. What works at the dock may not work underway. The design has to function in a multitude of

1

1 *Dos* is the right number to share *Numero Uno*'s hot tub after a day of marlin fishing near Mexico's Cabo San Lucas. The sexy 85-foot sportfishing yacht is of cold-molded construction, built by the Barattucci Brothers in California.

2 The white foredeck of *Awesome*, a 70-foot speedboat owned by Keith Williams of Hamilton Island, Australia, can be hard to look at on a bright day, but then who drives 50 mph without wearing sunglasses? The blue accent stripe saves the deck from disappearing.

3 Deck color is important in suppressing glare and in the overall color scheme of the hull and deck. Shannon Boat Company uses a traditional beige for the molded nonskid pattern of their full-keel fiberglass sailboats.

4 Rubber pads glued to the deck make for the surest footing, but are abrasive on bare skin. The brown nonskid on this Broward coordinates nicely with the varnished brightwork.

5 Carol Hasse, a sailmaker in Port Townsend, Washington, painted the deck of her pretty Folkboat a distinctive color to set her apart from the rest. It is surprisingly soothing on the eyes.

6 Built by Fife in Scotland, the classic yawl *Cotton Blossom IV* has teak decks to provide superior traction and good looks.

situations and weather—calm, angry, and changeable. The cockpit table that so elegantly performed its duty while anchored for lunch may become a terrible safety hazard at sea; the step in the side decks that was so easily negotiated during daylight could on a dark night trip crewmembers moving forward; and the flush foredeck that seemed so ideal for sunbathing when it was level transforms into a slick slab of tilted ice when the boat rolls. This is why fair-weather boat tests cannot possibly give the potential buyer a whole or exact picture of the vessel he is considering.

Besides safety, deck design has a lot to do with the beauty of a boat. As mentioned in Chapter 1, deck design contributes to overall style. A flush deck has a much different look than a conventional trunk cabin with side decks and foredeck. Let's first consider the form and function of deck design from a bird's-eye view.

COLOR

The first thing you might notice about a deck is its color. It is doubtful that the deck is white, which though cool reflects too much sunlight and is hard on the eyes. Soft shades of blue, gray, green, buff, and beige reduce glare; these subtle colors may cover the entire deck or just the nonskid areas. The color may be painted on, molded in the first layer of a fiberglass laminate, or selected from a color chart of rubber-type products that are glued on with a waterproof adhesive. Laid teak decks are easy on the eyes and provide excellent traction. The selection of deck color and material should be made at the same time as choosing hull colors, superstructure colors, and accents such as boottops, cove stripes, and supergraphics.

If you decide to change the topside color of an existing hull, you may want to change the deck color, too, for compatibility. And because

2

3

nonskid (whether molded-in fiberglass, rubberized pads, or painted on) eventually wears thin, this is a good time to restore traction. Marine paint companies market specially formulated granules to mix with deck paint for improved nonskid; you'll have to remove deck hardware, fill cracks, and carefully tape off the various sections before painting. Rubberized pads affixed with contact cement are more expensive than paint, but the time saved in deck preparation will probably pay for the product. Replacing teak decks is a major job; you can prolong the life of wood decks by avoiding chemical cleaners that eat at the grain. An attractive feature of wood decks is that their color is compatible with just about any hull color.

DESIGN FOR PEOPLE

The second thing you will probably notice about a deck is the amount of open space. Does it look clean and uncluttered, or does it seem strewn with dinghies, tanks, sailboards, and hardware? Will walking forward or aft require dodging objects as though you were running in a steeplechase, or will it seem as easy as strolling a boardwalk?

A deck must be negotiable by people; that is, movement fore and aft should be easy and safe. The side decks must be wide enough for you to walk without stumbling over your own feet. On some sailboats the rigging shrouds are fastened to chainplates in the middle of the side deck, thereby causing a serious obstruction. Even when the chainplates are bolted outboard, the angle of the lower shrouds can cut across the side decks at head height, requiring caution, especially at night. And many motoryachts have such wide cabins that side decks are sacrificed for interior space. Worse, the bowrail terminates too far forward to be of any use to the crew climbing out of the cockpit. Handholds on the side of the cabin are the only concession to safety. Granted, it's not often necessary to go forward on a powerboat except to sunbathe, anchor, or dock, but even in seemingly benign conditions accidents are possible.

1 *Quintus* has a bowsprit with cranse irons, chain pipe, and twin samson posts to tie off lines.

2 *Wahoma*'s horizontal windlass has both a wildcat and drum to handle chain and rope rodes.

3 The boat that anchors out must have provisions for carrying and retrieving anchors and rodes securely and conveniently. The tiny Sand Hen has a functional bow roller to keep the plow anchor from dinging the bow or topsides, and a chain pipe to stow the rode below.

with Jay Benford

On motoryachts with more than one deck we try to create a paint line to give more long horizontal lines to the boat, which helps reduce apparent height. Sculpting for shadow lines helps, too. For example, a thick, molded-rubber fender establishes a working-boat look and creates a strong shadow, which does the same thing as paint. We might also box in a large window area.

The one thing you shouldn't do with a full-width house is have vertical sides—they've got to have tumblehome. This is for aesthetic as well as practical reasons. If the boat is tied to a dock, piling, or another boat and begins to roll—and all boats roll—you don't want the house sides to hit. How much tumblehome depends on the design. The tenderness of the hull is a factor. My designs tend to be stiff, so we get away with less tumblehome. And if

you don't increase tumblehome then you've got to make the fender stick out farther—do something to solve the problem. Generally speaking, the higher you go, the more each successive deck is set in, and the greater the tumblehome. The idea is to keep the cabin from looking tall and boxy, give it some length.

The sheerline and line of the second deck are often parallel, but not in every design. Sometimes the two will be parallel for two-thirds of the boat, but if you break the sheer for a high bow, you can't follow that line on the second deck. It would look like a caricature and make standing in the pilothouse awfully difficult.

*—Jay Benford
Benford Design Group
St. Michaels, Maryland*

The Florida Bay Coaster, designed by Jay Benford, is built in steel in various lengths. She is intended as a versatile, shoal-draft coastal cruiser with luxurious accommodations.

4 Large yachts require powerful windlasses to set and haul large ground tackle. The seat at the front of the cabin is a handy place for crew to wait while the boat swings to—that is, if the owner isn't looking!

The foredeck should be protected by a bowrail, and ground tackle should be placed so that the crew can raise and lower anchors inside this safety net. Often bows are so cluttered with windlasses, cleats, anchor chocks, and vents that it is difficult to find secure footing at the stem to observe the anchor and rode coming aboard.

Clear sunbathing space is always appreciated. And because sunbathers frequently fall asleep, it is wise to plan for the eventuality of an unexpected roll that could dump them overboard. Stanchions and lifelines help, as do bulwarks and handrails. Some sort of seat forward is useful, too, whether for crew waiting for the boat to back down on its anchor or simply as a getaway from a congested cockpit. A cushion is a bonus.

CLEANING AND DRAINAGE

Few designers give sufficient thought to the cleaning and maintenance of the deck. Deck camber or crown not only adds strength and looks, it also sheds water faster than a flat deck. Stanchions set close to toerails and bulwarks are frustrating dirt catchers and knuckle-busters; scrubbing is easier if there's room to swing a brush. Look at the nonskid pattern, too; some catch dirt more readily than others.

And do not forget drainage. Scuppers may be placed at the lowest points on the designer's drawings, but after the boat is loaded with fuel and supplies it is not unusual to find water collecting somewhere else. Be sure that deck fills for water or fuel tanks are not located in these areas. Scuppers and toerail cutouts must also be big enough to move large volumes of water without becoming clogged with debris. Scuppers led to through-deck plumbing eliminate dirty stains on the topsides but add to construction costs.

Drainage of the cockpit is of course most important, because of the tremendous potential weight of water filling it. At sea, the cockpit—especially a large one—is without a doubt most boats' Achilles' heel. Calculate the potential weight of a boarding sea by multiplying the volume in cubic feet by 64 pounds. Even on a boat with a small cockpit, a pooping means thousands of pounds of water attempting to sink the stern. It is imperative that water in the cockpit be returned to the sea as fast as possible. Sailboats should have at least two scuppers with straightline discharges no less than 2 inches in diameter, and powerboats with open cockpits that extend to the stern and rails should have large over-the-side freeing ports. Preferably, decks and cockpits should drain when heeled or when powering with the bow up as well as on the level.

A good way to help keep water out of the cabin, and open up space inside, is the bridge deck. Full-length athwartship seating, perhaps under the protective visor of a dodger or perhaps wide and open enough for sunbathing, is afforded. Despite an unfortunate yacht-design trend toward making companionway access easier, bridge decks can be successfully incorporated into both traditional and modern designs. Strong bridge deck lines with good camber on the surface juxtapose the perpendicular fore and aft lines of the footwell and cabin and create an interesting structural network.

A not-so-wise development of the conventional bridge deck is the Swan-type bridge, in which the entire forward end of the cockpit is elevated a half step to provide headroom in the aft, under-the-cockpit cabin. This increases the distance between the companionway and the cockpit so much that in bad weather a crewmember traversing the bridge may have little or nothing to hold onto should the boat suddenly roll or a wave wash over. Robert Perry calls it "Hell's Half Ride."

Aft cabins aside, the bridge deck opens up usable space under the cockpit for electronics, binoculars, safety gear, and anything else that

Critical Deck Measurements

Item	Measurement
Side-deck width	15 in. minimum
Lifeline height	30 in. minimum
Seat height	16 in.
Backrest—height	12 in. minimum
—angle	10 deg.
Seat width	18 in.
Cockpit scuppers	2-in. diameter
Freeing ports	2 in. × 6 in. minimum
Toerail height	1½ in. minimum
Cabin tumblehome	1/4 in. inward : 1-ft. height
Deck crown	1 in. : 30 in. to 1 in. : 20 in.

must be quickly accessible from the companionway. The space lost is generally unused corners of the engine room anyway. See Chapter 14 for more information on cockpits, bridge decks, and companionways.

DOCKING

Many boats suffer from undersized or too few mooring cleats. In fact, a few years ago a major boatbuilder exhibited a racer/cruiser sailboat at the Newport International Sailboat Show without any cleats! The mooring lines were tied to stanchions, shrouds, and sheet blocks. This was a case of carrying weight savings much too far; the builder was irresponsible, pure and simple.

As a minimum, there should be cleats or bitts at the bow and at both stern quarters. Midship breast cleats make rigging spring lines

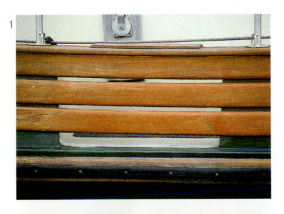

1 The tall fiberglass bulwarks of the Fisher line of motorsailers are interrupted by freeing ports so that large amounts of water can quickly run overboard. Teak strakes give continuity to the lines of the topside.

2 Scuppers in the toerails should be located at strategic low points to clear the deck of water. This one is so small it will clog easily, but the stainless steel lip is a classy touch.

easier and can also be used in conjunction with an anchor to hold the boat off a dock in a strong crosswind, but they should be placed outboard where they won't be tripped over. The size of a conventional cleat is determined by the size of line that will be used with it— about 1 inch of horn length for each 1/8 inch of line diameter. Cleats should be mounted at an angle between 15 and 25 degrees to the lead of the line. The distinctive CloverCleat, with four quadrant-shaped horns, is an innovative development that uses less space than other types.

While many modern boats aren't delivered with chocks, hawseholes, or half-round antichafe bars, there is no doubt that these are seamanly. Properly designed fittings have smooth, radiused edges that minimize chafe and prevent the line from jumping out. Without some means of being controlled, mooring lines run the risk of fraying from rubbing against abrasive surfaces such as wire stays and aluminum toerails or destroying brightwork. And with the rise and fall of the tide, the lines may cut across the deck, forcing the crew to step over or under. Not only is this unsafe, but it also just doesn't look neat and orderly. Adding or changing cleats is an easy job. Stick with one type—stainless steel, bronze, etc.—as mixing materials will make the deck look like a table at a marine flea market. Use liberal amounts of bedding compound, clean up carefully, and don't forget the backing plates.

Boarding and disembarking can be a real nuisance without lifeline gates or gangways. It is one thing for a teenager to leap from the cabintop to the dock, but less agile people appreciate conveniently placed steps to get off and on. This is especially true when carrying bags and boxes, and since all supplies come aboard by hand it is important to have an unobstructed passage from the gate to the cockpit.

If cruising to the Mediterranean or other region where stern-to anchoring is the custom, some sort of stern gangplank is required. A custom arrangement might include a gate in the stern pulpit and a hinged aluminum gangplank that can be raised and lowered from the cockpit; small wheels on the quay-end allow it to roll with the boat.

1 The hefty stainless steel bollard-type cleat on an aluminum ketch is unusual but certainly serviceable.

2 Placed inside the toerail near a hawsehole, a hinged retaining bar prevents a belayed line from coming adrift.

3 Deck cleats should be selected and placed for maximum function and with a view to style. This clever stainless steel casting incorporates both a cleat and chocks in one piece.

4 A simple wooden cleat looks best on a traditional boat.

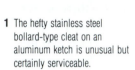

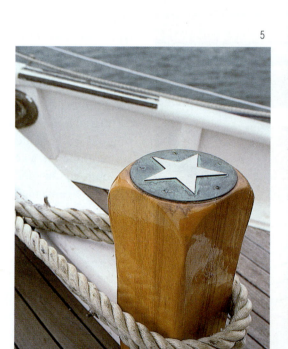

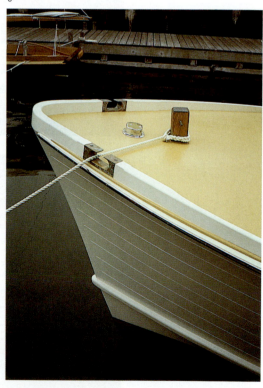

OTHER HARDWARE

It should go without saying that everything on deck must be very strong. A good test is to imagine a 200-pound crewman falling, kicking, or otherwise walloping a piece of gear—will it withstand the blow? If not, perhaps it doesn't belong on deck, for as surely as the wind blows, someday someone will step on your solar panel, trip on a Dorade vent, or fall against the bowrail.

The likelihood of accidents or damage can be minimized by intelligent placement of deck fittings. Walkways should be kept as clear as possible; this is undoubtedly easier on a boat with a trunk cabin, as hatches and vents can be mounted on the cabintop. However, there is no escaping the installation of these items on flush-decked boats, and common paths fore and aft and athwartship must be imagined when laying out the deck.

Fair mooring line leads are important on all boats, but more important are sheet and halyard leads on sailboats. The current practice of leading all mast halyards aft to the cockpit may reduce the number of times the crew will have to go forward, but these lines, fairleads, and linestoppers can create potential hazards. Lines should be kept low to the deck to prevent tripping; this is not difficult on a flat deck, but could be dangerous on a stepped deck. And while all of these taut, color-coded lines may look racy, they are cluttersome.

Sheet winches should be mounted for maximum convenience and strength; winching on the knees robs the grinder of bracing points and forces him to rely on upper-body strength alone. Blocks and fairleads should let the line run true to the winch or cleat for maximum efficiency. On racing yachts it is not uncommon to find that when adding innovative new gear and experimenting with different sail handling systems, some of the deck hardware must be moved to make the crew's work easier and faster. Old through-holes are difficult to repair and match with the deck color and nonskid pattern. Think through the project and consult experienced sailors before buying and installing hardware.

7

5 The traditional samson post, secured below to the hull or chain locker bulkhead, is an extremely sturdy point to belay rodes and docklines. The star is not only decorative but protects the end grain.

6 Bronze chocks set flush in the toerail control docklines, and stainless steel half-round on the rubbing strake prevents chafe.

7 For safety at sea, wide side decks with tall lifelines or rails are essential. On *Numero Uno*, a substantial bulwark reduces the height of the tapered stanchions for both appearance and strength.

1

2

3

4

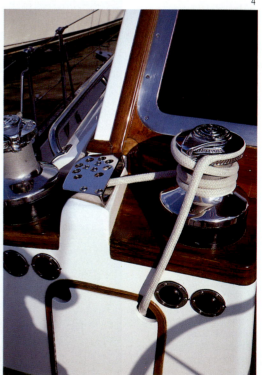

5

STOWAGE

When the stowage space below fills up, all manner of gear finds its way on deck: jerry jugs, fishing poles, tool kits, portable generators, buckets, extra lines, fenders—everything but the galley sink. Like some high-tech campers, there are "worst case" skippers who feel insecure without a tool or spare part for every possible breakdown.

The flip side is the Good Time Charlie who is so afraid of boredom he loads up the deck with all his favorite toys: sailboards, surfboards, bicycles, Jet-Skis, and scuba gear and compressor. That it might get in the way, rust, or break loose is of far less concern than having to sit in the cockpit with nothing to do.

Fortunately, innovative naval architects and boatbuilders are incorporating clever on-deck stowage ideas in their plans. Of course the bigger the boat the easier it is to conceal large objects such as dinghies and mopeds. Trends in yacht design toward longer waterlines, greater beam, and higher freeboard facilitate this task. Cavernous sailboat cockpit lockers can suck up folding bikes, gas grills, fishing rods, and surfboards as well as the usual cleaning supplies, life jackets, fenders, and sail bags. Here they are out of the elements, out of sight, and probably wedged in so tightly they don't need lashing. Some builders have designed space below the cockpit for stowing dinghies and sailboards; this "garage" is accessed through a door in the transom, often a "sugar scoop" with steps leading down to a swim platform.

Curiously, a powerboat of the same size may have fewer belowdeck options for stowing these sorts of recreational vehicles. This is because (1) the cockpits are larger for fishing and entertainment, (2) engines and baitwells may occupy much of the space, (3) the boats are seldom taken on long ocean passages where small cockpits are necessary safety features, and (4) designers are not accustomed to allowing space for bulky sail bags and miscellaneous cruising gear. Cabin space of course is allotted to living quarters—who wants a bicycle tied above his bunk?

But the resourceful owner will make do. Fishermen through-bolt large fiberglass deck boxes in the cockpit to hold bait, ice, and tackle; rods are stowed in overhead racks under the flybridge or inside the cabin; and outriggers are carried like lances at the cabin sides, ready to wage battle. Fender racks clamped to the bowrail at a raked angle are not unattractive, especially when clean terry-cloth fender covers are sewn over them. Likewise, there are off-the-shelf stanchion clamping systems for sailboards now available; they don't get rid of the problem, but at least they eliminate bothersome lashings.

Spinnaker and whisker poles are most often stowed on the side decks, hooked onto special deck fittings at each end. Naturally they're in the way. With a sliding car on a mast track, poles can be partially raised to get them off the deck. As a bonus they're also ready for use. Another alternative is to hang them on the lifelines. The French builder of Amel cruising sailboats incorporates two special stainless steel rings welded into the lifeline stanchions that keep poles off the deck and out of the rigging.

1 Wooden blocks, parrel beads, and belaying pins are all relics of the Golden Age of sail, before the development of lightweight, corrosion-resistant metals and high-impact plastics. They still function fine, and can put wanderlust in a dreamer's eye.

2 Warren Luhrs, president of Hunter Marine, has enough linestoppers on his race boat *Hunter's Child* to open a chandlery. If you can memorize the color code you can probably memorize the New York phone book, too!

3 Simple bronze fairleads on a sloop built by Oregon's Heritage Boat Works organize sheets and halyards led aft to the cockpit.

4 Instead of messing up the cockpit, sheet tails on the Mediterranean 86 are stowed in a handy locker with hinged door.

5 Racing sailboats today make frequent use of deck-mounted sheaves and line organizers to lead lines aft to the cockpit, thus centralizing crew work.

On-Deck Stowage Options

Item	Location
Propane tanks	Deck box, lazarette, Marine Energy Systems patented container, special molded compartment in deck or backrest
Sail and surfboards	Stanchion hangers, deck mounts, under cockpit
Fenders	Bowrail hangers, deck box, lazarette
Lines	Belaying pins on rigging, deck box, gallows, lazarette
Dinghies	Davits (stern or side deck), deck mounts, cabintop
Life rings	Cabin sides, lifelines
Life rafts	Canister on deck or cabintop, special compartment under cockpit or coaming
Spinnaker poles	Deck mounts, mast tracks, lifeline stanchions
Fishing rods	Coaming holders, cabin overhead racks
Anchors	Bowsprits, bow rollers, indeck wells (bow or side deck), deck chocks

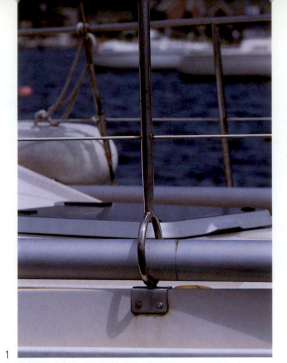

1

2

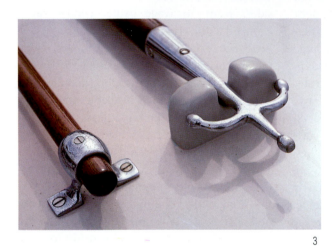

3

1 In the Amel line of cruising
ketches a ring is welded into
the lifeline stanchion to hold
the spinnaker pole.

2 The Mason 63 sailboat,
designed by Al Mason and
built in Taiwan, has lovely teak
decks and flush-mounted
stowage compartments,
including this anchor well.

3 On a proper yacht such as
Jessica, everything has its
place—even the lowly boat-
hook. The 75-foot Consolidated
commuter, built in 1930, has
been skippered by the same
man, Captain Raymond Tombs,
for more than 43 years.

4

TRANSOMS

Transom designs have evolved rather quickly in recent years. Probably the first reverse transom was on the 1962 America's Cup 12-meter yacht *Weatherly*. In effect, the counter was cut away merely for the purpose of reducing weight. IOR racers picked up on the idea. Form followed function and soon reverse transoms were seen on nonracing sailboats and powerboats as well. Later, as beam was increased and carried farther aft, transom sizes also grew larger. Suddenly it was feasible to fit a gate in the stern pulpit, mold steps into the sloping transom, hide them with a sugar scoop, and presto!—a convenient swim platform and boarding system was born. And a rakish new style.

Large motorsailers and motoryachts with aft cockpits have less need for such designs because hinged transom gates and ancillary swim platforms are easily incorporated. This means that freeboard aft must be kept low, which to many eyes is also far more pleasing than the aft cabin motoryacht, which seems top-heavy and incredibly boxy. Access to dinghies and swimming ladders in those designs is pretty much restricted to ladders hung from the deck, which is such a great distance you feel like a mountain climber rappelling down the face of Half Dome. The only other choice is to mount the ladder at a midship break in the sheer—common on aft cabin motoryachts—where the freeboard is at its lowest.

The reverse transom is being seen more frequently on powerboats, as the cross-pollination between sail and power sends the best ideas over to the other side, even though many designers hate to admit the influence. Just as it works on sailboats, the sloping transom makes access to the water much easier.

Tumblehome in the after part of the topsides of sportfishermen is not a new idea, but following a period in which they were squared off, some designers are reviving this practice. Whether it is more attractive is a matter of fashion trend and personal taste, but serious deep-sea fishermen find that the side-deck overhang in the cockpit, which results from tumblehome, gives the person working the leader a surer foothold.

5

4 The barndoor rudder on the Marshall 22 catboat *Tim-Tam-Too* has a bronze step, as does the transom, to help swimmers climb aboard.

5 The twin transom steps on *Executive Sweet*, built in Canada by Philbrooks Boatyard, provide easy access to and from the swimming platform.

1

2

3

4

1 The French-built Amel Sharki comes standard with a Mediterranean-style gangplank for stern-to mooring, a common practice in those waters. It stores against the lifelines when not in use.

2 The Elite 50 *Impromptu II* has an interesting stern platform that serves a multitude of uses, not the least of which is supporting a retractable swim ladder.

3 The 90-foot Martin Francis–designed maxi cruising sloop *Diablesse*'s reverse counter transom has teak-faced steps to facilitate boarding from a dinghy or retrieving a man overboard.

4 *Aquel II,* a 122-foot aluminum sloop designed by Ed Dubois and built in New Zealand, has a "garage" under the cockpit for stowing everything from fenders and lines to Jet-Skis, dive gear, and an inflatable. Hydraulics are used to control sails, anchors, and boom vang.

HANDHOLDS

It is either the curse or the blessing of naval architecture that style must ultimately yield to safety. The conscientious designer will find a way to make bedfellows of these two strangers. Handholds are a prime example. They are essential to keeping the crew on board. "One hand for the boat, one for yourself." No other piece of gear—lifelines, toerails, or jacklines—is as strong and easy to grab. Handholds should be placed along the coachroof or sides of a cabin at a height that doesn't require much if any stooping. On a flush deck, handholds are of limited utility and should probably be dispensed with in favor of high, fixed rails at the gunwale.

Handholds can be made from wood, plastic, or metal, and should always be through-bolted with large washers or backing plates. And they don't need to muck up the look of the boat. In fact, on many production fiberglass boats, teak handrails add a nice natural touch, especially if they are oiled or varnished. Stainless steel pipe is found more frequently on powerboats and is representative of the inherent styling differences between power and sail. Of course there is no rule that says you can't put stainless steel handrails on a Tahiti ketch, but other adjustments would have to be made to keep them consistent with the otherwise funky style. A bold project might include removing all other wood from the deck, painting the cabin and decks gray, and custom-welding the handrail end fittings and supports to avoid the off-the-shelf powerboat look. What you'd be striving for is a theme to justify an incongruous piece of gear—a *Star Wars* or Transformers look, for example. You might as well paint on rivets, too, but unless your cruise is intergalactic, why bother?

1 This black anodized handrail follows the curve of the tinted windows and in profile is hardly visible, which was the intent of the builder.

2 The edge-lit Lucite rails on *Time*, designed by Tom Fexas, produce a glamorous nighttime effect.

3 Stainless steel rails and handholds without baseplates give a clean, sporty look, but how much weight can they hold?

4 Teak handholds on deck have long been popular. They are not only strong, but the warm wood grain is a nice accent on the otherwise vast wasteland of white fiberglass, especially in the Privilege 48 catamaran built in France.

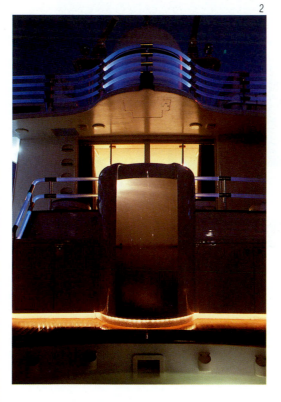

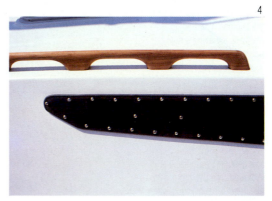

ARCHES AND GALLOWS

In an effort to copy the spoilers used on Indy-type race cars, yacht designers are drawing dramatic spans over the cockpit that look like small-scale models of the St. Louis Gateway Arch. They may be raked forward or aft, and are most representative of the modern Italian influence. In fact, American sailboat designer Robert Perry jokingly referred to them as "linguini struts" when he specified one on his own South Pacific 42 design. Most often, however, they are seen on high-performance powerboats. In keeping with the American tradition of exploiting good ideas *ad nauseum*, radar arches are creeping onto the superstructures of lumbering motoryachts and slovenly trawlers. It is true: Nothing succeeds like excess. One cannot help but fear that after a few years the arches will become as superfluous as the runabout fins that mimicked Detroit's automobile designs in the 1950s.

The saving grace of the arch is that it is not entirely decorative. It is an ideal location for mounting radar and radio antennas, setting deck and cockpit lights, fastening canvaswork to shade the cockpit, or, as Perry planned on the South Pacific 42, installing stereo speakers.

Ocean-racing sailboats have utilized arches as platforms for solar panels and wind generators and as catchalls for lines, horseshoe life rings, and more. Powerboat designer Tom Fexas even designed a complete helm station inside a bridge arch, and put another antenna arch on top of that!

A wholly functional antecedent of the arch is the boom gallows, whose purpose is to support the boom when the mainsail is furled. Not only does this remove the load from the mast (which a topping lift does not do), but it also protects the helmsman and cockpit crew in the event of the topping lift parting or a dismasting. And in a fierce gale it allows the boom to be lashed to something fixed so it won't slop wildly back and forth. Like the arch, it is a convenient point to attach canvaswork, provides a firm handhold in the cockpit, and when cruising the tropics is the logical place to hang ripening bananas.

While boom gallows have traditionally been fabricated from bronze or stainless steel stanchions and wood crosspieces, arches are typically made of aluminum or fiberglass so they can be given streamlined, airfoil shapes. Hence drag is reduced and a high-speed look instilled.

5 The radar arch, or "linguini strut" as designer Robert Perry likes to call it, is a stylistic trademark of the 1980s. A product of sexy Italian sportboats, Perry saw in them a utility as well, specifying one on his South Pacific 42 to house stereo speakers.

6 On *Golden Delicious*, a 95-foot Jack Sarin design for apple grower Bill Gammie, the radar arch is a logical mount for horns, antennas, lights, and satellite communications.

5

6

The boom gallows on the schooner *Brilliant*, owned by Mystic Seaport in Mystic, Connecticut, has three leathered crotches to lash the boom in a gale, plus a hinged board with leathered crotch to secure the boom higher at anchor. She was designed by Olin Stephens in 1930 and built by Nevins at City Island, New York.

CANVASWORK

Considering the present emphasis on slick, polished surfaces, it is amazing to note how much canvaswork is added to the decks of both power and sailing yachts. Certainly the soft look is at some odds with hull and superstructure material, but in tropical climates canvaswork is deemed essential to on-deck comfort. And its versatility and light weight make canvas the ideal material for temporary, collapsible structures such as cockpit dodgers and spray hoods.

The flybridges of trawlers and motoryachts are often rigged to be completely enclosed by canvas during inclement weather—see-through plastic windshields, canvas side curtains, and overhead biminis. It is not unlike steering the boat from inside a carefully fitted tent. Sailboat cockpits may be fitted the same way, often with the addition of an awning over the boom for increased shade while at anchor.

While biminis, dodgers, and awnings are essentially designed to protect the crew in the cockpit or flybridge from rain and sun, canvas has other equally practical applications on deck. Hatch scoops to funnel air below as well as awning flaps to keep out rain can easily be made of canvas. Opening windows and portlights can be given rain hoods or "visors" for shade. Deck boxes, especially those constructed of wood, are well protected by custom-fitted covers with snaps to hold them in place. The same is true of steering consoles, binnacles, windlasses, winches, and any other deck gear vulnerable to the elements. In fact, you will occasionally see the entire brightwork of a boat—caprails, coamings, flag staff—custom-fitted with color-coordinated canvaswork just to lengthen the life of the varnish, or rather to stay the day the crew has to take sandpaper in hand, don knee pads, and begin the hateful task of "bringing back" the yellowed, flaking finish.

Actually, the fabrics used today are seldom real canvas but are acrylics, which have chemical resins added to minimize fading due to the attack of ultraviolet rays from the sun. Design of the enclosures, color, and placement of windows are the principal elective elements. Shape, of course, is partly a function of the aluminum or stainless steel support tubing, and whether it is fixed or collapsible. Expert measuring and sewing skills are required to ensure a good fit. With experience, boxy-looking structures can be avoided in favor of more interesting shapes that work harmoniously with the lines of the boat. Strong colors—blue, brown, red, black, and green—are preferred to weak colors such as pastels, which will soon fade into oblivion and look dirty or washed out. Windows should be strategically placed for good visibility, but since the plastic tends to grow brittle and become scratched—especially when repeatedly rolled and unrolled—it is wise not to build the entire enclosure of it.

When and if protective overhead canvaswork begins to leak, it may be waterproofed with commercially available sealants that brush on. Periodic applications are necessary, and one should apply the sealant to a small patch first to note any darkening of the colors.

Despite the admitted practicality of on-deck canvaswork, too much of it may seriously detract from the boat's overall appearance, making it look more like a Bedouin's caravan than the yacht it was meant to be.

INTERVIEW: Designing Canvaswork

with Karen Lipe

Dodgers should attempt to re-create the boat's critical profile lines—the slope of the house or windshield, for instance. The dodger should also follow the camber of the house, which is fairly easy because the frame mounts on the house sides. Think about how the dodger dimensions, color, and shape will affect the boat's lines, and how it will fold down. If there is a splash rail on top of the house, the dodger should fold into it.

Dodgers are too complex for most do-it-yourselfers. The craftsman who builds dodgers is an artist, too. Don't put restrictions on him, such as requiring standing headroom underneath; there's no way he can make it look pretty. A good canvasworker will measure you and your crew's height to make sure the aft bow of the dodger doesn't hit you right in the eye.

Many of the biminis I see on powerboats are horrendous. The Euro-designed windshields and bridges are really swept back, and then someone builds a bimini that goes straight up. The go-fast look is destroyed by one badly designed accoutrement. I see the same problem with hardtops and side curtains; if the upright brace for the top is 45 degrees, then the side curtain zippers should be 45 degrees, too—not 90 degrees.

If the house is white, then in my opinion the dodger should be white also. Using blue or black or other strong colors breaks the lines the boat's designer so carefully put there. Dark colors, however, filter more ultraviolet rays and tend to last longer than white canvaswork. The difference in temperature on your skin is imperceptible. It's a compromise. Some people just like color. But if you want your bimini or dodger to disappear, try to match the color of the cabintop.

Aluminum frames are too soft; once bent they kink. The first time a person grabs the frame it's gone. Stainless steel is more expensive, but there's no reason it shouldn't last for the life of the boat.

The shape of the frame is important for aesthetic and practical reasons. A lot of small canvas shops can only make 90-degree bends. A good custom shop has special jigs to make those pretty curves. The forward and aft bows of a dodger or bimini should be slightly lower than the middle bow to prevent water from collecting. And, of course, the sides should be lower than the center. Acrylic leaks if it puddles.

I recommend that all vinyl glass windows be zippered so they can be removed during the off-season. Roll them carefully in warm weather; fuss with them in cold weather and the glass shatters. When the canvas starts to rip, take it in to the shop before it loses shape; once that happens you can't take a good pattern off it and you'll be faced with having to pay for an entire new one. Canvaswork not rigged tightly wears out much faster and detracts from the beauty of the boat.

—Karen Lipe
yacht broker and
founder of the Coverloft
Annapolis, Maryland

In the tropics, protection from the sun is important to health and comfort afloat. The bimini on *Swept Away* is cleverly divided around the mainsheet.

1 *Harbinger*'s deck awning is designed so that the boat can still be sailed with headsails and mizzen.

2 Side curtains with zippered opening windows convert the afterdeck of *Francis Marion* from an open-air "porch" to an all-weather enclosure.

3 *Coffee Break*, a Bertram sportfisherman, shows off a variety of canvaswork, including a cockpit awning, flybridge side curtains and T-top over the tuna tower.

MAKING CHANGES

It is much easier to envision changes to a boat's interior than to the deck, as if the latter was a *fait accompli* courtesy of the builder. Nothing could be farther from the truth.

Deck color can be changed with paint or nonskid rubber-type pads. Bulwarks can be removed or added; they can be constructed of aluminum, fiberglass, or wood, painted or left bare. A bonus of bulwarks is the concealing of cluttersome hardware, hence the presentation of a cleaner look to your "audience." Stanchions and lifelines can be replaced with newer models or by wood or stainless steel rails. Deck boxes can be removed as part of a simplification program or added for increased stowage space. New canvaswork, perhaps of a different color, complements a new paint job and improves the overall appearance of a boat. Cabintops can be lengthened or shortened, though this involves major structural work.

Take a long, hard look at your deck. What works and what doesn't? Is there nonessential hardware and other gear that could be removed without sacrificing boat handling or safety? Beyond function, what sort of look are you after? If your boat is traditionally styled, you might want to stay with wood as a feature: cleats, rails, deck boxes. Laying teak decks is a big job but one that will greatly alter the appearance of your boat. If your theme is modern, you might replace wooden handrails and toerails with stainless steel, paint the deck with a contemporary color, and upgrade clunky cleats and chocks with types that are more stylishly sculpted.

SUMMARY

Good deck design involves the careful integration of form and function. Unlike a house, a boat is a moving vehicle that consequently mandates certain safety considerations. Clean, uncluttered lines look best, and the installation of necessary gear should be planned at the time of initial design. Ergonomics, color, water drainage, stowage, canvaswork, and boarding convenience are important elements in the attractive, workable deck plan.

CHAPTER FOUR

Interior Arrangements

When the day is done, and the wind and sea have taken their toll on the apple-cheeked crew, a quiet haven is found in the cabins belowdeck. The sound of the wind is muted, motion is subdued, and comfort is found in a soft seat, a favorite jazz band playing on the stereo, a cold drink in hand. It is not exactly like your living room at home—certain conveniences are missing perhaps—but in many respects the saloon is better appreciated, for it is a movable, self-contained world that serves faithfully in any port you wish to enter.

No doubt one of the most appealing aspects of life aboard is the small, compact scale of the cabins. This almost primal attraction may be traceable to romantic memories of childhood, of building forts with blankets draped over chairs, and by extension, perhaps to cave living and the womb itself. It is no wonder we are drawn to warm, secure, and familiar rooms to relax, rooms where we can enjoy loved ones

and forget about the hectic, fast-paced world we've left behind the door.

Indeed, except for the multimillion-dollar megayacht, boat cabins are smaller than rooms in houses. This presents certain problems for the naval architect and interior designer, not the least of which is accommodating the five- and six-foot frames of men and women in restricted space. As designer Jon Bannenberg has noted, "The human form does not reduce in volume when it steps aboard a boat. There is no logic in reducing the size of door handles, fittings, chairs, closets, or cupboards." The trick then is to know what to leave standard size and what to reduce. The most obvious reduction is in the number of persons to be accommodated in a given hull volume. This is why sage old skippers advise keeping crew to two or three in a boat up to about 28 feet long overall (LOA), and no more than four up to about 40 feet. Sure you can squeeze in more, but stowage

A secondary entrance in *Black Pearl* offers direct access to the handsome aft cabin. The Nautical 56 ketch has two cockpits, a large one with the helm and a small one aft, equipped with captain's chairs, that functions as a private rendezvous for guests.

space is overtaxed, elbows knock, and privacy vanishes. In fact, many experienced seamen are adamant in the conviction that privacy is impossible aboard small boats, and to try to build it into the boat with extra bulkheads and tiny, claustrophobic staterooms is senseless. The solution, they say, is to cruise only with family and close friends who won't be appalled by the sound of a toilet flushing.

The well-planned interior is modest in its expectations and does not sacrifice the galley, navigation station, or head for berths that will seldom be used. It permits the free flow of persons forward and aft without unnecessary obstructions, allows light and air to enter and circulate, and is finished with materials—both hard and soft—that are pleasing to the eye and easy to maintain.

In this chapter, we'll look just at some basic principles of designing and building yacht interiors. We will leave the details to the chapters in Part II.

ENTRANCES

Stepping inside or belowdeck requires different physical movements on different boats. On a large motoryacht it may simply involve turning a door handle and stepping inside as easily and graciously as if the doorman at the Ritz had thrown his cape over a puddle and opened it for you. Entering a small sailboat may require you to descend backward through a small, dark hole as if you were lowering yourself down a coal chute. Obviously, companionway requirements vary according to the size, type, and style of boat, so it is impossible to describe a right or wrong arrangement.

But what happens once inside? By their very nature, sailboats—especially full-keel, displacement designs with cabin soles below the waterline—sit *in* the water, while planing and semidisplacement powerboats sit *on* the water. The lower the sole, the greater the distance between it and the companionway sill. On a sportfisherman the cabin sole is on about the same plane as the cockpit floor, or even a foot or so above it to allow for engine space below. Sliding glass doors are typical, and no special structure or movement is required for ingress and egress. On a full-keel sailboat with

a bridge deck, however, a five- or six-step ladder with handholds must be fitted inside the companionway. This means entering backward onto steps negotiated easily without looking. An intelligent improvement on conventional ladder design utilizes steps angled up on each side of the horizontal centerpiece, so that when the boat is heeled there is still a horizontal surface to step on. In aft galley designs the ladder may terminate on the galley counter or be eliminated altogether; this is a less desirable arrangement, as the foot is not captive between the side pieces of the ladder and could slip in a seaway, and there is the danger of putting a foot into the cook's quiche!

These principles should be observed not only in the main companionway but also at the port and starboard wheelhouse doors of trawlers and motoryachts, at forward and aft cabin entrances, and on sailboats with twin companionways in which one connects the cockpit to the owner's stateroom and another, forward under the boom, provides access amidships to the galley or saloon.

While the size of a boat may limit the number of entrances to one, there are obvious benefits in having a secondary means of entry. When crew are sleeping near the main companionway, it's nice to be able to leave or enter without disturbing them. And on larger vessels with separate crew's quarters, a separate companionway whereby they may come and go unnoticed by the owner and guests is logical. A second entrance/exit also provides an additional means of escape from fire or flooding.

In any case, the mechanism of entry should not intrude on cabin space, where it could become an obstacle to free movement and could occupy valuable space that is better used for square dancing and introspective pacing.

LAYOUT

General arrangement plans, which locate the saloon, staterooms, head, galley, and navigation station, have a critical impact on the beauty and livability of a yacht. Possibilities would seem finite—"there's nothing new under the sun"—yet as in any artistic endeavor, variations are almost limitless. As the novelist is advised, "It's not so much what you say, it's how you say it."

1 *Brigadoon,* a Lord Nelson Victory tug, has a solid Dutch-style wheelhouse door for improved visibility, ventilation underway, and keeping spray away from the controls.

2 A contemporary trend in companionway ladder design is the angling of the ends of the steps for level footing when the boat is heeled.

3 The traditional booby hatch on *Woiee*'s foredeck affords protection from the wind and spray while giving headroom to the person entering or leaving the cabin below. She is a 65-foot ketch-rigged motor-sailer conversion of a Down East commercial fishing boat.

4 The twin companionways on *Jan Van Gent* are possible in a boat of great beam. Such an arrangement, either athwartship or fore and aft, means that the crew's quarters or master stateroom can have its own private entry.

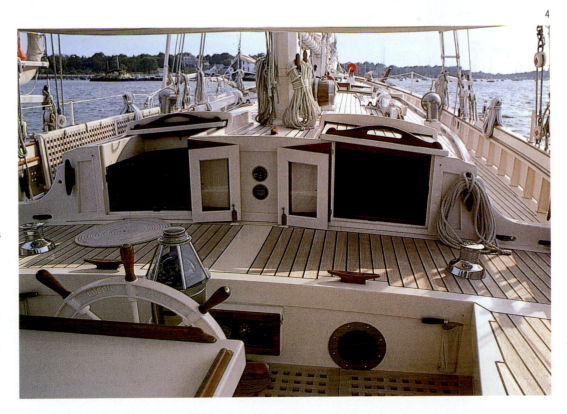

Sail. Again, boat size is a governing factor. Under about 50 feet, a two-stateroom plan requires that one be located forward and another aft. For example, V-berths in the bow effectively utilize this difficult, triangular shape. In center cockpit designs the second stateroom can be placed aft, isolated from the main living area; in aft cockpit designs, the second stateroom can occupy the quarter area under a cockpit seat. Indeed, a current trend on small boats is to use the entire under-the-cockpit area for a double berth; headroom is of course restricted, and you may need the supple joints of a contortionist to get in and out, but it does provide a second, private "stateroom" in a hull size that allows few other options.

Above 40 to 50 feet or so the V-berths may be pulled aft, offset from the passageway, and the V section used for a head, hanging locker, workbench, or sail stowage. High-low single berths in the same offset cabin are also possible, as are twin mirror-image cabins port and starboard of the centerline passageway, forward or aft.

Pushing the staterooms to the ends of the boat dictates placing the other cabins amidship. Because the saloon is the cabin where the greatest number of persons congregate—at dinner, say—it makes sense to utilize the area of greatest beam. Preferably, the galley should not obstruct movement forward and aft when the cook is at work. But if it is moved too far outboard or into a quarter, there is the problem of keeping the sink near the centerline where it will drain at heeling angles, and of providing sufficient swing room for a gimbaled stove/oven.

Unfortunately, the navigation station is often treated as the ugly sister, relegated to some inconvenient nook that only a stunted Ichabod Crane could slide into. Some owners prefer to dispense with the noble desk altogether in favor of another berth or entertainment console, believing they can spread charts all over the dinette table. But when room is available, navigation is a sufficiently important function on any oceangoing boat to merit its own, sacrosanct space. Where else will you

---

General Arrangement Plans for Sailboats

Space planning for yacht interiors requires an understanding of geometry and the human form as well as a creative knack for attractive, innovative solutions to design problems. Nevertheless, the dictum of "what works" has resulted in several conventions that loosely describe most sailboat cabin layouts. 1) Ted Brewer's one-cabin plan for the 26-foot Lubec Boat succeeds by not attempting to cram too much accommodation into a small space. Essentially a two-person boat, the berths double as settees; the dining table tilts up out of the way when not in use. No attempt has been made to give the toilet its own enclosure, which would have taken a lot more space than shown. The galley and hanging lockers are aft, eliminating the possibility of quarter berths. 2) Bill Luder's Sea Sprite 30 is representative of the typical aft cockpit layout: V-berths forward, settees in the saloon, and aft

galley. A formal dinette would have severely restricted traffic flow; the fold-down bulkhead-mounted table is a satisfactory solution. 3) The McCurdy & Rhodes Hinckley Sou'Wester 51 has a

voluminous interior divided by a center cockpit. Three private staterooms are featured as well as two heads, large galley and dinette, and generous stowage compartments.

(1)

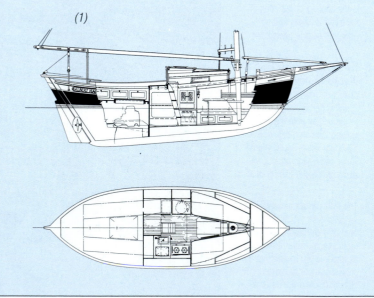

stow charts, binoculars, dividers, and hand bearing compass, or mount the Loran, Decca, SatNav, and radar screens?

The saloon, galley, and navigation station may be rotated around the midship area on paper or mocked up to see what works best for you. Certainly yacht designers have experimented with every conceivable permutation to achieve a "different look." But just as a cliché was once an original saying whose veracity was never doubted, the conventional cabin layout has become conventional simply because it works.

Altering the layout to satisfy personal requirements is certainly possible, but should be carefully considered. An individual or couple may feel too much space is wasted on berths, and so may decide to convert a cabin or bunk to a work space for sewing, typing, or shopwork. Moving structural bulkheads should be done only after finding other ways to handle rigging, wave-induced, and other loads. But within the framework of a given cabin, it is possible to alter or relocate furniture

foundations: lengthening berths, perhaps through footwells in bulkheads, widening berths by means of sliding shelves, removing an icebox in favor of a self-contained refrigerator, adding a chart table over a berth, and cutting a "window" in a bulkhead for improved circulation of air. If the V-berths are not used for sleeping, they might be removed for more stowage space or a workbench, or the toilet might even be relocated forward, leaving the head compartment for a desk, small galley, shower stall, or what have you. Bear in mind that, should you ever wish to sell the boat, eccentric interior plans will probably reduce its value. At the same time, your boat should be a satisfying place, especially if you cruise or live aboard.

Power. Arrangement plans on small, planing powerboats have more in common with sailboats than their larger cousins: V-berths forward (usually a double), head, dinette, and galley amidships. Where they really vary is in headroom and under-the-

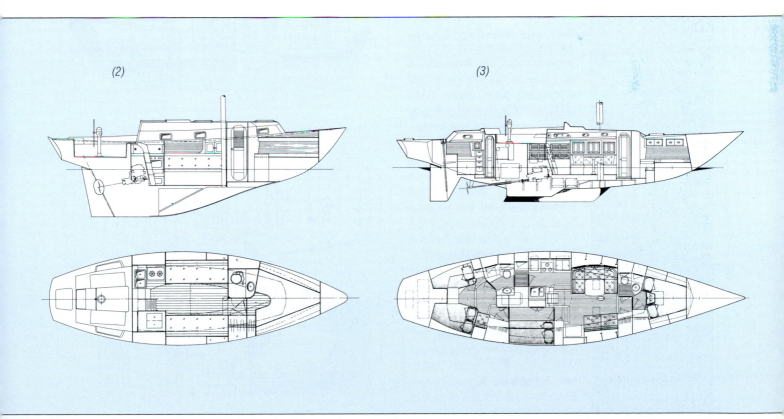

(2)

(3)

cockpit accommodations: the powerboat may have fewer because it has a flat or V-shaped bottom without a keel. Such shapes lessen the chance of fitting a berth under the cockpit (which most likely won't have fore-and-aft bench seats to add height to the quarter area) or locating the galley under a bridge deck.

A greater sense of spaciousness can be created aboard small boats by keeping the interior as open as possible: You can separate cabins with partial bulkheads and privacy curtains, mount mirrors on bulkheads or behind seats to create the illusion of greater space, forgo the fully enclosed head, stick with light colors, and bring in plenty of light via opening transparent or translucent hatches, portlights, and deck prisms.

The displacement hulls of the Down East "lobster" yacht, tug yacht, and trawler easily surpass the narrower and finer-ended sailboat hulls for interior volume. And because the cabin and superstructures are comparatively high, multiple levels allow some interesting opportunities for creativity. Usually the V-berths and head forward appear sunken in the bow; from there it's a few steps up to a wheelhouse or steering station at the forward end of the saloon. An elevated wheelhouse gives good visibility over a high bow, especially if there are bulwarks. An off-watch bunk in the wheel-

Floor Plans for Motoryachts

*T*he interiors of displacement and semidisplacement motoryachts possess tremendous volume. Space planning is somewhat easier than most sailboats since the hull sides tend to be more vertical and the sterns more nearly square. The frequent incorporation of protected wheelhouses and more than one deck permits a wider variety of floor plans. 1) The Nordhavn 46 long-range cruiser has a guest stateroom forward with head in the forepeak, owner's stateroom amidships under the wheelhouse, and a saloon with dinette, swivel seats, and adjacent galley. Access to the wheelhouse is by stairs either from the saloon or passageway outside the staterooms. 2) Though the forward V-sections of most high-performance sportboats are a limiting factor, the accommodations of the 60-footer built by the famous Italian firm of Cantieri Navali Di Baia are more than ample, thanks in part to a beam of almost 18 feet. As is common in this type of yacht, much space is given to conversational seating and lounging areas. 3) The Blue Seas 31 is a Down East "lobster yacht" with dual steering stations. The flared bow narrows sharply at the water, compressing the V-berths. The saloon has a settee that can be converted to a guest berth, but otherwise there is little room for visitors; the cockpit is a trade-off against increased accommodation. 4) Several floor plans are possible in Ocean Yachts' 53-foot motoryacht. Two decks dramatically increase the designers' options. The plan shown has a guest stateroom forward, owner's stateroom aft, and a third abaft the engine room. The galley, saloon, and several seating areas are situated on the main deck.

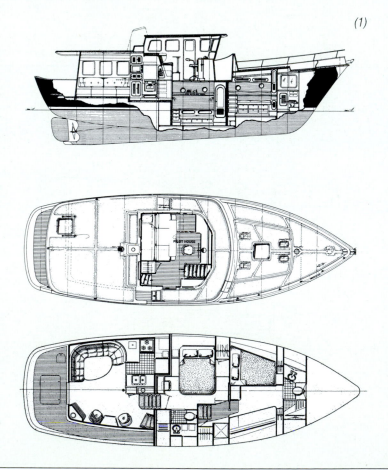

(1)

house is useful on night crossings or for kids who want their own space away from grown-ups. There may be room beneath the wheel-house for part of the head (a shower stall, for example), stowage, generator, or, as in the case of the Portsmouth 42, children's berths. The aft saloon may be a step down from the wheel-house and may encompass the galley, settees, and dinette or sofa bed.

Accommodation plans become far more complex on large yachts. Usable space on a 100-foot motoryacht can equal the square footage of a four-bedroom house, so there are numerous possibilities. A major distinction is that you can't create an L-shaped floor plan with wings running out over the sea! Two or three deck levels are partial compensation for this restriction, however. Imagine planning the interior of a narrow, three-story Baltimore rowhouse: Should stairways be kept at the ends of the house, or would a central stairway zigzagging upward among half-levels and rooftop decks be more interesting?

A review of several megayacht accommodation plans will reveal some standard ideas. Crew's quarters will probably be kept in the bow, separated from the aft owner's and guests' cabins by the galley and crew's luncheonette. On the main deck you may find the saloon, furnished with comfortable chairs and

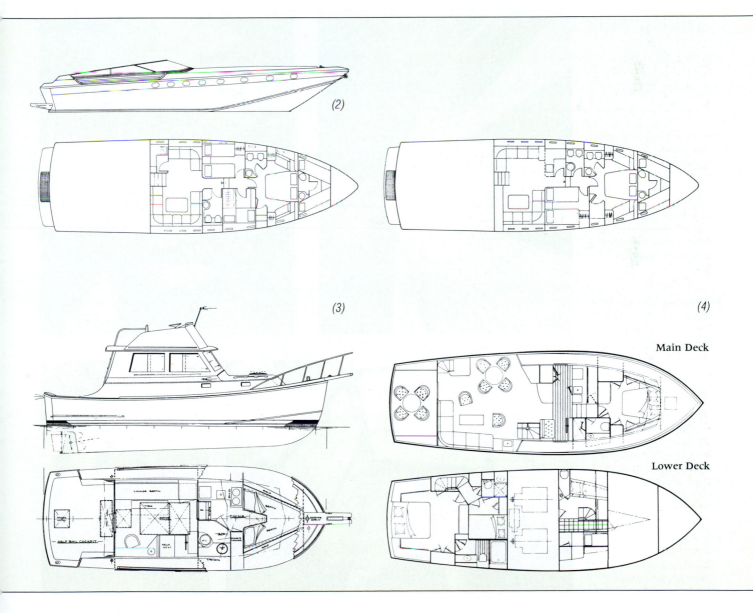

sofas, plush carpeting, or tiles. There will probably be a "dining room" easily accessible from stairs leading to the galley below, or perhaps there is a second galley on the main deck. A well-fitted bar is a must, and perhaps a game table as well. Forward is the wheelhouse running the full width of the superstructure for best visibility, and there is space for both standard and sophisticated electronics: satellite navigation and communications, several radars, weather facsimile recorders, navigation computer, fuel monitoring systems, and much more. A comfortable helmsman's chair and behind it a comfortable bench seat for observers are also included.

The saloon may be pushed to the sides of the yacht, thereby eliminating side decks; the trade-off is interior volume versus outside passageways, plus the added difficulty of cleaning windows from the outside and hanging fenders from the second deck. Even when the full beam is utilized aft, there will probably be exits at the forward end of the saloon to side decks that run past the wheelhouse to the foredeck.

Efficient traffic patterns fore and aft and between decks are vital. There will be more than one stairway or ladder between decks, planned for convenience and to ensure the privacy of living quarters. The crew will seldom use the main stairway; they will have their

1 No matter how large the yacht, there is always the temptation to carry the interior all the way to the rail, increasing space but eliminating the side deck. On *Golden Delicious*, the side deck forward stops at a door amidships, forcing some line handling and fender hanging to be done from the deck above.

2 The polished spiral staircase on *Double-O-Seven*, a 110-foot Denison-built megayacht, is an elegant transition between decks.

3 The stairway connecting *Record*'s deckhouse with the living quarters below is surrounded by painted steel pipe that wraps around the well to give the impression of being one piece. The rugged, simple rail also belies the boat's heritage as a commercial Norwegian ferry.

4 On *Bermbee*, a carpeted stairway lined with tongue-and-groove leads between the saloon and guest quarters below.

1

2

3

4

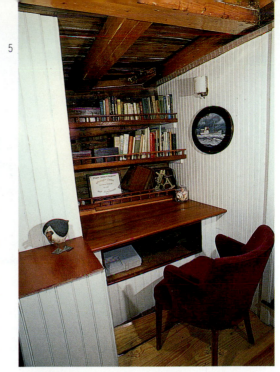

own inconspicuous access to the deck from their quarters. Spiral staircases, despite requiring more steps than a conventional stairway, don't take up much space and add interesting circular lines to a structure often beleaguered by square corners and long, unbroken straightaways. "In a fairly sedate cabin," designer Chuck Neville says, "an elegant staircase is sure to make people look and say 'Oh!'"

Hence a key to good design above and below deck is ease of movement. It should be possible to move between any two points on the boat quicky and without bothersome obstructions. After all, if you have to look at your feet every time you stand up and start walking, sooner or later you'll wind up on your fanny.

DESIGN WITH A PURPOSE

The way in which an owner uses his boat has a lot to do with cabin planning. Living aboard and extended cruising presuppose a given number of berths or staterooms; entertainment of business associates, as in the corporate yacht, dictates particular attention to conversational lounge areas; and the man or woman who makes his yacht his office as well as his home must borrow space for desk, computer, files, and the like. Likewise the professional captain of a charter yacht must think about his clients' privacy and comfort, gear for fishing, scuba diving, and watersports, and his own personal needs as well. Identifying your requirements becomes easier after owning several boats and learning your habits and routines.

The cruising boat must have comfortable accommodations for the number of persons normally aboard, plus provisions for occasional guests. The Pearson 37 sailboat, introduced in 1987, was aimed at the couple who mostly cruises alone, and seldom offshore. The only berth is a large double forward with foot space on either side for getting in and out of bed. Because motion is greatest in the bow, and because there are no hull sides or lee cloths to lie against, the designers assumed owners would not be making overnight passages but rather would spend the night at docks or at anchor. A "window" in the main bulkhead opens up the interior and improves ventilation;

this is a significant departure from the two-stateroom boat in which privacy is purchased dearly with sacrifices in light, air, and elbow room. In the saloon of the Pearson 37 are two rotating easy chairs flanking an entertainment console with stereo, television, and videocassette recorder, for a homelike feeling. And the galley and navigation table are large. The designer who knows that only one couple will sleep aboard has considerable freedom to play with space that in more conventional layouts would be assigned to additional berths. At the least, each of the basic functional areas can be expanded to create unusual roominess.

The couple who cruises with children has different needs than the couple who cruises with clients or friends. They may want young children nearby for safety reasons and may

5 *Record*'s desk, with bookshelves, armchair, and large work surface, rivals most home offices and is almost cozy enough to make you want to pay bills and write thank-you notes.

6 The desk in *Jan Van Gent*'s master stateroom is convenient to the berth, a sensible arrangement for the skipper who is sometimes moved to leap from bed in the middle of the night to compose love sonnets for his sweetheart or plot outlines for future books.

prefer an open interior because privacy really isn't necessary. On the other hand, the charter boat must have enclosed staterooms far apart so that honeymooners and lovebirds can feel alone when they want to. Aft cabin models of sail and powerboats serve this purpose well, and whether the passage connecting them to the saloon is inside or outside is an individual decision. The same choice is true of catamarans, in which staterooms are located in both hulls and may or may not have inside companionways leading to the saloon that lies between them on the bridge.

Ocean cruising requires safe sea berths and narrower sole space so crew won't be thrown great distances in violent weather. Conversely, cruising in protected and coastal waters justifies more double berths and enlarged sole area. Also affected are portlight and companionway sizes, location of the galley and head, and amount of space devoted to workbenches, chain lockers, and navigation stations. Excepting the custom yacht, rarely does one find a boat that suits him to a T. Here the all-wood interior is at a definite advantage over fiberglass pans and inner liners, because the wood interior can be unscrewed and rebuilt with comparative ease—berth height and width can be adjusted, tables and counters added, galleys expanded, and so on.

Large corporate yachts are not the only boats whose design is predicated on the functions of entertainment. High-performance speedboats and sportfishermen with maximum cockpit and minimum interior accommodation are geared to the daytime pursuit of pleasure, be it sunbathing, swimming, waterskiing, angling, light meals, or happy hours.

Features that in other boats would be belowdeck are found in the cockpit or bridge area; U-shaped lounge seating and small hors d'oeuvre tables, all built of weather-resistant materials, are open to the sun with a good view of the water and are designed for crew hanging out in swimwear. The cabin's main function is to furnish a private lavatory, and belowdeck berths are intended for occasional overnighting, though many seem aimed at whetting the sexual fantasies of hot-blooded owners. Candid designers will tell you in discrete asides that they consider the muscleboat cabin, with "soft walls" and overhead mirrors, nothing more than a "fornicatorium." South Florida is full of them.

The serious fishing machine has just one purpose, and that is catching fish. Steering towers enable the driver to spot fish, expensive fighting chairs dominate the cockpit, and the cabin appointments have only to sleep the crew on overnight trips to the fishing grounds and keep the beer cold. The more time spent in the chair, the better.

Of course, large sportfishermen have interiors that are quite opulent—if you've got the bucks, why not have it all? At the same time, Wellcraft designer Kurt Mizen notes that fishermen don't want interiors that look fragile, as sportfishermen are perceived as men's workboats.

The dockside liveaboard boat is a bird of a different feather. The owner who works aboard or ashore needs not only all of the amenities of an apartment or house, but space to work as well. Boatbuilders talk of unusual clients such as the couple who worked for IBM and specified 20 feet of hanging lockers for

2

1 The Pearson 37 stirred a controversy with its one-couple interior. Critics decried the absence of sea berths, but Pearson's intention was to accommodate the lone couple who has no intention of going offshore. The only berth is the double forward, though the dinette seat to port could function as a guest berth for a lone child.

2 The afterdeck of a motoryacht is a good spillover area from the saloon, offering conversational seating and fresh air when weather permits. *Crystal*'s afterdeck features nonskid Treadmaster and an ice cream maker.

with

Susan

Fox

We opened up the interiors of several models by engineering an innovative three-piece deck. We moved away from traditional deck support systems because we didn't want to interrupt the wrap-around window with bulkheads. In addition to the new deck, we used compression posts so you can still see through space. We wanted to create a barrier-free design.

Conventional galley cabinet fabrication has always seemed visually heavy to me. In a house you're working with 36-inch countertops with 8-foot ceilings; here we're limited to 6 feet. Our solution was to borrow principles used by Frank Lloyd Wright in his Falling Waters house, in which cantilevered beams extend over space to float part of the house. The galley cabinets are now cantilevered off stringers in the hull, which gives them a much lighter feel.

We also wanted to open up the aft cabins, which seemed claustrophobic and poorly lit. Again we replaced bulkheads with compression posts to support the deck, and were able to very effectively float

stairsteps off the stainless steel post. But the main benefit was eliminating the barrier between the main and aft cabins. A curtain gives visual privacy, which is all you can ask on anything but a very large boat. On a small boat, you're not going to get sound privacy even with a bulkhead.

Color and texture were also important in this project. We did not want color to dominate this barrier-free space; after all the effort we'd made, we didn't want to clobber the nice natural light with strong color. Instead we used atmospheric background color and placed more emphasis on texture. We used a color scheme called the Grand Canyon series, in which the color dilutes itself as you look into the distance. It goes away from you instead of coming forward. These are not bright colors, because the more color you put into a boat, the smaller it looks. On seeing these new interiors, the first reaction of our dealers was, "God, it's so big in here!"

—Susan Fox
Wellcraft Marine
Bradenton, Florida

suits and dresses—on a 38-foot ketch! Or the architect who needed an aft cabin large enough for his drafting table, and the computer programmer who had his hardware built into the cabinetry of his "office" cabin. Such customizations are highly specialized, and resale value may suffer for the eccentricity of their design, but the point is that with a little imagination anything is possible.

UNDERSTANDING SPACE

A common fault of novice yacht designers is the drawing of more accommodations than the hull will accept. The temptation arises when studying the general arrangement plan, whose perimeter represents the maximum beam of the boat at the rail. Beam, of course, is narrower at the water, so the designer is not working with a cube shape, but rather an inverted, three-dimensional triangle. Space that may appear available in the arrangement plan view simply does not exist in section view. The consequences of such errors include berths which may have to be pulled inboard toward the centerline, under-the-deck stowage bins with less

volume than intended, and perhaps the relocation of equipment such as pumps and plumbing. Boatbuilders sometimes complain that the designer's drawings are simply impossible to build. Even for experts, conceptualizing space is sometimes difficult. As a rule, the slower, displacement hulls have more interior volume than the faster, planing hulls.

More often the persons who fail to understand the space limitations of boats are the owners. Space diminishes toward the waterline not only in section view, but also in the bow and stern, where even modest overhangs dramatically reduce interior volume. Furthermore, not all interior furniture can be installed parallel or at right angles to the centerline. In a small galley, for example, the sink may have to be placed at a 45-degree angle so that it faces the point where a person stands. This means potentially lost space behind it; a pot and pan stowage area might be incorporated here, but the reach is often too great for it to be functional.

Planning the interior of a boat is like building furniture inside a bowl. The boundaries are all curved, and the only flat surfaces are bulkheads and the cabin sole, which is never as large as it appears on paper. As a result, berths taper at the foot, bins narrow at the bottom, and outboard book racks vary in width as they follow the curvature of the hull. Unlike houses, where everything is theoretically plumb and square, conceptual confusion is inherent in boat design, where the shapes of the trapezium, ellipse, and quadrant are the rule.

Experienced designers and builders are frequently in the unenviable position of having to help the owner develop more realistic expectations. They often bear the brunt of the owner's frustrations when told there really isn't room for a washer-dryer combo in the hanging locker. Alack! Fortunately, most boat owners are civilized enough not to shoot the messenger.

Beyond the geometric reality of a given space, there is a perceptual aspect that influences how we react to an interior. Sometimes the way things *seem* to be is more important than how they really are.

THE FEEL OF OPENNESS

On stepping aboard a small boat, the first impression of guests is frequently one of wonderment. "Everything is so compact!" "Every bit of space is used." "Everything has its place." What they seem to be saying is, "It's cute, but how can you live in such a small space?" Anyone who has lived aboard knows that neatness and orderliness do count. But there are design tricks that enhance the feel of openness.

The use of color has tremendous power to influence the perception of space. Too much bright or intense color is overwhelming, making objects seem larger than they actually are by stimulating the retina and attracting the eye's attention. An entire area treated in one of the cooler colors makes the space seem larger than it actually is, whereas a warmer color tends to make the space seem smaller. On smaller boats, off-white, gray, and beige are good, conservative choices that, while not exciting, probably won't turn anybody off either. Imagine the interior of a 33-foot sport cruiser representing the trend away from high contrasts to a more monochromatic look. Partial bulkheads separate but do not close off the double berth forward from the saloon with dinette and sideboard galley. Carpeting is a short pile with a medium gray color, furniture bases are off-white, seat cushions are a metallized graphite color that matches the galley countertops. Window curtains are light gray with a shell design that includes a few other quiet colors, barely noticeable. By itself, this interior might seem a little dull. But add a splash of lemon yellow with four or five toss pillows and the interior jumps to life.

But put those same pillows in a tan or beige scheme and they will look entirely different, maybe even dull and dirty. Why is that? Probably because the yellow color is in the same

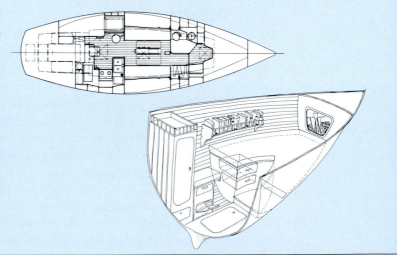

The Geometry of Space Planning

Because there are few square shapes inside a boat, furniture foundations and stowage compartments assume some peculiar geometric shapes. The fine entry lines of both sailboats and powerboats are particularly challenging to naval architects, and oftentimes downright unfathomable to the untrained eye. The space that appears to be generous in the accommodation or floor plan may not be there at all when viewed in cross section. Notice how the V and round shapes of these hulls produce oddly shaped lockers and berths.

family as the tan or beige. Colors affect one another and therefore look different in different surroundings. For a successful scheme it is important to have some sense of color theory, be it learned or intuitive. When in doubt, nothing works better than trying large samples in the areas they are intended for.

Sometimes the designer will alter standard shapes for the sake of jazzing things up and adding interest. Exaggerated curves may seem gratuitous, however, and should be used with restraint; unusual features without any purpose often look funny. This seems to be the case with some production muscleboats and a few sailboats whose designers seem bored with straight lines and subtle turns. Still, it is not necessary that every table and settee be square; that too is rigid and dull.

Textures and patterns play an important role. Excessive busyness is distracting and can contribute to seasickness. On large surfaces, avoid strong patterns with large visual repetitions and strong directional lines; instead, favor the subtle effects of surface variation in softly ribbed or tucked upholstery, pleated shades and miniblinds, and plastic laminates or tiles in the head or galley. Like strong colors, strong patterns should be used as accents, not background. Be especially wary of patterns that seem to "move," as they can promote queasiness underway.

Again, mirrors seem to double space by reflection. Entire bulkheads and doors may be mirrored to divert attention from, say, storage closets, and to emphasize the furniture, colors, and patterns they reflect. A similar effect is achieved with lacquered woods and the discreet images they bounce back to the observer. Megayacht interior designer Terence Disdale says he prefers gloss lacquer to mirrors on overheads, to elevate ceilings.

The tendency toward compartmentalization naturally stops the eye and contributes to a trapped feeling. Both small and large yachts benefit from partial bulkheads or sliding doors that allow a flow of "events"—as designer Joe Artese calls them—from one area to another, thereby shifting attention from the normal lines of demarcation.

One or two accents in an area, whether they be high-contrast colors, unusual shapes, or unexpected objects, are sure to grab attention. But too many focal points distract and confuse the eye.

1 The saloon in *Ilinga*, a 1956 Huckins, appears larger than it really is because of the oversize windows, which permit panoramic viewing even when seated. Such windows would pose a safety hazard offshore, but that was never the intent of the Sportsman 40. The owner is fastidious, abhorring extraneous gear and knickknacks.

2 Designed by Philip Rhodes and built by the Burger Boat Company, *Anadarko*'s master stateroom makes effective use of mirrors across the aft bulkhead to increase the sense of spaciousness. Light cream colors help, too. The changing seats inboard of each berth are a thoughtful touch.

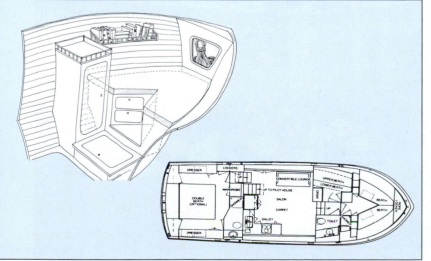

*A*ll our powerboat designs are deep-V planing hulls. We begin our work with an overall concept of the boat. We tell the client he can have all the speed he wants, but here's where the engines are going to go, and here are the sacrifices in accommodations.

Machinery space is top priority. For high-performance boats the center of gravity must be about 60 percent of the length of the waterline aft. Tanks, generators, hot-water heaters, and other fixed weights are generally installed aft of the engine. Inboard/outboards and surface-drive propulsion systems, however, enable you to locate the engines even farther aft, which makes our life easier. High-performance boats up to about 60 or 70 feet run best with the engines all the way aft. This gives you about three-quarters of the length of the boat to play with for interior accommodations.

Faster speed means finer entry, and finer entry means starting the accommodations farther aft. If a client wants a walkaround queen-size bed and huge head, you either have to give the hull a wider entry, which hurts performance and increases pounding, or talk him into increasing boat size by 10 percent.

with John Kiley

It helps if you can sense early an owner's inclination to stuff his boat with goodies.

There seem to be more possibilities in powerboats than sailboats because the soles are wider and the topsides more vertical. Foam-cored stringers are critical in handling the slamming loads of a hull, and give us quite a bit of freedom in locating transverse bulkheads. Plus you don't have to worry about masts and rigging.

Aft of about station three, there isn't much difference in accommodations between high-performance and more conventional hulls. Once the machinery and stringers are fixed, I draw the sole lines and countertops so we have a realistic place to start the accommodations. When looking at the plan view, it's surprising how many people, including some designers, think the sole can extend to the sides of the boat. But a boat is not a house, and a lot of people have a problem understanding the difference.

—John Kiley
C. Raymond Hunt Associates
Boston, Massachusetts

1

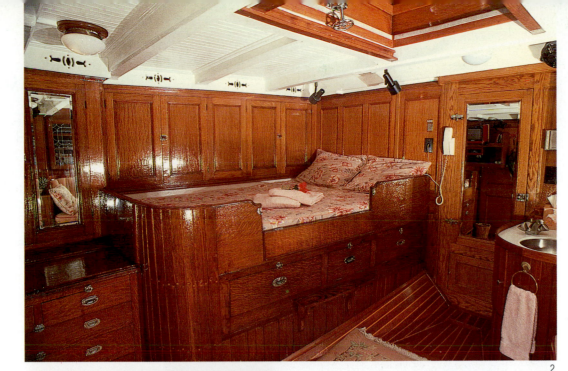

Harbinger

The 117-foot double-headsail, bowsprit ketch *Harbinger* was built by Stowe and Sons of Shoreham, England, between 1913 and 1919, no doubt delayed by the kaiser's ambitions. She was commissioned in 1920 for a Scottish duke and Royal Yacht Squadron member. Today, still fresh from a five-year rebuild, she sails in the Caribbean charter trade, a cassette deck in each stateroom and a color TV and VCR in the saloon (amidships) and the master stateroom (aft). What would the dour duke think? Probably he'd console himself with a glass of Glenlivet and the fact that she remains one of the most elegant traditionally styled yachts on the world's oceans.

1 The saloon paneling is mahogany and lacewood. Dark-green velvet settees surround the dining table, and deck chairs supply additional seating.

2 *Harbinger*'s master stateroom is paneled in oak and has a large double berth, a private head with shower, and a small wash basin en suite, a nicety missing on many modern yachts.

3 A voluminous linen closet is cleverly concealed behind an ornamental cut-glass cabinet in *Harbinger*'s master stateroom.

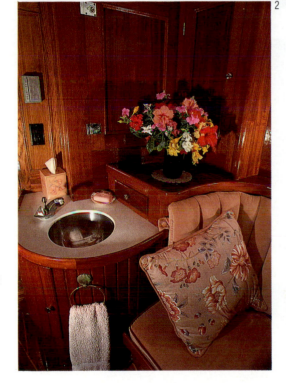

2

3

SUMMARY

Interior layout and design integrate elements of both function and beauty to produce a harmonious whole. Accommodations must remain full size yet not appear too crowded. Movement from deck to cabins should not require strenuous effort, and traffic patterns below should provide convenient access to all areas without annoying distractions. A custom interior plan takes into consideration how the yacht will be used and by whom. A good understanding of space is a prerequisite of designing, as is knowledge of the use of color, patterns, and other "tricks" to impart a sense of spaciousness.

1 One tried-and-true theme uses neutral colors for carpeting, bulkheads, and upholstery, with selected focal-point accents such as the colorful throw pillows in *Lady Frances*'s saloon.

2 The saloon table is a common gathering place. In *Tiana*, a Swan 76 built by Nautor of Finland, dropleaves convert the unit from a coffee-table centerpiece to a full dining table. The base makes a logical stowage compartment. Flame stitching on the seat upholstery is distinctive though busy. The red threads pick up the color of the wood grain.

Light, Air, and Color

Comfort afloat requires more than soft cushions and cold drinks. Light not only facilitates everyday activities such as cooking and reading, but also has a profound influence on emotional moods. Like gloomy weather, dark interiors can be depressing, making one feel incarcerated or as though he lives in a perpetual state of fog and cloud. Generous natural light brings the outdoors inside and effectively neutralizes the oppression of close quarters. Color is intimately tied to light, and it too plays an important role in the comfort of a cabin or room.

Similarly, a poorly ventilated boat often seems like a tomb and is prone to condensation and mildew. Especially in the tropics, cooling ocean breezes must be brought below and freely circulated throughout the cabins. Whether the boat cruises Alaska or Baja California, the key to comfort is the ability of the crew to control light and air to suit conditions. It is more difficult than in a house, but with intelligent planning, good results are possible.

LIGHT

Unlike Shakespeare's rose, not all light is the same. Foremost is natural light, which varies with the weather from harsh brilliance to weak gray. Portlights, hatches, and companionways determine how much gets below and at what angles. Artificial light is created by the designer, either for general illumination, atmospheric lighting, or task lighting.

NATURAL LIGHT

The sun is truly the source of life. Without it, the earth would be a cold, airless planet devoid of plants and animals. At the same time, the sun's ultraviolet rays can damage human skin and be generally debilitating. Controlling the amount of sunlight belowdeck is vital to health and pleasure on board.

Windows, portlights, skylights, deck prisms, hatches, and companionways are the six main gateways through which sunlight can be introduced below. Their number and configuration vary with the type and style of yacht. The large, sliding windows of a motoryacht would be both impractical and aesthetically repugnant on an ocean-cruising sailboat. By the same token, the small bronze portlights required for safety on a circumnavigating sailboat would look terribly out of place on a motoryacht. As always, homage must be paid to Mistress Style. But the safety factor cannot be overlooked: Frames must be strong and glass able to withstand the crushing power of a boarding sea or a

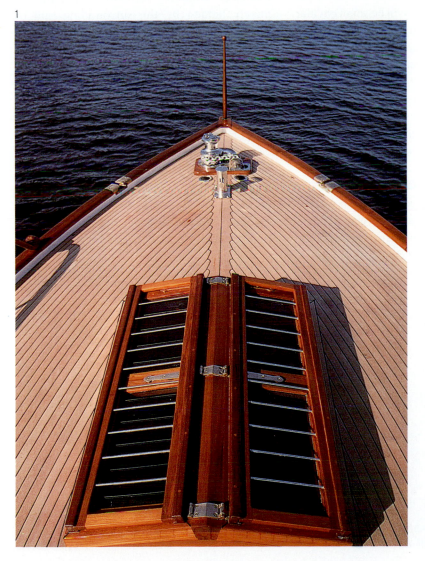

1

2

guest thrown off his or her feet. More than one boat has gone to the bottom because windows failed.

Windows—if we may call them that—are less common on sailboats because of inherently lower freeboard and lower cabin structures. The closer the water, the smaller, stronger, and more waterproof the windows must be. Even on a two-deck motoryacht, the windows near water level will be small circular or rectangular portlights; the saloon and wheelhouse 12 or 15 feet above water level may be permitted the luxury of larger fixed or opening windows. Sailboats with elevated saloons amidships may have larger than normal windows to permit expansive views from the dinette. Clever design work will provide water views from both standing and seated positions.

Extruded aluminum frames look cheap and are not very strong. Better choices are welded or cast aluminum, welded or forged stainless steel, and cast bronze, perhaps chromed for looks and maintenance. Plexiglas is not much

used as a pane material any longer because of its tendency to craze and turn milky under the violent attack of the sun. Lexan, tinted or clear, is the fabled bulletproof material used on heads-of-state limousines. It is not as scratch-resistant as glass, but is more so than Plexiglas and is incredibly strong. Safety glass, as used on automobile windshields, gives the clearest viewing and can be used on boats wherever the likelihood of being hit by waves is remote.

For their light weight and buyer's value, plastic-framed portlights have grabbed a hefty share of the small-boat market. These range in quality from poor to fairly good. A distinct advantage of them is that they won't rust; they have neither the strength nor the appeal of good metal portlights, however.

A simplistic treatment is the so-called frameless window. Actually the frame is merely hidden by the surrounding hull or cabin side. Common on many powerboats and some sailboats, frameless windows are featured by the Henry R. Hinckley Company as a design trademark. The look certainly is clean, and if the pane is recessed and the lower lip angled outboard, window visors probably won't be necessary to keep dripping water out.

Obviously opening windows and portlights provide an important means of letting breezes in. But as size increases, so must pane thickness. At some point the opening feature becomes impractical if not downright unsafe. Hence, other ventilation methods are necessary.

1 The traditional skylight is an excellent means of introducing light and air below. A good boat carpenter also finds the skylight a conspicuous showcase for his joiner skills. Poor design, craftsmanship, or maintenance often results in irritating leaks.

2 The forward-facing bronze opening portlight on *Irene*, the last yawl built by Concordia, introduces much more air than the same portlight on the side cabin. It also permits a view forward without sticking one's head out a hatch, a feature difficult to achieve on swept-back cabin faces.

3 *Antipodean*'s large round windows seemed to violate all rules when Jon Bannenberg's design was first introduced. From inside, one has the sensation of viewing the world through the window of Captain Nemo's *Nautilus*, and from outside the vertical hemi-spheric dividers create interest.

4 Aircraft bubbles, popular among long-distance ocean racing sailors, enable the crew to observe sails and weather conditions without leaving the safety of the cabin. The woodwork and almost viscous plastic, not to mention the added light below, make the viewing/steering dome a worthwhile feature in its own right.

3

4

Hatches serve several purposes, of which ventilation and light are probably the most valuable. (Others include functioning as emergency exits and as ports through which to pass up sail bags and other gear.) Hatches are available in most shapes and all sizes, each employing some means of keeping it in the "up" position. Better models permit opening to any position, enabling the hatch to function much like an adjustable vent in a home heating or automobile air-conditioning system. Sailcloth windscoops rigged above the hatch are particularly effective on hot, airless days. Check the locking mechanism for strength and ease of operation. Four-way hatches are cleverly designed and of great utility when lying beam or stern to the wind, as often happens at a dock. Tinted Lexan is an ideal pane material— strong and cool.

Another way to control sunlight is by installing a curtain on double tracks or a sliding panel that hides behind the overhead. This thoughtful touch is especially appreciated over a berth, where the early morning sun can surely turn a hangover in the wrong direction!

Traditional skylights are double-opening pitched hatches usually constructed of wood, paned with glass, and protected with brass rods. Sometimes the entire structure is hinged to facilitate the passing through of gear and provisions. While indeed quite handsome, they are prone to leak and can be an obtrusive presence on deck. But on a boat of the right character, an old wooden schooner for instance, the skylight is an integral element of its personality.

Deck prisms are small rectangular glass pieces set in a frame in the deck. Their purpose is to shed small amounts of natural light in dark corners. They are seldom specified on new boats nowadays, partly due to the availability of low wattage electrical lights, which are more effective.

Last, light is admitted belowdeck the same way people are—through the companionway. Saloons and wheelhouses that are otherwise short on light sources are well served by glass doors, or at least wooden doors with windows. One or more sailboat weatherboards can be duplicated in Lexan, or one can be constructed as a screen to provide ventilation as well as light.

5

5 Hatches need not be square. This small round hatch with window glass and protective bars is an attractive alternative. The boat is a 27-foot 1959 Chris-Craft cabin cruiser.

6 The smoked Plexiglas hatch on *All Is Best*'s foredeck typifies contemporary hatch styles, especially those of European influence.

7 The versatility of a simple wooden hatch on a Concordia yawl is doubled by adding two small elliptical skylights that echo the shape and style of the cabin portlights.

1 Hatch shades drawn from inside are a much appreciated method of blocking light, especially for late sleepers. The Privilege 48 catamaran has two pullout shades of different density—light and dark. Also possible is a panel that slides between the deck and overhead so that it is not seen when not in use.

2 Vertically drawn custom-pleated Roman window shades with battens can be styled to match other colors, fabrics, and textures in the same cabin. Depending on the material chosen, such a treatment may look heavy, but that's not a problem on the small window in *Destiny*'s guest stateroom.

3 Traditional curtains were chosen for the master stateroom on *Deluxe*.

4 A slightly raised deckhouse over the saloon of the Ocean 71 *La Cosa Real* allows for windows all around with Levolor blinds for privacy. On either side of the forward passageway are mahogany cabinets with additional freezer capacity.

5 Blue Verosol-pleated shades were chosen by interior designer Blanche Bloomfield for *Deluxe*'s saloon and dining area. The material resists staining, and a special sun-screen coating helps minimize fading. Although they must be either raised or fully lowered, they are translucent and pass enough light to keep living areas bright.

6 The elliptically shaped aft ends of the saloon windows in the Ocean 53 motoryacht are squared off with fixed, pleated curtains so that Levolor blinds can be used over the rest of the glass.

4

5

6

1

2

3

1 The skylight above the staircase on *Part VI*, a 150-foot
   Oceanfast, provides needed
   light to the stairwell.

2 Prisms mounted flush in the
   deck are a sensible means of
   lighting otherwise dark corners
   below without compromising
   the strength of the deck or
   lines of the vessel.

3 The bronze kerosene lamp is
   hard to beat for atmospheric
   lighting. Its soft glow and
   radiant warmth are appreciated
   on chilly nights.

4 Tiny overhead quartz lights,
   similar to slide projector
   lamps, are the primary lighting
   source in *Hawkeye*'s saloon.
   Some reading lamps would
   probably be appreciated, but
   clearly the idea is to keep the
   space open and uncluttered.

ARTIFICIAL LIGHT

Natural light is of little help at night, of course,
and even during daytime it may be too dim for
tasks such as reading and navigation. Before
the invention of the long-life storage battery,
first whale oil and later kerosene were common lamp fuels. A handsome brass kerosene
lamp is still a nice feature swinging above the
saloon table; its light is soft, and the warmth it
gives off is appreciated in chilly weather.
Kerosene is smelly, however, and despite the
use of smoke bells it will soon smudge the
overhead. And in the tropics the added heat
source is intolerable. Electrical lighting is the
universal answer. A basic lighting plan should
include the three types mentioned above: general lighting, atmospheric lighting, and task
lighting.

As you develop your lighting plan, think in
terms of these basic fixture types: uplights,
downlights, spotlights, table and floor lights,
colored lights, and recessed lights. Imagine
where the light from each fixture will fall. Will
it cover the desired areas? How much overlap
between fixtures? Will there be an attractive
balance between the various types? What
effect will the lights have on the colors you've
chosen for upholstery, hull coverings, bulkheads, carpeting, and window shades?

General Lighting. At night or on cloudy afternoons you will want to light each cabin with general utility lighting. These may be as simple as 12-volt incandescent bulbs with shades. They might be strategically mounted on the bulkheads for maximum lighting. Incandescent light is considered a warm light, as it has a comparatively large red component. Alternatively, you might opt for fluorescent bulbs either hidden behind trim pieces or covered with plastic lenses. One advantage of fluorescent lighting is that it draws less electricity than incandescent bulbs. Several types, each throwing off different shades of light, are available. Fluorescent lamps designated "warm" emphasize yellow, orange-red, and red-purple colors in fabrics and other materials. "Cool" lamps accentuate blue-purple, blue, blue-green, and yellow-green. Sometimes the most successful lighting is a combination of incandescent and fluorescent bulbs.

As at home, some general lighting may be placed overhead, while other fixtures should be fixed lower for a softer effect. Dimmer switches save electricity and adjust light intensity and mood at the same time.

Atmospheric Lighting. Atmospheric lighting lends a touch of elegance and romance at night. This type includes a variety of indirect light sources such as small footlights to gently illuminate stairs and furniture foundations, strips of micro-illumes or rope lights around vanities, and fluorescent fixtures hidden by coves and valances. The purpose is more to set a mood than perform a specific job. Footlights and subtle cockpit lamps also can be used on deck, not only for safety but to create an understated ambience as well.

Task Lighting. Task lighting usually involves narrow beams of light for facilitating specific activities. For example, a high-tensile lamp, perhaps with an adjustable red shade, over the navigation table enables the navigator to read charts without disturbing the rest of the crew. The cook will want lighting fixtures that eliminate dark corners and brighten up key areas of the galley evenly, especially the stove and countertops. And don't forget lights for food, utensil, and pot stowage lockers; a small bulb triggered by a switch coupled to the cabinet door will keep your flashlight in its drawer.

4

In the staterooms, adjustable narrow-beam reading lamps should be positioned over each berth.

An interior yacht designer will give considerable thought to a comprehensive lighting plan when working on a new vessel or renovating an older one. But nonprofessionals undertaking the job themselves may overlook its importance until late in the game, when the switches are flicked and to everyone's dismay some areas are poorly lighted and others suffer under a harsh glare. Every part of the boat requires light, but not necessarily the same type. Develop a cabin-by-cabin plan, consider the activities that will be performed in each, try to anticipate how your lights will affect the color and visual texture of fabrics, and read manufacturers' catalogs to familiarize yourself with the fixtures available. Identify lighting needs early, for the electrician's benefit if not your own.

You can correct some problems simply by replacing fixtures with a different type. For instance, if your incandescent lights aren't flattering the new cushion covers you've sewn, try changing to a fluorescent fixture. Or if one area has two wide-beamed general lights serving it, you could replace one with a narrow-beamed task light for reading convenience, or perhaps with a muted light fixture merely for the ambience. Lamp fixture styles, especially the shades, seem to date quickly, and you can alter or update the look of your cabin quickly by buying new fixtures or shades. And, of course, you can add additional new lights to an electrical circuit with an electrician's kit (wire, connectors, stripper, etc.), a hand drill, and a screwdriver. If you have dark corners that seem to defy illumination by existing lights, this may be your best course.

1 The handsome interior of *Flying Goose* utilizes various lighting schemes, including polished brass task lights over the chart table and settees.

2 The instruments on *Bermbee*'s bridge, including a 72-mile color radar, provide soft atmospheric lighting of their own. Night vision is always a factor in planning lighting on the bridge.

3 *Bermbee*, an 85-foot motoryacht designed by Jack Hargrave and constructed of aluminum by Palmer Johnson, looks just as good at night with carefully planned deck lighting. She is lying at Lyford Quay, Nassau, Bahamas.

4 Valance and footlights in *Golden Delicious* create a warm, inviting atmosphere, especially after hours. The complex lighting system relies heavily on incandescent fixtures on dimmers.

5 *P'zazz*'s forward lounge combines spot downlights with neon-lit coves overhead and rope lights around the bar. The counters are black marble, the furniture is upholstered in black leather, and the bulkheads are pony hide.

1

2

3

4

5

AIR

One of the great advances in 20th-century technology is the ability to at least partly control our environment. Sophisticated heating and air-conditioning systems in our homes and cars thermostatically regulate temperature to suit personal requirements, and air-exchange systems can replace stagnant air inside with fresh outside air on a timed cycle. Environmental control methods are of necessity simple on small boats, but with increased size and power comes access to computer-controlled equipment that can make the interior of your yacht as comfortable as the most complex office building.

NATURAL AIR SOURCES

Obviously the most convenient sources of fresh air are the breezes that blow across the water. The principle of how to harness them is as simple as erecting a windmill or flying a kite—open a hatch in the right direction and it will scoop the air and redirect it below. Vents perform the same function, though the volume of air moved is generally smaller. By necessity, such devices are deck-mounted, except

The original Dorade vent, shown here on the yacht *Dorade*, was designed by Olin Stephens to provide ventilation for the 1931 Transatlantic and Fastnet races. A small box with a trap inside prevents water from entering the cabin below. Theoretically an all-weather air source, the design does not circulate a great deal of air.

portlights in the hull, which are mostly small and may not be operational underway on windy days.

It makes sense to develop a ventilation plan from the bow aft, because underway or at anchor, the apparent wind will come from forward; berthing at a dock or quay, however, requires different solutions. Also, it is one thing to introduce air and another to expel it. The principle of air exchange is to provide an intake upwind and a discharge downwind. Consequently, the function of some vents and ductwork is merely to get rid of bad air. It might seem a waste of gear, but there must be a relief valve or escape hatch.

It is highly desirable—though not always practical or possible—to circulate air throughout every part of the boat, including bilges and engine compartment. The possibility of condensation and mildew is reduced, musty smells are eliminated, and if there are wooden floor timbers, the potential of dry rot is minimized as well.

Begin at the bow, in the forepeak or chain locker. Ventilation here is perhaps not as critical as in other areas, but consider the smell of moist mud and seaweed on the anchor rode—whew! Worse, it's at the foot of the V-berths. A low-profile deck vent such as a small cowl or mushroom type on the foredeck is often sufficient to dry out smelly substances. To move this air out, it may be feasible to install flexible ductwork under or outboard of the V-berths and into the bilge, where it in turn may be expelled by a bilge blower.

Moving aft, the forward stateroom requires good ventilation for sleeping comfort. Fortunately, this cabin is perhaps the easiest to keep airy and cool. Overhead hatches with adjustable arms allow considerable control of how much air is allowed to enter. On still nights, some sort of cloth windscoop suspended over the hatch captures whatever traces of breeze are blowing. Side-opening portlights introduce air in beam winds, but also function as exhaust ports when the wind is on the bow. The action of wind passing by the opening will suck out the air inside just as an open car window sucks out cigarette smoke.

Special attention should be given to the head compartment, as toilets and plumbing are

with Danny Greene

*W*hile it is relatively easy to achieve good light and ventilation on a boat in port, especially if it is moored or anchored and thus head to wind, it is extremely difficult to do so when sailing. When the weather is hot and rough it can be almost impossible.

Dorade vents are, I think, overrated and almost useless. If they admit a significant flow of air, they also admit a significant flow of water, whether it is heavy rain, spray, or solid water on deck. Deck hatches are also of little use in rough weather.

The best solution I know is a large companionway hatch protected by an extensive dodger. The rigid dodger on my 34-foot ketch Brazen *extends about 2¹/₂ feet aft of the hatch and so allows me to leave the hatch open in all but the most severe weather. And since it has large windows on three sides as well as the top—which is removable—it also contributes a great deal of light below. This companionway arrangement, combined with a wide-open interior, makes conditions down below quite comfortable even in rough weather in the tropics.*

A light color interior—gray in my case—and good-size portlights in the cabin sides also help the situation, especially when the dinghy is stowed over the main cabin deck hatch.

—Danny Greene
Naval architect and contributing editor to
Cruising World
living aboard in Bermuda

---

natural sources of foul odors. An opening portlight is a minimum fresh air source, but an overhead vent is recommended. The head is a good place to try a solar-powered exhaust vent; this is a low-profile mushroom-type vent with a fan inside.

Because of the difficulty of ventilating hanging lockers and drawers, the best solution is to keep them open to the cabin interior. Caning and louvers permit decent circulation. Small plastic building vents such as those used to ventilate the eaves of houses can be put to good use in the backs or sides of lockers where other types of screened openings are impractical. And perhaps the best way to keep clothes fresh and vegetables from rotting is to stow them in sliding, plastic-coated wire baskets.

The main cabin or saloon, the dinette, and other midship living areas require the most ventilation, partly because of the heat generated by people and the galley, and partly because this area is not as exposed to prevailing breezes as the forward parts of the boat. Again, opening portlights, hatches, skylights and Dorade vents will help bring in air. The main companionway is an excellent exhaust. Large, fixed windows can be fitted with smaller, opening portlights, though they tend to look strange. Depending on the deck layout, it may be possible to add an opening hatch in the overhead of a poorly ventilated cabin, but care

should be taken that the structural integrity of the deck isn't compromised. Still, chances are good that some form of artificial ventilation will be required, and we'll examine that in the next section.

Quarter berths and under-the-cockpit berths are notoriously stuffy. The minimum solution is to install an opening portlight in the cockpit footwell of sailboats and small powerboats; on larger boats it may be possible to have a portlight in the hull side. Overhead vents are indicated where feasible, but often there is simply no available deck space. A side benefit of forced-air heating and air-conditioning systems is the ductwork that connects the cabins and helps circulate air even when the heater isn't in use.

Aft there should be exhaust vents connected to the bilge by ductwork. A blower is required equipment aboard gasoline-powered boats, and is worth considering even on a boat with diesel engines.

A drawback of deck-mounted ventilating gear is the obstructions they create. Polished chrome Dorades certainly look good, but they are line-snaggers and foot-trippers, and they make it difficult to stow dinghies on deck or even to sunbathe. Some builders have developed innovative solutions such as mast vents that funnel air into the cabins below, but options are limited on small boats.

1

2

3

4

5

1 The custom hatch awnings aboard *Parenu,* a Valiant 40, keep sunlight from heating the cabins, protect the varnish on the hatches, and keep out light rain and drizzle while admitting air. They also can function as windscoops, and underway the material folds into itself to keep water off the hatch seals.

2 A windscoop fixed over the forward hatch is capable of directing below great volumes of air. Canvas or acrylic withstands the chafe from buffeting winds better than lightweight nylon.

3 In good weather, the most efficient air source is an open window!

4 Solar-powered mushroom vents can be mounted just about anywhere on deck. A small fan moves air whenever the sun shines; even at night some air still enters through the screen.

5 Mildew is the nemesis of every boat owner, and it is especially virile in closed lockers. Basket weave, caning, and decorative cutouts are attractive methods of circulating air through small enclosed spaces.

ARTIFICIAL AIR SOURCES

Certainly natural ventilation is to be preferred over artificial, but the reality is that there are muggy days and still nights. During those times, the crew that can flick a switch to activate a fan or air-conditioning unit will be infinitely more comfortable than poor souls trapped in a stagnant cabin—especially when there are mosquitoes cruising outside!

The time-honored fan is the mainstay of cabin ventilation—at least in smaller boats. Twelve-volt fans are available in 6-inch "personal" sizes—ideal for mounting over berths—and in larger sizes capable of cooling an entire cabin. Many are oscillating.

Motoryachts and large sailboats with auxiliary generators will likely opt for the sybaritic comfort of central air-conditioning. The manufacturer can help you determine the size of unit required. This will be based on Btus (British thermal units). As a rule of thumb, belowdeck cabins will require a unit with a Btu capacity about 60 times the square footage of the cabin, and above-deck cabins, because they are not as well insulated by the surrounding water and are more exposed to wind, will require a unit with a Btu capacity about 120 times the square footage of the cabin. (For example, 500 square feet × 120 = 60,000 Btus.)

Most units run on 110- or 220-volt electrical power, which is provided by the generator. Ductwork carries the forced air to registers mounted throughout the cabins, often on the foundations of furniture or perhaps in the sole (floor). The registers, of course, should be adjustable to direct or curtail air flow.

For an added cost of about 15 percent, most air-conditioning units can be fitted with heating coils to provide warmth in cold weather.

In addition to the heating and cooling benefits of such equipment, there is the bonus of circulating air whenever the unit is on. Boat cabins are for the most part small spaces, and because they are designed to be watertight and hence airtight, there is considerable potential to trap cooking, smoking, and other smells. If you've ever wondered why the couple who lets you smoke in their house won't let you smoke on their boat, this is why. The only other explanation is that they love the boat more!

DESIGN FOR MAXIMUM LIGHT AND AIR

The tendency to compartmentalize boat interiors not only closes up the available space, but also works to the detriment of good light and ventilation. Especially on smaller boats, the demand for privacy results in numerous bulkheads that create dark, hard-to-light areas and impede the flow of air between cabins. Half-bulkheads and privacy curtains offer flexibility: With curtains open the cabin feels more spacious, light diffuses, and air circulates; with curtains closed, privacy is ensured, yet some amount of air can still pass through and around the material. Curtains are also soft, and that is always a pleasing effect in a structure composed mostly of hard materials.

6

Much of the accommodations in displacement hulls are at or below the waterline, so that only by standing can one look out a window at the scenery. On some boats there may be portlights in the topsides, but these will probably be small for safety reasons. An elevated deckhouse generally provides larger windows with seating arranged to take advantage of them; an inside steering station may be located at its forward end, and there may be a small dinette for lunches. Such a bright and airy cabin, nevertheless offering protection from the sun and rain, is sure to be one of the most popular places on board.

And lest we forget, if it's light and air you're after, it's hard to beat the cockpit and deck. Like the porch at home, a good cockpit is half

6 Where auditory privacy is impossible, visual privacy is the best that can be hoped for. In *Jan Van Gent*, a 50-foot Shpountz 44-40 by French designer Daniel Bombigher, partial bulkheads are supplemented by privacy curtains. The cabins are effectively separated at night, but when the curtains are tied back the interior opens up magnificently.

1

inside and half out. Some sort of hard dodger or canvaswork in the form of a bimini, dodger, or awning shields the sun to a degree, yet leaves the sides open for freshness. During inclement weather side curtains can be dropped wholly or partially. The key again is the ability to *control* how much sun and wind you receive on your body.

COLOR

Everything we perceive has color. Even black, which is sometimes defined as the absence of light, is a color easily discernible to the human eye. Color has a powerful symbolic and emotional influence on people, and so it is little wonder that color is an important creative tool of the decorator.

Ancient cultures attached great symbolic importance to colors. The Greeks believed in four primary elements in the universe—earth, fire, water, and air—and each had its own color in paintings and other illustrative depictions. The Hindus too used red for fire, white for water, and black for earth. The Chinese, on the other hand, depicted the earth as yellow. American Indians had a color for each point of the compass: yellow symbolized north, red the south, white the east, and green the west. While we of the 20th century may not be as superstitious nor so immersed in the symbolic use of colors, we still associate red with fire or passion, yellow with cowardice or the bounty of the earth (as in corn and other grain), green with envy, white with innocence, and black with evil.

No doubt you have favorite colors, as well you should. "Color travels in a ten-year cycle," says Blanche Bloomfield, a Pompano Beach, Florida, interior decorator. "We all react to colors. It is said that introverts like cool colors and that extroverts like warm colors."

Though your choices may be somewhat limited by current market fashion, don't feel tied to the High Point market predictions—you'll never keep up. For example, in late 1988 Bloomfield said, "Jewel tones, so popular last year, are fading. Earth tones such as rust are in. Plaids are popular, as are sweet pastels such as lilacs and other dainty colors. Chenilles are coming back and leather is always big. African patterns and Southwest moods are holding their own."

Like the rest of the fashion industry, color is a fickle and fascinating business. Color selection has a major impact on any decorating job, so take advantage of this creative opportunity and make choices that reflect *your* personality and taste.

A cabin's color scheme is established by the treatment of its main and secondary areas. Accents are important, as they complete the general effect—the finishing touches, so to speak. Consider the main areas of your cabin first—the bulkheads and hull sides, the soles, and the overheads. On entering a cabin, your eyes are often drawn to a beautiful sole, and this is perhaps a good place to begin. Next select colors, patterns, and textures for the secondary areas such as bunks, window treatments, and large furniture. Last, consider minor areas: lamps, pillows, and accessories. They must all work in harmony, whether your plan is to stick to one color or hue, to two complementary colors, or to several different hues in the same color. Any number of approaches is possible.

As you would at home, obtain sample swatches of materials and colors you like and place them on the boat for a few days. Note how they change during the day. Where does the light fall, and what does it do to the color? Darks, for instance, may turn black in dark, shadowy corners, yet become washed out in bright direct sun. How can you control the natural light? And how will you use artificial light to retain the original color you selected?

1 The deck awning on *Ring Andersen*, a 115-foot Baltic ketch built in 1948 in Svendborg, Denmark, extends from the mainmast to the stern, cooling and sheltering the deck and interior. Large awnings, though expensive and clumsy to stow, are important gear for the tropics.

2 *Margin Call*'s saloon is predominantly blue and pink, both of which are potentially troublesome in dark wood interiors: Dark blue absorbs light, and pink may clash with the color of some woods. The windows appear yellow because storm shutters are installed outside.

3 *Margin Call*, a Little Harbor 75 sloop designed by Ted Hood, powers through the U.S. Virgin Islands.

with
Blanche Bloomfield

You hear so much talk from interior decorators about "exposure," you'd think they'd alter the Earth's orbit if they had half a chance. But the angle and intensity of the sun's rays do indeed play an important role in how a room should be furnished. Climate figures in, too. Favored colors, textures, and materials vary from the tropics (cool colors with smooth surfaces to offset frequently bright, intense sunlight) to the American Pacific Northwest and northern Europe (warmer colors on rougher surfaces compatible with the many cloudy days, and weaker sunlight). Northern houses are designed with dramatically sloping roofs and vast banks of windows to capture the prevailing light. Greenhouses are affixed to the wall with the right exposure. Paintings are placed in the living room with a thought to the light that comes through the nearest illuminating window.

So where does this leave the yacht interior decorator who must tackle a beast with no permanent exposure?

"Don't let exposure influence you at all," says Blanche Bloomfield, president of Sea and Sky Interiors in Pompano Beach, Florida. "Forget north, south, east, and west. The only way you could rely on exposure is if the yacht is berthed at the same slip for three months, but of course that's silly. Choose colors that work for you. And control the light that plays on your colors with window treatments: window tints, tilting blinds, and the old standby, drapes.

"Keep colors light in the south. Dark colors and small spaces don't work. Blue is very popular with men, but it absorbs a lot of light, and no matter how good the dye is, it tends to fade easily. You want a moderate tone for boats that move from north to south. Pea green is bilious. Blue-greens and turquoise tend to spread because the ocean tends to take up on those colors.

"Anything with a pattern retains its practicality in terms of cleaning and interest. But don't use a multitude of patterns, and be careful of their scale."

SUMMARY

Interior design is the key to enjoying time spent aboard a boat, whether an afternoon or a lifetime. The ability to control both natural and artificial light and air ensures a more comfortable climate, and the color, pattern, and textures of materials such as cabin soles, overheads, hull ceilings, and fabrics help create a psychologically pleasant atmosphere as well as an aesthetically pleasing environment. While marine conditions impose greater restrictions on the designer than the land-based home, changes can be made to your boat that increase its value and improve the quality of life afloat.

2

3

Part II

The Division of Space ∎

CHAPTER SIX
Common Cabins

n every yacht there is a cabin or area where the crew congregates during the off-watch or when day is done. In a Rozinante canoe yawl it may be the only cabin on the boat, furnished simply with two opposing settees performing double duty as berths. In a larger motoryacht there may be two or even several common cabins—a saloon and deckhouse, for instance—where people can relax, eat meals, watch television, listen to Ahmad Jamal on the stereo, or simply observe the crests of passing waves.

A brief analysis of the space available in a given hull should suggest the rough dimensions of the common cabin and its size in proportion to other cabins such as staterooms and galleys. Whereas the stateroom need be little larger than a double berth, the common cabin must provide seating, stowage, entertainment centers such as bookshelves and stereos, room for the restless to stand and stretch, plus sole space for the flow of traffic through and about

the cabin. Since the majority of waking hours belowdeck are spent in common cabins, the decoration of these areas sets the tone for the rest of the interior.

WHERE THEY ARE, AND WHY

SALOONS

During the golden age of passenger liners, the ornate cabin used by passengers for socializing was called the *saloon*. It is the cabin where Phileas Fogg played whist during an ocean leg of his journey in *Around the World in Eighty Days*. In smaller yachts today it is the equivalent of the living room in a house, a public area where the family reads and plays and where guests are entertained. The saloon or main cabin is the heart of the vessel, centrally situated in the accommodation plan and convenient to all other parts forward and aft.

1 *Weatherly*'s saloon is simple and expansive. A small galley and a nav station are forward, and beyond the privacy curtain is a large forepeak with folding "basket" berths. *Weatherly* is a 12-Meter racing sloop converted for day charter. Skippered by Bus Mosbacher, she won the America's Cup in 1962. She competes in the annual Classic Yacht Regatta in Newport, Rhode Island.

2 *Southern Cross* is a converted navy launch whose 50-foot hull was built in 1943 by the New York Naval Shipyard. Her recently renovated saloon features an attractive dinette, painted overhead, and brass fixtures. The lighthouse photograph is mounted on a hinged door that hides a television.

1

2

A Saloon is a Saloon is a Saloon—not a Salon

The evidence is mounting. We're seeing it almost every day now. Somebody around the waterfront has mighty sticky fingers and has been running off with one of the os from the saloons of our boats, leaving us with a lot of unseamanlike and shore-bound salons.

We're not sure who's responsible, but recent reports cause us to speculate that the Carry Nations of our lives—the ones wearing black bonnets and carrying hatchets—have spirited our o away and chopped it into commas. What they overlooked is that the Demon Rum has nothing to do with it.

Drinking establishments got the sobriquet saloon after some enterprising 19th-century barkeeper— in Denver, Colorado, we've heard—dressed his joint up to look like the fancy main cabin of an ocean-going passenger ship—a saloon. Not the other way around.

Here, we'll go on using the double o, double-good word saloon for the main cabins of our boats. The difference between the two is as plain as the difference between a reef knot and a granny.

—George Day
Cruising World

1

DECKHOUSES

Among the distinct advantages of raised deck-houses are the larger windows and great views of the seascape they afford. Forward-facing windows, aft windows and large companion-ways, and windows port and starboard intro-duce light on all four sides of the cabin. Being able to see outside while seated surely helps set a more joyful and liberated mood aboard ship. And in the morning, when you huddle over a cup of freshly brewed coffee and watch Canada geese lift from the wetlands and honk noisily into the sky, the panorama of 360-degree viewing makes you feel almost a part of their vast migration without having to wet your bot-tom on the dew-covered cockpit seats.

The deckhouse may not be the only com-mon cabin, but it will certainly be a favorite. Whether planned as a primary or secondary gathering spot, seating should be arranged to take advantage of the window heights. If space permits, canvas-backed captain's chairs com-plement the standard seating and can be folded up and stowed when not in use. A sofa bed or convertible settee converts the deckhouse into a guest stateroom. Window treatments and cushion fabrics should be carefully selected to retain their colors and patterns in bright sun-light as well as at night, and should contain

ultraviolet inhibitors to prevent fading. There will be fewer dark corners needing special lighting, hence neutral background colors can be darker in tone than in other, lower cabins. But at the same time it may be best to keep the ambience light with soft tones and invigorating colors.

Creating a deckhouse where none existed before would certainly be a significant under-taking, the likely success of which would depend to a great degree on the layout of the predecessor structure. Simply raising the cabin sole and cabintop of a midsize boat is seldom the answer; not only would such a move prob-ably destroy the exterior lines, but it might also dangerously alter the center of gravity.

The possibilities increase with boat size. A large sailboat with generous interior volume might tolerate a raised coachroof aft with an elevated sole; an inside steering station, small conversational seating area, and perhaps a navigator's berth might be possible. A feature sometimes seen on older sailboats is to extend the coachroof over the forward end of the cockpit (thus lengthening the line for the sake of proportions) and to create a sheltered hard-top that more or less obviates the need for can-vas dodgers.

1 *Lotus*'s saloon features beige UltraSuede wallcoverings and original 19th-century oil paintings. At a time when most large motoryachts are marked by glitz and eccentricity, *Lotus*'s interior seems tastefully quiet and simple. The Burger Boat Company built the 72-foot *Lotus* in 1971 for comfortable cruising. Top speed with her twin Caterpillar diesels is 15 knots.

2 *Bermbee*'s afterdeck provides an alternative gathering place for guests. The hinged leaves on the coffee tables serve as fiddles in rolling seas.

3 *Obsessed*, an 85-foot Ed Monk, Jr. design, features a large and bright galley with full-length windows on each side, a center island counter with wine cooler, and spacious wraparound seating.

4 *Record*'s deckhouse, though small, affords tremendous views through curved windows aft and through doors port and starboard.

2

3

4

GREAT CABINS

In some yacht designs the common cabin is located aft of a center cockpit. This arrangement works best when the beam is carried far aft and the buttocks are full to provide good interior volume. A U-shaped dinette aligned fore and aft works well. Adequate lighting can be a problem because the cabintop is likely to be low, compressing the size of the portlights. A flush afterdeck effectively increases space, but this will mean small portlights mounted in the topsides. Fixed windows or opening portlights in the transom provide a welcome view from the dinette but should be engineered very strongly to survive following seas. In any case, wide hatches will be counted on to introduce light and air, especially if there is no companionway to the cockpit. On larger yachts there might be an aft companionway leading to a small private cockpit, but this tends to change the definition of the space from great cabin to simply an aft cabin.

Sometimes the galley will be located at the forward end of a great cabin. In such cases the staterooms forward of the cockpit are necessarily pushed forward of the midship line, where they are subject to more motion and hence are less than ideal as sea berths. Still, the immense volume of a great cabin is impressive, and 270-degree viewing, especially aft, imparts a unique feeling and evokes the captain's quarters on a 17th-century galleon.

1

2

3

1 *Anadarko's* saloon is warm and inviting. The light colors, informal patterns, large throw rug, easy chair, and tables make it a casual, pleasant place to entertain.

2 The great cabin is rarely seen, occupying as it does much of the aft end of a sailing yacht, thus forcing the cockpit up or forward. In *Rangga,* the great cabin is fitted with an unusual V-shaped table. Emergency access to deck is via the bulkhead steps and hatch at the stern.

3 The forward lounge on *Crystal* has a panoramic view forward over the Jacuzzi with a plush, winding sofa and built-in seats straddling the video station.

DESIGN AND DECORATION

LAYOUT

Space restrictions have a lot to say about layout, but there are always options. A common cabin dominated by a large dinette has the drawback of forcing everyone to sit in one place, and runs the risk of "trapping" persons on the inside seats. If possible, more than one seating area is desirable for sheer variety as well as for allowing guests to break into smaller conversational groups.

Draw the cabin to scale on a piece of graph paper and sketch in your ideas. Remember that in most boats the cabin sole won't extend to the maximum beam, and you aren't dealing with all-square shapes (see "The Geometry of Space Planning" in Chapter 4). It may be helpful to cut scaled cardboard figures of a man and woman, preferably with articulated joints, so you can see the space occupied by persons standing, sitting, and lying (see the accompanying "Ergonomic Factors of Furniture Design").

Custom boatbuilders may be able to mock up various interior arrangements in cardboard and cheap plywood on the shop floor so you can test your ideas in three dimensions. Have several people sit and move about the cabin to give you an accurate idea of space. Move seating, tables, and entertainment centers until you are satisfied. Pay special attention to traffic flow.

Every conversational area should have a focal point or "center of gravity." This may be a pedestal table, coffee table, or simply an imaginary spot around which the seating is arranged. It is unlikely you would want to position seats to face directly out windows; rather, one looks across the centerline and out windows on the other side. While scenic views are not possible in all boats, they certainly are a treat if window and seating heights are agreeable.

Ergonomic Factors of Furniture Design

*T*he dimensions of berths and seats are determined by the human body in its various natural positions—standing, sitting, and lying. Though certain arbitrary distances have become standardized for the "average" size man (6 feet 1 inch, or 73 inches) and woman (5 feet 3 inches, or 63 inches), persons who are unusually tall, short, or wide-bottomed should adjust the suggested average measures below according to what's comfortable for them. Why suffer insomnia because the bunk is too short? Why develop a backache from a straight backrest? Why do head butts with a low overhead?

Seatbacks that are slightly angled and rounded are more comfortable than flat, vertical backs. Seat and cushions should firmly support the underside of the thighs. And be sure there is enough footroom under the table. Chart tables often double as work desks, so plan lighting, seating comfort, bookshelves, and other features with more than navigation in mind.

SEATING

Of primary importance is adequate seating for the entire crew. This may take the form of settees; U-shaped, L-shaped, or circular dinettes; swivel chairs fixed to the sole; or couches and sofa beds. Much is dictated by the type of boat: sail or power, planing or displacement hull, high or low freeboard, wide or narrow beam. Seating can be moved farther outboard in beamy, flat-bottomed boats, creating more open space, but this is not necessarily a good thing on smaller boats that pitch and roll, and it may not be the most efficient use of space where other needs such as stowage must be considered. Furniture will be built in on sailboats and small powerboats; sportfishermen and motoryachts, however, have the space for conventional items such as sofa beds, end tables, and lamps, though these must be fixed to prevent sliding. Upholstery and other finishes should be suitable to the marine environment. A sure way to drive a professional crew nuts is to load the boat with all manner of lamps, vases, and knickknacks that must be wrapped and stowed every time it leaves the dock.

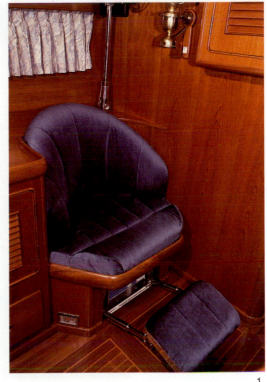

1

2

1 *Blue Star*, a Little Harbor 53, is fitted with an unusual built-in chair with adjustable footrest.

2 *Jennifer*, a Beneateau Oceanis 500, uses cabinets and countertops as a space divider between galley and saloon.

1

3

2

TABLES

Tables tend to be congenial gathering spots, if by no other virtue than providing a place to rest elbows, set down drinks, or spread books and navigation charts. Large, fixed tables are less versatile than smaller tables, especially ones that fold away, change size with dropleafs, or lift out for stowage or use elsewhere, as in the cockpit or on the sun deck. If they are to be used underway, fiddles help keep small objects from sliding off, though they are a nuisance for dining. Removable fiddles are a clever solution.

Pedestal and folding tables are sometimes prone to wobbling. Worse, many cannot withstand the force of a crewmember bracing or falling against them. There is no substitute for rugged construction, ingeniously complex folding mechanisms notwithstanding. And no sharp corners, please.

COVERINGS

In recent years tremendous advances have been made in the field of marine textiles, as mills fight for market share with high-volume boatbuilders as well as for after-market sales. Fabrics are more durable, ultraviolet- and mildew-resistant, and colorfast.

How the boat is used is an important factor in selecting upholstery material and color. A boat used for corporate entertaining will certainly have more elegant and costly coverings than, say, the family boat in which children in wet swimsuits clamber about. These are important considerations in choosing between expensive upholstery and washable slipcovers. The range of available fabrics is wide, including leather, synthetic leather and suede, cotton, woven synthetic fibers, and wool. Each mill has its own version of a product and marks it with a trade name, such as Springs Industries' UltraSuede HP.

Slipcovers with heavy-duty plastic zippers over 5- or 6-inch foam allow for easy periodic cleaning. And when the mood to redecorate strikes, the process of replacement is less disruptive than reupholstering. Piping gives a tailored appearance as well as adding strength. Use open-cell foam (which is softer) in dry areas and closed-cell foam in wet areas. Interior designer Anne Brengle recommends upholstery where a more formal look is desired. She says that with busy patterns finish detailing should be kept fairly plain. On the other hand, if the pattern is plain, finish detailing can be more elaborate, such as pleating and button-and-tufting. Synthetic threads, most often polyester, should be used for strength, durability, and colorfastness.

New cushion and furniture covers have an immediate impact on the look of an interior. If you've bought a boat with soiled or dated fabrics, this is a good starting point for your redecorating project. And if you're just trying to buy time before the funds or plans for a more ambitious renovation project materialize, inexpensive slipcovers should do the trick.

SOLES

Entry to the saloon may be from the companionway ladder, aft sliding glass doors, or a weathertight door on the side deck. If possible, materials here should be waterproof, such as a sole covered with tile, sheet vinyl, or water-resistant carpeting. Varnished teak and holly veneers, cork tile, and parquet are traditional treatments but may be slippery when wet. Doormats and throw rugs, to pick up dirt or accent the sole, should have some sort of non-skid backing.

Carpeting may be necessary to cover an all-fiberglass sole, which is cold and tends to transmit engine noises. On a wooden boat, however, a carpet may prevent the bilges from breathing and promote dry rot. In any case, carpets should be removable for bilge inspections.

Most marine carpets are synthetic: polypropylene, polyester, or nylon. The use of wool is pretty much restricted to high-end megayachts. Carpets can be cut pile, closed loop, woven, or needle-punched. It is important to use carpeting materials with polypropylene backing rather than jute, which rots. Make sure that steel staples and tacks are not used in binding and installation, as they will rust. Ultraviolet stabilizers and the use of the solution-dyeing process make today's carpets more fade-resistant and colorfast than products of just a decade ago. The color range is unprecedented in the history of the industry, so you should have no difficulty finding just the right carpet for your boat.

1 The pedestal-mounted saloon table in *La Cosa Real* can be raised and folded out for dining, or folded in and lowered for lounging. A half-rotation locks it into position. The backrests and seats are one piece and hinged in front so they can be tilted forward for access to storage space behind and underneath.

2 *La Cosa Real*, designed by E. G. Van de Stadt, is an Ocean 71 built in Poole, England, in 1976. The double-headsail ketch rig offers many sail combinations to guarantee good performance in all weather.

3 Aboard the 61-foot *Trashman*, a custom cruising sailboat designed by David Pedrick and built by Narragansett Shipwrights in Newport, Rhode Island, the best place to read is in this built-in chair with bookshelves and integral "end tables" to either side. The veneers are butternut and the trim is teak.

Type of Table	Surface size	
	Length (in inches)	Width (in inches)
Cocktail	24	14
Work or writing	30	18
Dining (4 people)	42	30

Minimum Table Dimensions

3

4

5

1 The saloon in *Gleam,* a 102-foot Ron Holland–designed motorsailer, has a casual elegance with lavender synthetic leather settees and wicker chairs.

2 Grand Banks trawlers are noted for their fine joinerwork. The dropleaf table is unobtrusive when the leafs are folded; the foundation contains several drawers and a top-loading stowage bin.

3 The dining table on the lean 65-foot Bruce Farr–designed *Lively,* a lightweight, flat-bottomed centerboarder, is by necessity lean, too.

4 The standard U-shaped dinette is given a different twist aboard the Whitewing 36 as it is oriented fore and aft instead of athwartship. The sculpted foam cushions provide good support to the back and legs.

5 *Crystal*'s glass dining table with crystal chandelier overhead gives the sportfishing boat a royal ambience.

HULL LINERS

Covering the inside of the hull hides a multitude of sins: scratchy fiberglass, chainplates, wires, and fasteners. Finely fitted yachts will likely have cabinets and other joinerwork obscuring much of the hull, yet rare is the yacht without some part of the hull exposed. The least expensive response is to use contact cement to glue on a vinyl liner. Snap-on or screwed panels covered with some type of fabric are possible where the surface is relatively flat. A traditional treatment is the wooden ceiling—generally tongue-and-groove planks or spaced battens fastened to vertical pieces bonded directly to the hull.

Fabrics that breathe and do not retain moisture cut down on mildew, and those with some sort of cushioned backing are especially comfortable to touch and lean against. Soft walls with a subtle pattern give a plush, warm feel despite the inevitable remarks about padded cells. Metal and uncored fiberglass hulls may be insulated from sound and temperature extremes by fitting fireproof insulation materials behind panel and ceiling covers. Wooden hulls are best left open to breathe.

FINISHES

Nowhere are the practical considerations of decorating more important than in surface finishes. Maintenance is a chore few enjoy, so washability, scuff and mildew resistance, and colorfastness are qualities to look for in selecting materials.

Old Paint didn't become a popular horse name for nothing, for certainly it is the standby finish. From alkyds to oil-based enamels to two-part polyurethanes, paint is a quick and easy way to spruce up a dinged and dirty surface.

Varnish is easy to clean and down below it might require only an annual touchup. Still, on a boat with a lot of natural wood this can be a time-consuming job. Avoid varnishing near sinks or other surfaces likely to get wet. Stainless steel galley counters are utilitarian and impart a sense of permanence.

Wood oil is an attractive but duller finish that also requires periodic maintenance. It is less impervious to mildew than varnish.

Natural wood veneers—in teak, mahogany, oak, spruce, and other woods—are rich-looking and can be applied over old plastic laminates or plywood bulkheads. Tongue-and-groove boards are rustic and informal treatments of bulkheads and furniture foundations, and are easy to install.

Today there is a wide variety of plastic laminates available in every color of the rainbow and in patterns from simulated wood, granite, and slate to bold geometrics. Plastic laminates must be cut close to shape and affixed with contact cement, with their edges then trimmed and filed. Most are scratch- and stain-resistant and clean easily. Plastic laminates often come in two thicknesses, one for countertops and one for vertical surfaces. Be careful that the laminate you choose is right for your intended application.

Mirrors create the illusion of greater space, reflect light well, and if etched with artistic designs or figures can be highly decorative.

4

1 Teak ceilings, screwed to vertical wood strips glassed to the hull, add warmth to the interior yet allow air to circulate freely.

2 Boatbuilder Sam Devlin's 20-foot Surf Scoter powerboat is constructed of marine plywood covered with fiberglass. The varnished ply veneer inside gives a handsome, seamless look.

3 Ash ceilings and teak bulkheads are combined in the Freedom 28's interior for an interesting contrast of wood grain and color.

4 The stained mahogany interior of the Laurie Davidson 40, though rich, seems in danger of disappearing in a black hole. Dark wood interiors work well in cold climates but don't play as well in the tropics.

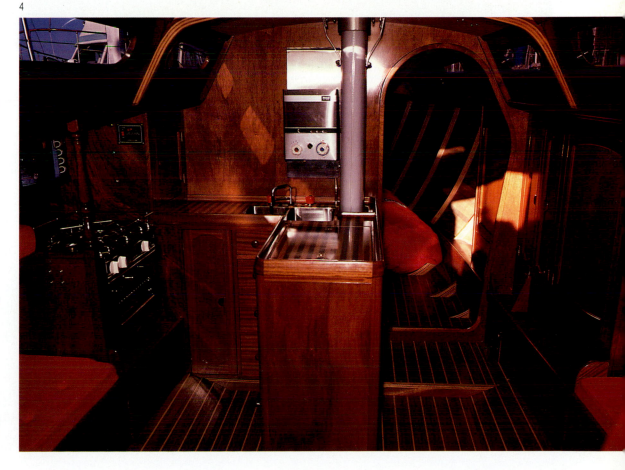

1

2

1 The interior of *Caroler,* a gorgeous custom sailboat, shows a lot of tradition in the painted deck beams trimmed with varnished mahogany, her brass bell, and skylight.

2 The light oak interior of *Lively* seems almost like an unfinished furniture outlet, yet sufficiently different from the norm to work. The boat is a contemporary development of the sharpie type in which light colors are consistent with the light displacement.

3 *Diva,* a steel boat designed by Grahame Shannon and Robert Perry, has a simple, clean interior with bulkheads covered by plastic laminate, Corian countertops, and padauk trim.

4 The 49-foot *Diva,* built by Dieter Pollack and Lauren Schmidt, shows crisp lines and a very fair radiused single-chine hull that is hard to distinguish from fiberglass.

3

4

STOWAGE

It is a common saying that there's never enough stowage on a boat, and it is equally true that expert joinerwork drives up costs. Prefabricated modular bins are typical of production boats, reducing material and man-hour costs, but it is precisely the joiner detailing of custom boats that helps set them apart. An intelligently planned boat anticipates the kinds of gear and belongings that must be stowed in each cabin and provides suitably sized lockers in the right places. Geometry dictates that much of this space be behind and below seats. Small bookshelves might appear obtrusive when mounted on bulkheads, which are perhaps best left for the mounting of clocks and barometers, paintings, and other decorative touches.

If stowage areas have been adequately provided in other cabins (i.e., clothes lockers in the staterooms, linen shelves in the head, tools in the engine room), the saloon will not have to accommodate clothing, charts, or tools. In any case, the saloon—being the largest cabin—must be designed to stow a goodly amount of gear.

There is a variety of clever solutions to insufficient stowage. Try to avoid relying too heavily on space under berths and settees, because it tends to dampness and poor accessibility—"Excuse me, you're sitting on top of the fruit cocktail!" If there is unused space behind the settee backrests, consider cutting access holes, hinging the backrest, and installing a shelf and dividers between the hull and backrest. There may also be space available for aircraft-type lockers in the overhead where the hull and deck meet, but be certain this won't interfere with headroom. Net hammocks and soft pouches slung under the side decks are easy to make, are functional, and can add a nice decorative touch.

MAKING YOUR MARK

The opportunity to turn an unfinished saloon into a cabin that reflects your personality and style is a rewarding challenge. Decorating, after all, is a creative process that puts your taste on display for others to admire.

Color, texture, materials, shapes, and layout must be integrated to work as a whole. It is important to understand basic principles and elements of design. The opportunities for expression may be limited by the size of the cabin and the need to work around certain givens such as bulkheads, built-in furniture,

1

2

1 *Quintus*, a 28-foot sailboat built in England by Cornwall Peninsular Marine, is Airex-cored fiberglass with teak and iroko trim. A Taylor kerosene heater is nicely tucked away in a compartment next to the settee.

2 Under-berth compartments are a good place to stow all manner of seldom used articles, including passports and cash in this hidden safebox.

3 Now you see it, now you don't! Which is exactly what you want of an on-board television. A sliding tray and pivoting mount do the trick.

and hull material, but even the smallest accent can have a big impact. Perhaps there is a print or painting you wish to highlight on a bulkhead. Or perhaps a Pueblo weaving or Colombian mola from the San Blas Islands. What is its theme? What are the dominant colors? A strong geometric pattern would clash with an unrelated, strongly patterned upholstery; a plainer fabric would be more suitable. A Winslow Homer print of fishermen working in a New England dory might influence your other choices of cushion covers and lamps—say, navy cotton duck and ornamental brass. Whatever your taste, your choices reflect your personality and set your boat apart from all others.

SALOON CHECKLIST

☐ Is there room for two people to pass each other without turning sideways?

☐ If the galley, navigation station, or other work area is also located in the saloon, will the person sitting or standing obstruct other activities?

☐ Is leg room adequate?

☐ Can stowage bins and cabinets be reached without undue stretching?

☐ Are the backrest angles comfortable?

☐ Can you see out the windows?

☐ Can you talk to other persons without twisting your body?

☐ What are the major activities pursued in this cabin? Reading? Entertaining? Sleeping? Eating? Games?

☐ Which way should cabin doors open?

☐ Is there adequate stowage space for books? Stereo? Cassettes? Magazines? Personal effects?

☐ What sort of locking mechanism will be installed on cabinet doors?

☐ Are cabinets ventilated?

☐ Where will natural light fall?

☐ Where will you install lights? What kind?

☐ Should tables fold away? Are they sturdy?

Shelf Dimensions for Books and Magazines

Book/Magazine	Shelf size	
	Height (in inches)	Depth (in inches)
Average paperback	8	5
Average hardcover	10	8
Large-format hardcover	14	10
Average magazine	12	9

YACHT
PROFILE

Top Secret

Ernest Bonnamy designed the bizzare interior of the 104-foot Top Secret. *Built by G. de Vries Lentsch of Holland and Merrill Stevens of Florida, the ash, oak, and teak interior is decorated with etchings, sculptures, and reliefs.*

Stained leaded glasswork shows the Saxon King Harold in full battle regalia defending England against the invading Vikings in 1066. The door handles are ivory.

The master stateroom is fit for a Viking king.

The bar stools are carved from solid blocks of ash, and the footrests are original bronze castings of gargoyles. The bar itself is topped with lead.

CHAPTER SEVEN

Staterooms

The word *stateroom* connotes a grandeur and elegance that is given short shrift on most small yachts. First used to describe an elaborately equipped and commodious apartment in a palace or mansion that was reserved for high-ranking persons of state, and later a cabin aboard a ship or train, the stateroom was traditionally fitted with a sink and toilet to make it a fairly self-sufficient living space. Aboard the great Victorian and Edwardian passenger liners, one did not expect to catch the Vanderbilts and Astors brushing their teeth in common washrooms!

Yet by virtue of its privacy, even the simplest sleeping cabin is a special place indeed. In a small cabin cruiser there is likely to be just one stateroom—the forward V-berths—but if it can be closed off by means of a door or curtain, it becomes a personal space where one can get away from the wind, noise, even guests who grow tiresome. More than a sleeping space, the private stateroom is a hideaway in which to read, dress, groom, and generally perform those desultory activities best done in solitude.

Of course the range of amenities is directly related to boat size and layout. Staterooms may be located forward, aft, port, or starboard. Some make good sea berths, others are useful only in port. Standing headroom is nice, but once reclined with bedcovers tucked under the chin, a weary soul is just as content in a crawl space.

The shape of the hull, as mentioned in Chapter 4, has a strong effect on available interior space, including sole area, headroom, berth dimensions, and stowage areas such as

A cut-glass etching of satanic orange eyes watches over a naked woman and the silk-covered bed in *Crystal*, a 129-foot sportfishing boat designed by Jack Sarin.

hanging lockers, drawers, and cubby bins. Because the largest and most useful space is usually amidships and allocated to the saloon, staterooms are frequently relegated to the ends of the boat. Unless the forepeak and lazarettes are totally obliterated, this is fair enough, since staterooms are used mostly for sleeping and therefore don't require as much sole space or headroom—unless the occupant is an inveterate sleepwalker or a worrywart who must pace to think. But that is what decks are for!

FORWARD STATEROOMS

In small boats the forward stateroom often consists of little other than V-berths that extend

1

outboard to the hull sides, forward to the forepeak chain locker, and aft to the bulkhead that separates it from the head. On larger boats, substantial forepeaks effectively push the V-berths aft, thereby broadening the base of the berth for more foot space. And it is possible to terminate the head of the berth forward of the bulkhead to provide some sole space for standing, bureaus port and starboard perhaps, a seat for changing clothes, and possibly a vanity for the lady of the ship. Alternatively, the vanity might be converted to a small writing desk or office with a typewriter or built-in computer.

Standing headroom at the head of the berth facilitates entry as well as clothes changing. On many boats it is impossible to retain headroom over the foot of the berth, but the only real inconvenience comes when changing the sheets. If the head of the berth does not abut a bulkhead, however, it is nice to be able to sit athwartship with your back resting against the hull; this requires a vertical distance between mattress and overhead of at least 3 feet.

Underway in any kind of seas, or at anchor in an exposed harbor, the motion can be jerky, making sleeping difficult. Forward staterooms do not make good sea berths. The flip side is that ventilation is best in the bow, where vents and windscoops can pick up faint breezes without being obstructed by cabins, masts, canvaswork, and other deck gear. In the muggy tropics, this cabin may well be the only one where you can get a good night's sleep.

OFFSET STATEROOMS

Boats about 38 feet and larger may have sufficient length and beam to locate a stateroom just forward of the saloon and to port or starboard of the centerline. It might have a double berth or high-low single berths, depending on space and crew requirements. On larger boats, there may be enough space to make this offset cabin the owner's stateroom, which is always assumed to be the biggest and best aboard. In cases where beam is lacking, there may be room only for high-low berths, which are deemed more appropriate to the ranking of crew and children.

French sailboat builders have popularized mirror-image staterooms port and starboard of the centerline, both forward and aft in the

2

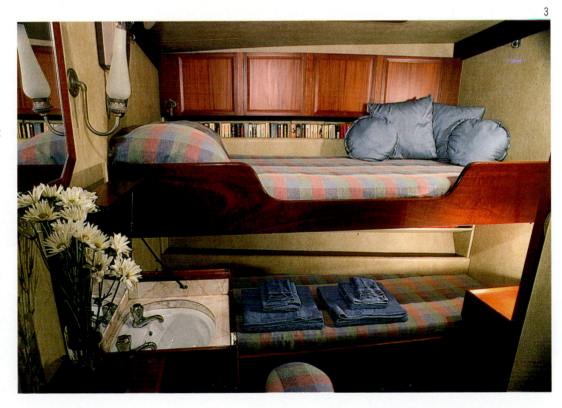

3

1 V-berths forward, as in the Little Harbor 46, is the standard use of this difficult area. An insert board and cushion over the changing seat converts the two singles to an extra-wide double berth.

2 *Southern Cross* has an offset double berth on the starboard side of the forward cabin, leaving room for a vanity and seat to port.

3 The port guest stateroom of *La Cosa Real* has high-low berths for twin accommodations, or the top berth can slide out to form a double. Beneath the lid of the built-in vanity is a porcelain sink with hot and cold water; a small hinged stool swings out from beneath the vanity.

quarter areas under the cockpit. This practice, however, makes it difficult to plan for hanging lockers, drawers, and miscellaneous stowage space for personal effects. With just one offset stateroom in the design, the logical place for clothes is "across the hall." Often the head is placed forward, in the fine sections of the bow.

Because air entering through hatches in the forward cabin will blow down the centerline passageway, ventilation may be a problem in offset staterooms. For this reason they require large hatches and vents of their own, preferably with intake and exhaust fixtures that encourage good circulation.

QUARTER CABINS

Sailboat quarter berths have long been acknowledged as the best sea berths. Because they are located just aft of amidships, motion is near a minimum; the hull and cockpit footwell provide surfaces to brace against, and they are convenient to the companionway ladder, making it quick and easy to get topside when called on watch.

As beam-to-length ratios have increased in recent years, the quarter areas have expanded dramatically, so that it is now possible to fit a double berth in this same space. And by constructing a bulkhead with door around the forward end of the berth, the entire area can be enclosed and billed as a private stateroom. Of course this barrier cuts off ventilation and necessitates installing large hatches and vents in the coachroof overhead. But the cabin's location aft means more deck and coachroof obstructions in the way of air flow, so the quarter cabin is likely to be the stuffiest cabin in the boat. They aren't called "coffin berths" for nothing.

Careful cockpit planning is necessary so as not to tamper with important seating dimensions; sometimes the cockpit seats and backrests are moved so far outboard (to provide headroom in the cabin below) that one's legs cannot reach the seat on the other side. When a sailboat heels, foot bracing is essential to safety and comfort.

Builders of both sailboats and powerboats have experimented with variations on the quarter cabin theme. These include mirror-image quarter cabins and berths directly underneath the cockpit. Some are ingenious,

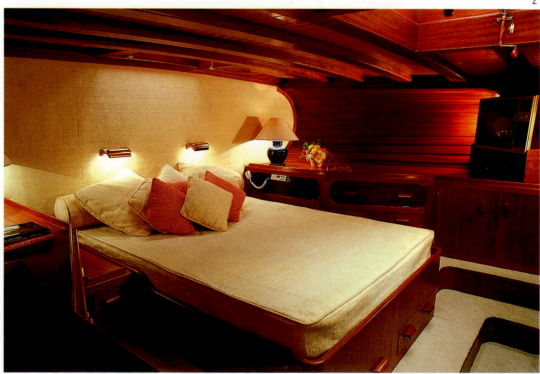

while others are so difficult to enter and have headroom so restricted that only children, with their penchant for making "forts," are likely to find them at all useful or entertaining. And as usual, there is a trade-off between gaining extra berths and losing valuable stowage space.

AFT CABINS

The tri-cabin motoryacht and aft cabin sailboat offer the owner the option of taking his stateroom to the stern instead of the bow. Beam is greater, hull sections are fuller, motion is less, and privacy is as good as or better than in the forward stateroom. The only drawback is somewhat poorer ventilation.

Because of the substantial beam aft, many different berthing configurations are possible: singles port and starboard, one double and one single, one double offset or one double on centerline. An advantage of the latter is easy access from both sides of the berth, eliminating the unpleasant possibility of landing a knee in your mate's groin as you climb over on the way to the head in the middle of the night. On the other hand, it makes a lousy sea berth.

Consider these other noteworthy features: Stowage space is generally excellent in after staterooms, as there is often space for hanging lockers, bureaus, and drawers beneath the berth. It is often the only stateroom on boats under about 45 feet in which a second, private head can be located, usually port or starboard under the cockpit. And good lighting is possible not only through hatches but from portlights in the hull sides and transom as well. Indeed, it is an exquisite pleasure to lie in bed and see through eye-level windows the wildlife, other boats, sunrises, and the general bustling of the harbor outside.

3

1 The 100-foot *Aile Blanche* sails across Penobscot Bay near Camden, Maine. Built in 1939 by Camper and Nicholson, her hull is teak on steel frames. Beam is 19 feet 6 inches, draft 13 feet, displacement 89 tons, and she powers at 9 knots with her 230-horsepower auxiliary.

2 The master stateroom in *Aile Blanche* has a double berth on the centerline, wooden overhead and hull ceiling, downlights in the quarters, and reading lights over the berth.

3 *Truant*'s aft cabin is offset to allow for passage to the aft companionway. This arrangement is sometimes a more effective use of space than a berth on centerline, but the person sleeping on the outboard side has to scramble over his bunkmate to get out. *Truant* was designed by C. Raymond Hunt & Associates, a Boston, Massachusetts firm known for its pioneering work with deep-V hull forms.

1

2

3

1 *Miss Marty*'s master stateroom says glitz with its black-and-white color scheme, mirrored bulkheads, and gold accent throw pillows.

2 The master stateroom in *Tiana* has a large double berth with stowage below, single berth, comfortable settee, vanity, and ensuite bath with tub.

3 *Tiana*'s two guest cabins each have two single berths; the starboard cabin has high-low berths, and the port cabin (pictured) has opposing berths.

BERTH TYPES

When the yacht designer turns his attention to berths, form definitely follows function. The basic dimensions of the human form must be respected despite restricted space—at least 6 feet, 2 inches long and 2 feet wide for the average person. Obviously, larger people require larger berths. In forward areas especially, the curve of the hull can encroach on the berth area, but with good planning this will usually be at the foot rather than at the head, since feet occupy less space than shoulders.

As is true of the entire accommodation plan, berth designs are necessarily influenced by boat size and layout. Permanent berths for the standard number of crew are desirable, though on small boats there may be no way to avoid sleeping some of the crew on convertible dinettes and pullout sofa beds. Few other interior features have received as much attention from designers as have berths, and indeed some clever solutions are possible.

Sliding berths.   A berth or settee that must be kept small to permit the passing of traffic can be expanded at night by pulling out a sliding seat board. The extra space may be filled by the seat's backrest cushion, or perhaps the unused portion of the cushion can slide and stow out of the way underneath the backrest, bookshelves, or cabinets.

Pipe berths.   Popular on pre–World War II sailing vessels, this berth consists of two strong steel pipes and a piece of canvas with sleeves sewn on each side. U- and Y-shaped wooden blocks mounted on facing bulkheads hold the pipes in collapsed and opened positions. When not in use, the pipe berth folds up outboard. This makes a good emergency berth, but its bedding must be stowed elsewhere. The saving grace is that it doesn't require a mattress; like the army camp cot, the taut canvas suspended between two pipes provides adequate support.

Pipe berths may be mounted over settees in the saloon, above single berths in offset staterooms, or, on large boats, above the workbench or sail bags in the forepeak. The pipe berth is an excellent means of adding a berth without making major changes to the interior.

Concordia berths. The Concordia berth, "invented" by the Concordia Company of South Dartmouth, Massachusetts, in the 1930s, is a unique fold-away arrangement. Among numerous other designs, builder Waldo Howland commissioned the German yard of Abeking & Rasmussen to build a number of 39-foot sloops and yawls, which were then shipped to the United States for finishing and fitting out. Known simply as Concordias, they are still much admired today. The saloon berths Howland designed for them were a development of earlier hinged berths used in other boats from his yard: a handsome slatted backrest that folds down over the settee. By giving a slight radius to the backrest, Howland was able to ensure that a thin mattress is sufficient for comfort. The beauty of the design is that the bedding folds up inside it—no muss, no fuss. Though boatbuilders today seem reluctant to put this much emphasis on saloon berths (everyone wants private staterooms), the simplicity and ingenuity of the Concordia berth has assured it a secure place in the history of yacht design.

Folding berths. Found mostly on motor-yachts with high freeboard and ample interior space, the folding berth operates much like the ironing board closet built into Victorian homes. A flat board is hinged on the outboard side and held up in the open position by two chains fixed to the inboard corners. As in the Concordia berth, bedding may be kept in place. Because the board is hard, some sort of mattress is required.

Perhaps a better idea is the "basket" berth, which is simply a lightweight, four-sided aluminum frame covered with canvas or containing a mattress. In years past root berths were commonly fitted to large forepeaks that doubled as crew quarters. Because they folded up, they weren't obtrusive and their light weight didn't seriously affect the trim of the boat.

Convertible dinette berths. On small to midsize boats where living space is at a premium, it is sometimes necessary to convert the dinette to sleeping berths. Almost any shape of dinette will do—U-shape, L-shape, circular, or

3

1 *Altair*'s traditional extension berth is a bit unusual in that it is a pilot berth rather than settee. Lee cloths give the sleeper security underway.

2 *Weatherly*'s pipe berth is suspended by two lines that lower it to a horizontal position over the saloon settee.

3 A pilot berth utilizes the space outboard of the settee under the side deck. With lee cloths or board it makes a good sea berth on board the Whitewing 36.

bench seats. The common feature is a table mounted on an adjustable pedestal or a set of legs. The dinette seats are fitted with cleats or a lip to support and secure the table in the down position. Backrest cushions are used as fillers. Due to the gaps between cushions and the retaining fiddles that hold the cushions in place, such berths are not the most comfortable. But removable fiddles eliminate hard spots, and Velcro tabs could help keep the cushions from shifting. Convertible dinettes are often larger than permanent berths in the ends of the boat and are easy to climb in and out of.

Sofa beds. Motoryachts and sportfishermen are most often designed without built-in saloon or deckhouse furniture, leaving the owner free to select home-style chairs and sofas. An athwartship sofa bed is an attractive means of obtaining extra guest berths. By day it is a cushy conversation seat, and by night an above-average bed. Upholstery fabric can be picked to match the cabin decor, and throw pillows can be important accents in the overall scheme of colors and patterns.

V-berths. The forward cabin is typically fitted with two single berths having a common foot. An insert and filler cushion convert the two singles to one double, though as mentioned above, fiddles and shifting cushions can be distressing—literally a pain in the butt.

A couple might decide to toss out the single-berth cushions and custom-cut a single foam cushion to fill the entire space. Because of the usual flare in topsides, it may be possible to make the berth larger by raising it a few inches, but there is a trade-off in lost headroom and distance from the sole. Because the head of converted V-berths is probably much wider than necessary, bookshelves or stowage compartments can be built into the corners without robbing sleeping space. Fitted sheets and plump pillows complete the transformation from cold single berths to a cozy, sumptuous double. There is no reason you can't be as comfortable sleeping at sea as at home—after a day on the water, everyone deserves a little hedonism!

Oversize berths. The owner's aft stateroom never looks so rich and inviting as when furnished with a queen- or king-size berth, especially if a home-type mattress set is used in place of foam. This is true luxury afloat. And with a standard-size mattress, sheets, blankets, bedspreads, and comforters can be purchased without worrying about custom fitting.

Oversize berths beg for a decorator's touch. By virtue of its sheer size, such a berth calls for attractive coverings to make the most of its large surface area; who'd think of covering a royal bed with army surplus blankets?

STOWAGE

It is only natural that people like to dress and undress in the room where they sleep. This means planning for clothing stowage in the stateroom—hanging lockers and drawers.

While it may be true that aboard a boat you won't need as many pressed and wrinkle-free garments as at home, entertaining and dinners out might require a pretty dress or presentable suit. Thus a hanging locker large enough to house conventional coat hangers (plastic doesn't rust!) is indicated. Louvered doors facilitate ventilation and cut down on mildew, which can ruin good clothes in a hurry. Lining the locker with cedar paneling isn't difficult and helps eliminate musty odors.

Most clothing can be stowed in drawers or bins. This is a much-preferred alternative to under-the-berth compartments, which are inconvenient, dirty, and prone to dampness and mildew. Unfortunately, on many boats drawers are small and too quickly filled with sweaters, pants, and the like. Drawers should have a catch mechanism to prevent accidental opening, and the facings should have some sort of opening—finger holes, louvers, caning—to

2

3

1 The Concordia berth is a trademark of the 39-foot wooden Concordia, developed by Waldo Howland. With the release of a simple rope noose, the settee backrest folds out and another line secures it into position through a fastening in the cabin sole.

2 Often the simplest innovation is the most likely to be overlooked. The beautiful bookshelf built above the V-berths on *Altair* serves as an anchor for the samson post. The hull ceiling is spruce.

3 *Sumurun*'s guest cabin has a very small vanity with sink and stowage at the foot of the berth.

4 *Royona*'s attractive aft cabin has two elevated single berths, a narrow settee, and bureau.

4

ventilate the insides. Plastic-coated wire baskets that slide on fixed runners are an excellent way to minimize mildew and mustiness.

Net hammocks have the same advantage and can be slung along the hull sides or in any other out-of-the-way place. Similarly, space-saving soft pouches made from a variety of vinyls or fabrics can be hung on the hull sides to stow clothing and personal effects.

Shoe stowage is best kept low in open bins, under the berth for instance, or perhaps below a hanging locker. Assume that every crewmember requires at least two pairs of shoes or sandals, and without comprehensive stowage planning they will be left about the boat where others might trip over them or will be shoved into clothing lockers where they can dirty clean apparel and accidentally tumble out.

It is the habit of many persons to empty their pockets before undressing. And unless you're Dennis the Menace with fatigue-type pouch pockets jammed with fishhooks, coins, toothbrushes, jackknives, magnifying glasses, and slimy pet frogs, it is convenient to have a catchall place to dump your pockets at night. On a boat this is often the dinette table, which soon resembles a flea market sale. A personal shelf above each berth is an intelligent solution.

MAKING MODIFICATIONS

Like walls in houses, most bulkheads in boats are structural and can't be eliminated or moved without careful engineering. They support the hull and deck in critical areas and on sailboats may transfer heavy rigging loads to the keel and hull. Nevertheless, there are opportunities for customizing berths and staterooms to better suit your needs.

It may be possible to cut out part of a bulkhead without seriously weakening it. Bulkhead "windows" can open up an interior, disseminate light, and circulate air. Footholes for berths can be cut into a bulkhead to increase leg room. For example, if you want to add a table or drawers at the head of a berth, you might be able to gain the space by pushing the foot of a berth "through" a bulkhead. Be sure the foothole is large enough to turn over in without catching your feet on the top of the box.

1 The vanity in *Tiana*'s master stateroom doubles as a writing desk.

2 When space is at a premium, there is no reason an entire berth must be open. The foot of the pilot's berth in *Record*'s wheelhouse is covered by a portion of the navigator's table.

3 The telltale compass is positioned over the skipper or navigator's berth so the off-watch can check the course at a glance.

YACHT PROFILE

Altair

Altair is a wooden gaff-rigged ketch built by Earle Barlow in East Boothbay, Maine, in 1973. Her interior is pine with oak and teak trim. Owner Derik Webb sails her out of Osterville, Massachusetts.

The saloon has pilot berths, a dropleaf table, brass lantern and bulkhead-mounted heater.

At anchor *Altair* resembles a Tahiti ketch.

Seating on all four sides of the small cockpit is comfortable, with high coamings and pillows. The steering system is rope wound around a drum and led through blocks to the outboard rudder. The transmission is controlled by simple nylon lines led from the engine room into the cockpit for the utmost simplicity!

Inside the companionway is an oilskin locker for hanging wet foul-weather gear.

As mentioned earlier in this chapter, V-berth insert boards and cushions easily convert two single berths to a nice double. A pipe or upper hinged berth can be installed above a settee without hacking up furniture foundations.

Speaking of foundations, all-wood interiors are much more easily modified than molded fiberglass pans or inner liners. Most wood interiors are constructed of plywood and are screwed together. It may be necessary to break some glue joints and fiberglass tabs to the hull, but splintering can be patched and hidden later. The fiberglass pan, on the other hand, must be cut out with a saber saw and new sections laminated to what remains. Great effort and skill is required to feather in the new "lams" so the surface is even; and new gelcoating seldom matches the mirror-smooth surface made in a mold.

Except for some of the best custom yachts and those built in Taiwan and Third World countries where labor is cheap, many boats lack the detail joinerwork that provides important stowage space. Robert Perry jokingly says of the Taiwan interiors that "even the corner moldings have corner moldings," and "if you open a drawer . . . you will find another little drawer." While cheap labor makes this sort of overindulgence in gingerbread and knickknack compartments tempting, it is equally true that there is seldom enough stowage space in a boat. Actually, it's *usable* space.

Everything from books to clothes, flashlights, eyeglasses, and loose change has to have a home somewhere, and the utility of almost any stateroom can be enhanced by the installation of appropriate stowage compartments, whether they are dovetailed drawers, filigreed shelves, soft pouches, or string nets.

DECOR AND DETAILS

Once the basic plan is drawn and the essential construction completed, it's time to consider the finer touches that make the stateroom a truly pleasant place to spend time. Atmosphere is important.

If the cabin is small, light colors will make it seem more open. The bulkheads may be painted white or another light color. (If they are covered with laminated plastic, e.g., Formica, a light sanding will help the paint stick, but results may still be marginal.) Sewing portlight curtains and installing hatch shades will control light, ensure privacy, and soften the effect of metal frames. And how about some plump throw pillows for back support and a change of texture or color?

Bare hulls are cold and uninteresting, so consider covering them with a patterned, foam-backed fabric or carpet, wood ceiling, or some type of vinyl-covered paneling. Except for gluing directly to fiberglass, it's a good idea for the covering to be removable, especially if there are fasteners behind that might require caulking, repair, or replacement in the future. Air spaces between the hull and covering function as insulation against heat and cold, and the conventional wooden hull's breathing requirements advise against closed coverings that restrict the circulation of air.

Plan your lighting by sitting and lying in the expected positions to see what works best. You may want separate fixtures for general lighting, reading, and night vision. A small fan will pick up the slack from less-than-perfect hatch, portlight, and vent arrangements. Refer to Chapter 5, "Light, Air, and Color," for more information.

Despite the seaman's predilection for early risings, the well-appointed stateroom should be a place in which you wouldn't mind passing a foggy day or recovering from the flu. As Sir Harry Lauder said, "Oh, it's nice to get up in the mornin'/But it's nicer to lie in bed."

YACHT PROFILE

Nena VIII

The owner of Nena VIII wanted a fast motor-yacht for extended cruising to the Caribbean and South America. The 109-footer has a top speed of 34 knots and a range (at 13 knots) of 3,000 nautical miles. Powered by MTU diesels and KaMeWa jet drives, she was built by Denison Marine.

Because some of the owner's children like disco dancing, a small dance floor was incorporated in the saloon, including a smoke machine, computer-controlled light system, laser light projector, and marble dance surface. Boat owners will go to any length to entice their children aboard.

The guest stateroom with high-low berths looks fit for a wizard visiting Emerald City.

The red-and-black VIP suite includes plush carpeting and overhead spots.

STATEROOM CHECKLIST

- [ ] Are the berth dimensions right for you and your crew?
- [ ] Can you comfortably sit up in bed to read?
- [ ] Are the lighting and ventilation adequate? Should you add spot lighting? A hatch? Deck prism? Portlight? Electric fan? Curtains?
- [ ] Is the mattress thick enough? Are pillows adequate? Do sheets fits?
- [ ] Is there stowage for spare linens?
- [ ] Is there a place for personal effects? Books? Flashlight?
- [ ] Is space for hanging lockers and clothes bins adequate? Is it well ventilated to prevent mildew? Conveniently located?
- [ ] Is the hull insulated to prevent condensation?
- [ ] Is the hull covering pleasant to the touch?
- [ ] Do you need a telltale compass so you can read the boat's heading in bed?
- [ ] Can you exit quickly if there is a fire? Reach a fire extinguisher?
- [ ] Can you lock hatches from the inside and outside?
- [ ] Can you turn off the stereo without leaving bed? Are there speakers in the stateroom?
- [ ] From the V-berths, can you gain access to the chain locker?
- [ ] Can you inspect all sections of the hull beneath the berths and other furniture?

Galleys

ood eating is one of the finer pleasures of daily living, especially at sea. There are many reasons why this is so. For one, the physical activity of running a boat and the exposure to wind and sun are tiring, making the appetite acute. Second, compared with the routine at home, on most boats the day-to-day character of cruising and fishing has elements of "roughing it," which puts an onus on the cook to keep mealtime at least semicivilized. You might be able to forgo your hot Jacuzzi and satin-sheeted waterbed for a week, but eating cold beans from a can is depressing. Last, life aboard a boat is frequently dull; indeed, on an ocean passage it might seem downright monastic. So it is not uncommon to hear the crew growl, "Let's eat!" when there is nothing else to do. Just as a fresh spice highlights the flavor of a dish, the ocean is the perfect accent for the appetite.

The galley, of course, is the cook's workshop. And here are found the tools of his trade: stove, sink, skillets, saucepans, spatulas, and spices. As with any trade, the right tools make the job much easier. The trick on a boat is to pare the frills and satisfy the basics in a small, workable space.

GOURMET OR SHORT ORDER?

Few parts of the boat are customized more than the galley. Depending on the owner's eating habits and how he uses his vessel, the galley always seems either too large or too small. Some people don't want to be bothered with cooking aboard, preferring instead to nibble crackers and sardines—anything to avoid lighting the stove. Others aren't happy unless there's *coq au vin* or *coquilles Saint-Jacques* on the table every night. Americans must have their meat, potatoes, and vegetables, the English their kidney pies, and the French their rich sauces. Of course much has to do with the skill and ambitiousness of the cook, which is why a good one has long been considered the most important member of the crew.

Production boat galleys range from portable trays that slide out of sight when not in use to expansive counters with ovens, microwaves, refrigerators, and freezers built into the cabinetry. As a general observation, however, most boats are short on counter space and food lockers, especially ventilated compartments for fresh produce.

The owner planning modifications to the galley should consider long and hard his requirements. For how many days must the

1

cook normally plan meals? Should there be three squares a day? Is baking required? How fancy should the dishes be? What number of crew is there to be served?

FUEL

The best kind of stove fuel is a conundrum generating endless debate, akin to the best sailing rig, hull material, engine make, and so on. It is interesting that for many years alcohol was considered the safest fuel because it allegedly mixes with water. But the flame is difficult to see, and if the Primus-type burner isn't preheated correctly, flareups result. And water, as it turns out, often just spreads the flame rather than dousing it. After a rash of injuries reported in boating periodicals, it seemed alcohol stoves were doomed to the fate of dinosaurs. Enter the Swedish company Origo and its line of nonpressurized stoves. Alcohol is absorbed in a cotton batting inside the fuel tank, much in the manner of a Zippo lighter. The flame is controlled by a simple sliding lid a la Sterno cans.

Thus inspired, Kenyon Galley now makes an alcohol stove with a ceramic wick to heat the vaporizer. With such devices, in which little can go wrong, alcohol can again be considered a viable stove fuel. However, it is expensive, doesn't burn as hot as other fuels, and is difficult if not impossible to find in many countries.

Kerosene, or paraffin, is seen less and less outside Great Britain, where old ideas are clung to with a tenacity forged in the London air raid shelters of World War II. This fuel is smelly, hard to preheat, and generally a nuisance. Same for diesel, which is only practical in Alaska and other arctic regions generally unfit for human habitation.

Propane (or LPG—liquefied petroleum gas), butane (LPG's cousin), and compressed natural gas (CNG) are more and more the choices of serious shipboard cooks. Because CNG is lighter than air, in the early 1980s it was predicted soon to surpass LPG in popularity. That hasn't been the case. LPG is easy to find, it occupies less space than CNG, the tanks are available in a wide variety of sizes and shapes,

1 Aboard *Volador*, an 81-foot cruising ketch, the galley has everything needed to turn out gourmet meals for the charter trade, including a large standup refrigerator, loads of stowage space behind the varnished cabinet doors, and good light and ventilation from two overhead hatches. The interior was designed by Pieter Beeldsnider.

2 *Gray Goose II*'s galley is situated to one side of the trunk for the lifting keel. The planking is oak and the overhead is UltraSuede.

3 *Pandora*'s galley is located on the port side of the aft cabin, opposite the stairs leading down from the wheelhouse. While compact, a flat cabin sole and wide house make it comfortable, and its sequestered location spares the cook interruptions from other crew.

4 *Pandora* is a 33-foot trawler, strip-planked with Honduras mahogany that is bronze-riveted to oak frames. The wheelhouse and cabins are constructed of white oak, mahogany, and fir, and her interior is pine and mahogany. She is powered by a four-cylinder 85-horsepower Perkins diesel. She was designed and built by Grant Robinson of Newburyport, Massachusetts.

5 The galley of the Pearson 28, a production fiberglass racer/cruiser, is situated in the port quarter area of the main cabin near the entrance to a small under-the-cockpit aft cabin. The two-burner alcohol stove and the icebox are outboard; the sink is near the centerline to facilitate draining on both tacks.

2

and more sophisticated leak alarm systems have made it much safer to use. In any case, all of the gas fuels burn hot and clean.

Electricity remains a good choice for motoryachts, especially those equipped with shore power and generators to power electric appliances. A prime reason is that motoryachts are more likely to spend the night at marina docks where 30-ampere and 50-ampere service is readily available, in which case the generator isn't even needed.

The stove fuel decision should be made in conjunction with selecting a refrigeration and hot-water system, if there is to be one aboard. Electric refrigeration, which requires a lot of power from a generator, makes choosing an electric stove/oven logical. If you have a propane fridge or hot water heater, it only makes sense to stick with gas for the stove. But if the fridge works off an engine-driven compressor and the hot water via an engine exhaust heat exchanger, then it really doesn't matter.

4

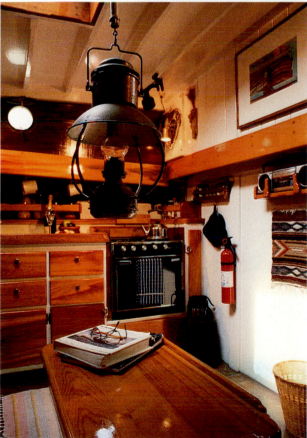

3

5

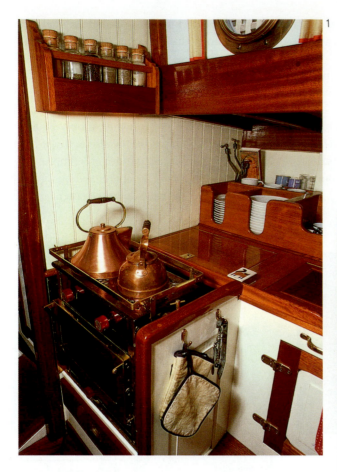

1 The handsome two-burner stove in *Jan Van Gent*'s galley is made by Taylor in England. It sacrifices some versatility for the virtue of compactness. The spice rack above is handy, but the countertop locker tempts the cook to reach over the stove.

2 The Hillerange propane stove and oven is a popular American model, gimbaled here aboard a Freedom 42. The cupboard doors hinge down, which is a bit unusual, and are useful as extra counter surfaces for food preparation.

3 The rugged Shipmate stove in *Iron Mistress,* a 41-foot steel cutter, seems ideally suited to the owner's long-range cruising plans. The stovepipe removes much of the heat generated by this appliance, which is an important consideration in the tropics. Cleaning underneath the stove will be easier than on most boats.

4 Microwave ovens are a logical choice in all-electric galleys, such as this one on the Rhodes-designed motorsailer *Sargasso,* as they conserve fossil fuels and won't heat up the cabin. Note the sunken knife rack behind the sink, intercom phone, and stained glass, which adds a dash of brightness to the space.

3

4

LAYOUT

The galley is generally located near midships and the saloon—that is, near the dining table. It may be U-shaped, L-shaped, a sideboard affair running under the deck port or starboard, or a bipartite elaboration with an outboard section and an inboard "island." A common reason for islands in sailboats, under a center cockpit for example, is so the sink can be installed on the centerline, thereby allowing it to drain when heeled on either tack. Powerboats don't have this problem, and designers are somewhat more free to manipulate the essential galley elements.

This business of heeling is also reflected in the shape of the galley, since it is assumed that the cook aboard an ocean sailing yacht must work underway at a 20-degree angle. Hence the popularity of U-shapes, which allow the cook to be literally strapped in between two hip supports. The situation is altogether different aboard a motoryacht, and the solution

thoroughly modern: Select a dinner from the deep freeze, slam it in the microwave, and nuke it for three minutes!

The sideboard galley is the least obtrusive configuration but often lacks counter space. And the sink won't be anywhere near the centerline of the boat. Hence the logic of L-shapes, with the long outboard section paralleling the centerline of the boat and the short section thrusting inward. Designers have a lot of fun figuring out how to make the short leg innovative: square as a draftsman's T to the centerline, running off at an oblique angle, or a swirling French curve. It may be open to the rest of the boat or closed off by bulkheads. On the serious cruiser the leg may be laid out purely for food preparation, and on the boat used primarily for entertainment you might find bar stools lined up on the saloon side. The engine may be positioned underneath the galley counter in some designs. The permutations are endless. In addition to the sink, should you have a refrigerator

Standard Galley Shapes

*O*ver the years, several standard galley shapes have evolved to meet the cook's requirements for handiness, stowage, placement out of traffic flow, appliances within arm's reach, and counter space for food preparation. 1) The L-shaped galley fits well in small corners of the cabin, though counter space often suffers and the refrigerator may be too close to the stove. 2) U-shaped galleys make a nice haven for the cook, provide support underway, and allow for better separation of appliances. 3) A galley "island," here under the cockpit, makes good use of an otherwise difficult space and increases counter area. 4) Sideboard galleys, most functional on nonheeling motoryachts, may force the cook to move some distance laterally to reach appliances and stowage bins. The opposing sideboard or island in this boat is an intelligent solution; however, the cook won't appreciate working in the passageway to the aft cabin.

(1)

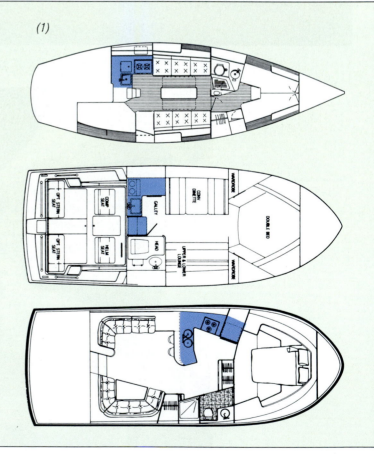

in the leg, a liquor cabinet, a waste trap, a chopping block, a trash compactor, or a dishwasher? Hard to say.

And what about overheads? The cabin overhead is an area often overlooked for stowage, though too much cabinetry up high stops the eye and compresses the sense of space. Racks for stowing charts and fishing poles are common in wheelhouses and deckhouses. In the galley, overhead racks for glasses represent a good use of space. Small cabinets may be fitted above the sink and stove for lightweight items such as placemats, paper plates, plastic cups, spices, and so forth. Naturally they should be positioned so that one won't hit one's head on them, and this often means placing them outboard under the side decks.

One of the most important criteria for galley layouts is to keep the cook out of everyone else's way, or should we say to keep the rest of the crew out of the cook's way? Dishwashing is

another chore requiring adequate space for a decent, easily accomplished job. Double sinks are helpful; a dish rack that fits over one side eliminates water draining onto the countertop. Overhead stowage racks for plates and glasses, mounted above the sink and beneath the cabinets, drain in place and save a step. A removable cutting board can be custom built to fit one or both sides of the sink for additional counter space. The same can be accomplished with the stove, which is not necessarily in use during the early stages of food preparation such as chopping scallions or blending batter.

Evaluate the utility of a galley by standing in the normal cooking positions and seeing if you can reach the stove controls, pot and pan stowage, cutlery drawer, spice rack, and so on. Do you have to reach over open flames? Will you hit your head on overhead cabinets? Is counter space adequate? How many plates can you lay out and still have room for the usual mess of saucepans and butter trays?

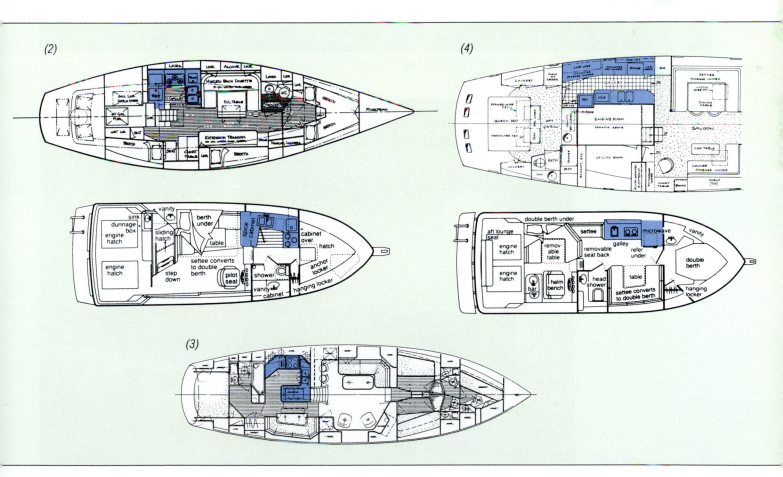

1

2

3

1 The light colors of *Lotus*'s galley and breakfast dinette contribute to its almost antiseptic look. The dinette has proven to be a comfortable gathering place for owner and crew as it represents neutral territory. The "island" contains the sink, dishwasher, and drawers. Overhead lighting is recessed. Glass racks are fitted inside the overhead cabinet.

2 The wooden motorsailer *Loon* has a traditional sideboard galley. There are large opening portlights for light and ventilation, a handhold overhead, a fan to keep the air moving, and a stainless steel countertop on the sink side.

3 *La Cosa Real*'s galley is a good example of the U-shaped layout, making maximum use of space and keeping crew out of the cook's way. Pot and pan recesses permit stowage close to the stove. The freezers are located under the counter, and a microwave disappears behind cupboard doors above. The refrigerator and dishwasher fit under the counter opposite the sink.

4 The Little Harbor 50 has a four-sided galley that virtually surrounds the chef. Tall fiddles with corner joints of contrasting wood keep dishes and pots on the countertops, but more open counter space would be an asset. A large double sink is located near the centerline to facilitate draining on both tacks. Cabinet doors are trimmed with teak and louvered for ventilation.

4

APPLIANCES AND COMPONENTS

Decide what you need in your galley, then sketch a layout on paper and draw in possible locations of appliances, stowage areas, and fixtures. Some ingenuity is probably required, and you may have to relocate some components outside the galley proper.

Sinks. At the heart of any galley is the sink. Not only is it essential for cleaning and peeling vegetables, serving as a receptacle for dirty dishes, and dishwashing, but it is often the most convenient place to wash your hands, launder a stained piece of clothing, or rinse cleaning sponges and rags. Go for the deepest one you can fit, preferably with square sides, even perhaps at the expense of under-counter space. Shallow sinks won't hold many dishes or keep water from slopping out. Round, contoured sinks are better suited to the head compartment. Again, consider a double sink.

Stainless steel is a durable material, and though prone to tarnish, it polishes nicely. Custom plastic sinks have the advantage of being molded in unusual shapes and in any color desired. For something really distinctive, a sink can be constructed of beautiful hardwoods and sealed with epoxy resin.

As you contemplate sink sizes and types, think also of fixtures and water supply. With pressurized water systems, home-style faucets are possible. You may also want a manual pump in case of emergencies, however, and of course one is required in the absence of a pressure system. When cruising in clean water, a seawater pump to rinse dishes saves fresh water for drinking and cooking. Foot pumps free the hands and are easier to operate. Filters in seawater hoses are critical to prevent clogging from seaweed and other junk. For cleaner and better-tasting water you may also wish to consider a home-type charcoal or membrane-type filter on the tank supply hose. A soap tray or vertically mounted liquid soap dispenser is handy, as are paper- and dish-towel racks.

Stoves. On small camp cruisers, good cooking can be accomplished on a portable two-burner stove, though the size of frying pans and pots may be restricted. Bread can be baked in a Dutch oven, and an inverted clay flowerpot placed over the burner flame will radiate heat on chilly nights—sort of. In any case, much is asked of the small stove.

Obviously, the more burners you have the easier it is to prepare elaborate meals. Unless you stick with one-pot stews and casseroles, the balanced diet of meat, starch, and vegetable suggests the utility of three burners. Four is just like the home kitchen.

Ovens don't seem to get a great deal of use aboard many boats, because of the heat they generate and the amount of fuel they consume. Then too, many people on vacation don't want to get that involved with their galleys. Still, there is no denying the advantage of baking your own bread and cookies; the aroma alone is worth the trouble.

In sailboats it is customary to gimbal the stove or oven so it remains level even when heeled. A heavy weight such as a slab of lead should be strapped to the bottom to dampen its rolling motion. The gimbaled stove is most often mounted athwartships, that is, facing the center or beam of the boat. But there are advocates of mounting stoves fore and aft, reasoning that if pots are thrown during a sudden lurch, they won't hit the cook. Either way, a strong bar should be through-bolted across the face of the stove to give the cook a firm handhold and to prevent his falling onto the burners.

On his 34-foot steel ketch *Brazen*, Danny Greene mounted his propane stove on a custom plywood foundation with a top that curves up at both ends. The stove rides on two tracks with roller wheels—in the manner of a roller coaster car—so when the boat heels the entire stove rolls port or starboard to stay level.

On powerboats and multihulls gimbaling usually isn't necessary, and this allows a freer hand in finding the ideal location, even catty-corner if that's what works.

Iceboxes and refrigerators. The icebox is a tried-and-true means of keeping meats, vegetables, and dairy products chilled. There are certainly no moving parts to break. The disadvantages are numerous, however, and include the hassle of hauling ice blocks, the likelihood of curdled milk and spoiled meat, and the huge interior volume, which on some boats requires

1

2

diving in head first to fish out the last can of beer. Without constant vigilance, bacteria and mold run rampant. The cartoon of a wary skipper cocking the trigger of his revolver as he opens the icebox lid is funny only during the slide show weeks after the cruise is finished.

Today there is a variety of refrigeration systems designed to work on all but the smallest boats. Some fit inside existing iceboxes and run off the ship's batteries, while others are complicated holding plate systems requiring engine-driven compressors, yards of hoses, and extra-large boxes. Motoryachts are often equipped with vertical, self-contained units with built-in compressors. Because the engine or generator runs for hours every day, such units don't require the thick insulation found on sailboat refrigerator boxes.

As a rule, top-loading boxes are more efficient, since cold air sinks and "falls out" of front-loading types. But the option of choosing between top and front styles gives the boat owner more latitude in designing his galley. As in the home with a secondary storage freezer, on large yachts it is common to install a front-loading refrigerator and a top-loading freezer.

To ensure the maximum efficiency of any icebox or refrigerator, keep it isolated from the stove and the engine compartment.

Custom-built refrigerators with varnished teak doors and stainless steel handles and locks impart an old-fashioned look reminiscent of the days when ice wagons made the neighborhood rounds. At the other end of the style spectrum, self-contained units come with a variety of decorator doors and facings so that colors can be matched with the rest of the galley. In contrast, the conventional top-loading box built into the galley counter is hardly noticeable at all, that is until you realize you must move four dishes, six glasses, two sauce pans, a

greasy skillet, and dirty kitchenware off the lid to scrounge for the cream you forgot!

Counters. Where space is a precious commodity, counters may seem like a waste—all that empty space just sitting there! Sure you're tempted to mount the television or radio direction finder there, or perhaps convert part of the galley to a chart table or magazine rack or liquor cabinet or God knows what else. But the odd thing about boats is that with such a high percentage of the interior already designed and earmarked for specific items, general surface space left open for a variety of activities is valuable indeed.

Galley counters are prime examples. One solution is to build removable or sliding extensions that can be pulled out during cooking and stowed the rest of the time. These might be cutting boards that slide out between the drawers and countertop, a fold-up extension at the end of a galley counter, or a board that slides out from under the deck or other structural horizontal surface. As mentioned, covering boards for sinks and stovetops can also provide extra working area.

Today most countertops are of laminated plastic, which is easily cleaned and available in decorator colors and patterns. A stainless steel section around the sink, perhaps recessed or angled slightly toward the sink, has the advantage of being scratchproof as well as able to shed water. Unfinished hardwood tops are traditional and look shippy, but must be kept dry and well-scrubbed (especially after cutting meats) to prevent mildew or salmonella poisoning. Decorative tiles, though heavy, are yet another possibility. Conventional grout between tiles will collect dirt and grease; epoxy grout, however, is tough and resists mildew.

1 The motoryacht *Truant* has a surprisingly small galley situated in an outboard corner of the saloon. The standup refrigerator is typical of powerboats that can generate the electricity required of such appliances. The large windows are delightful.

2 An icemaker, providing a virtually endless supply of cubes for cocktail hour, is a special treat aboard a boat, especially one the size of the Freedom 42.

1

2

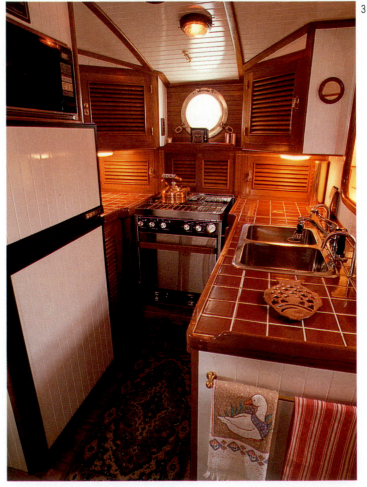

3

1 Built by Able Marine in Maine, the 50-foot *Palmyra* has stainless steel countertops, which are waterproof and tough. Unlike plastic laminates, stainless steel won't chip, peel, or burn.

2 Owner Chris Page chose white for *Caroler*'s bulkheads and overhead, and white plastic laminate countertops for the galley. The cabinetry is Brazilian mahogany with 10 coats of varnish. Built in below the sink is a counterbalanced swing-down drawer that utilizes the small space between the sink and the cabinet face.

3 The red ceramic tiles and white grout on *Gatsby*'s galley countertop are easily cleaned and give a warm, decorator feel to the interior. The overhead paneling is carried down the refrigerator door to establish a theme.

4 The composite epoxy resin (Corian) countertop on *Diva,* a cheerful blue with a random speckle pattern, resembles granite but weighs much less.

YACHT
PROFILE

Gatsby 39

The Gatsby 39 is a Taiwan-built replica of a classic motoryacht designed by Jim Backus. The outside steering station is a simple arrangement consisting of a bulkhead steering wheel and twin deck boxes doubling as seats. The raised afterdeck increases space belowdeck.

The outside steering station is abaft the wheelhouse; the flush afterdeck gives good visibility over the house. The bronze steering wheel with teak spokes reflects the 1920s styling of the boat.

Gatsby plies the waters of Puget Sound, Washington.

The deck of *Gatsby* is clean and handsome, with teak planks following the rail line, traditional skylight, polished brass Dorade vent, and a nice camber.

Gatsby's bar features brass rod over leaded glass doors, marble counter, and brass rail. There is a lot going on in this interior, including several kinds of wood, simulated tongue-and-groove overheads and bulkhead coverings, red velour upholstery, and decorative brass. The San Francisco bordello theme seems a little too precious.

Stowage. Designing stowage areas for the myriad kitchenware is a difficult task, especially since each must hold its contents in place, without breakage, when the boat rolls. Here are a few ideas:

- Glasses—underdeck cupboard with holes drilled in bottom slightly larger than glass bottoms (stack glasses to save space); bulkhead or overhead boards with holes for dropping glasses in. Wine glasses can be stowed upside down with the bases sliding between two thin boards standing proud of the overhead.

- Plates—underdeck bins built to size of plates—dinner, salad—with vertical cutouts to show the plates and permit removal. Also, four dowels fitted into holes drilled in a shelf will hold a stack of plates in place.

- Utensils—drawers, hooks, bin sunk in counter or bulkhead mounted near stove.

- Cutlery—drawers, bulkhead-mounted bins.

- Pots and pans—large drawers or bins under galley; bulkhead hooks. Pots should be kept from swinging.

- Packaged food—large bins under galley or saloon seats; lazy Susan with fiddles under galley; counter-level and overhead cupboards; pantry locker. Keep cans low.

- Fresh food—refrigerator; net hammock; wire baskets hung in pantry locker. Keep fresh food away from heat sources.

- Spices—bulkhead rack; counter-level cupboard near stove.

- Beverages—refrigerator; bins under galley; bilge.

- Garbage—compartment under galley counter with trap; under sink; trash compactor.

The style of the galley is determined to a great extent by the cupboard facings. Sliding tinted Plexiglas panels are a modern treatment, while hardwood doors are traditional. Bins with no doors at all have a lean, simple look, and on multihulls and other performance boats the weight savings is desirable. Louvers, caning, basket weave, and distinctive handcut fingerholes such as fish and dolphin shapes state a theme as well as increase ventilation. Positive locking devices should be standard.

The galley is one of the most heavily used areas of the boat. When the cook is off-duty the sink, cutting boards, and counter space are the platforms for activities that range from brushing teeth to repairing fishing reels, soldering wires in a broken radio, cleaning paint brushes, cutting sewing patterns—you name it. An attractive, well-organized galley is a satisfying place to be, even if you're not the cook.

1 Shelf-mounted wooden posts provide plate stowage on *Iron Mistress*. This simple arrangement saves the weight of a cabinet, and the shelf will be easy to clean. If new plates of a different size are purchased in the future, the posts can easily be moved.

2 The space under the companionway steps is frequently wasted; not so on *Altair*. Dry goods and other galley wares are stowed in each compartment. A ventilator above helps combat rot, rust, and mildew.

1

2

There are compact wine and glass racks behind *Capricious*'s settee. The galley is well equipped with a polished stove, built-in microwave oven, double sinks (mounted on centerline to facilitate draining on either tack), and cabin fan.

*F*or many owners, boats represent novel ways to entertain friends and associates, formally or informally. Clever liquor storage cabinets, fancy glass racks, and wet bars all further the cause. It is undeniably more civilized and satisfying to serve brandy in a snifter than a plastic tumbler with a rubber nonskid base!

The spirit locker aboard the Freedom 42 has a wine rack overhead and a mirror mosaic to distort reflections only enough so you won't recognize yourself when pouring that "just-one-more" nightcap.

The wine cellar and liquor locker on *Golden Eagle* is discreetly hidden beneath a galley cabinet. The laminated bird's-eye maple veneer is stunning, but a little goes a long way.

Spiritual Dispensation

154

All the plates, cups, and glasses are within arm's reach in *Jan Van Gent*'s simple galley. The round copper sinks are attractive but perhaps too small for serious galley work; the covering boards, however, are a good way to increase counter space when the sinks are not in use.

The laminated teak wet bar on *Numero Uno* has a slim, unobtrusive presence in the saloon, owing much to its crescent shape and shallow countertop. There is a stainless steel accent band running the length of the backboard. A sink, refrigerator/icemaker, and cupboards are built in.

No need to feel that you can't buy a drink on *Nena VIII;* her bar is as complete and exotic as any landbound watering hole. From the padded bar rail to the intercom, beveled mirrors, bison sculpture, and neon lights, this is a place you can figure on meeting someone fun!

1

2

1 A conventional dish stowage method consists of overhead bins with face cutouts.

2 The small drawers in the galley of the wooden ketch *Moondrift* are handy catchalls for small utensils and cutlery. Fancy drawer pulls dress up the simple, solid wood construction. Ventilation cutouts in the opposing door are of a plain though effective design.

3 The decorative tiles on *Record*'s galley island set off a traditional-looking cabin. The staving around the smokestack makes a handy mount for cutlery containers and stereo speakers.

4 Above the motoryacht *Bermbee*'s entertainment console are overhead racks for showcasing the crystal.

5 The simple pine ceiling of *Rosalind*'s galley incorporates an all-purpose shelf for stowing baking supplies and condiments.

3

4

5

GALLEY CHECKLIST

Consider these essential features of the well-equipped galley:

- ☐ *Good, flat sole space for the cook to stand on*

- ☐ *Kick space under cabinets so the cook can get close to his subject*

- ☐ *Nearby seat for cook*

- ☐ *"Seatbelt" for cook on sailboats; safety bar in front of stove*

- ☐ *Surfaces to lean against underway*

- ☐ *No stowage bins behind stove*

- ☐ *Adequate drawer space for cutlery*

- ☐ *Large drawer for spatulas, blenders, cleavers, etc.*

- ☐ *Paper- and dish-towel racks*

- ☐ *Large bin for pots, pans, and skillets low in boat*

- ☐ *Generous counter space for food preparation, cookbooks, etc.—avoid using icebox lid as counter space*

- ☐ *Deep double sink with cutting boards over*

- ☐ *Three-burner stove and oven*

- ☐ *Refrigerator with icemaking capability*

- ☐ *Cabin fan*

- ☐ *Spot lighting*

- ☐ *Opening hatches and/or portlights; overhead vents*

- ☐ *Ventilated stowage for fresh produce*

- ☐ *Dry stowage for cans and beverage bottles*

- ☐ *Dry stowage near stove for cardboard-packaged goods and spices*

- ☐ *Convenient bins for plates, glasses, etc.*

- ☐ *Secure glass bottle stowage*

- ☐ *Shelf for cookbooks*

CHAPTER NINE
Heads

Use of the word *head* to signify the toilet compartment is not so curious as it may seem, shortened as it is from the word *bulkhead;* on a sailing ship the main bulkhead is generally forward under the mast and separates the saloon or main cabin from the toilet in the bow. It is also interesting to note that *Webster's International Dictionary,* which lists 36 definitions for the word "head," gives one as "the seat of intellect." Of course it is the brain's housing that is referred to here, but it is equally accurate to think of the toilet seat as a place of intellect or meditation, a "throne," "altar," or "porcelain god" where some of our best and most serious cogitation occurs.

Despite the efforts of pundits to dignify the toilet through humor, there is really nothing divine about it. Nevertheless, a well-appointed and private head is bound to put blushing visitors and diffident crew more at ease. On boats without a good head it is not uncommon to learn that your guests have been constipated for three days, more from fear of using the toilet than from any change of diet. Those little plaques sold in chandleries that threaten misusers of the bowl and plumbing with a walk down the proverbial plank don't help.

Operation of the somewhat complex apparatus of the toilet need not be so daunting as it often seems. The best course is to purchase a good toilet—the quality will repay the owner many times over in troublefree operation. Anyone who has had to clean clogged hoses at sea knows the wisdom of these words.

LOCATION

Since little time is actually spent in the head, it only makes sense to locate the compartment in some distant, oddly shaped corner of the boat. Options are limited on small boats to portable toilets under the forward V-berth, or with a small increase in length and beam, to a stall behind a partial bulkhead and thence to a fully enclosed closet between the saloon and forward stateroom. The advantages of this location are its accessibility from both forward and aft, and the fact that the user is less likely to disturb others who are sleeping.

Above about 30 feet, alternative locations are possible. If the V-berths have been pulled aft and offset port or starboard, the forepeak is available. A toilet there will be difficult to use

1

when bucking head seas, however; thus the sign that admonishes "Men and boys please sit to pee."

The quarters are areas of more gentle motion, which is why sea berths are often located there. Good headroom is possible if the compartment isn't pushed entirely under the cockpit seats, but then of course it encroaches slightly on the saloon.

Aft cabin designs suggest two heads, as a single toilet forward is hardly convenient to persons sleeping in the stern. The aft stateroom head is almost always situated forward of the berth, under the cockpit or deck.

2

FEATURES AND FIXTURES

Regardless of its location, the well-designed head incorporates these features:

- Privacy—visual and audible
- Ventilation—hatches, vents, and portlights to circulate air
- Roominess—sufficient space to stand, sit, and turn around without knocking elbows
- Light—electric lamps to illuminate the compartment for shaving or applying makeup and to aid in cleaning
- Mirror—for introspection of the facial kind
- Toilet—for reasons that need not be stated
- Sink—for daily ablutions
- Stowage—for toilet articles, medicines, towels, and perhaps linens
- Floor drain—to remove water even if there is no shower
- Waterproof bulkheads—to prevent mildew and delamination of plywood and veneers, and to aid in cleaning
- Handholds—to provide security underway
- Artwork—to stare at when it's too rough to read!

WATERPROOFING

While fiberglass pans may restrict customization elsewhere in the boat, it is the ideal material for heads. Especially if a shower is installed in the head, a one-piece fiberglass unit eliminates seams where water can cause cosmetic if not structural damage. Sinks overflow and toilets leak.

Unfortunately, a one-piece fiberglass unit may be impossible to install in an existing boat. An alternative is to coat all horizontal wood surfaces with clear epoxy, paying special attention to seams, which may be filled first with a mixture of epoxy and filler such as Cab-O-Sil or microballoons. More difficult would be to construct a false floor with generous vertical flanges to hold water. Once waterproofed, the head is also an excellent oilskin locker for dripping foul weather gear and other apparel.

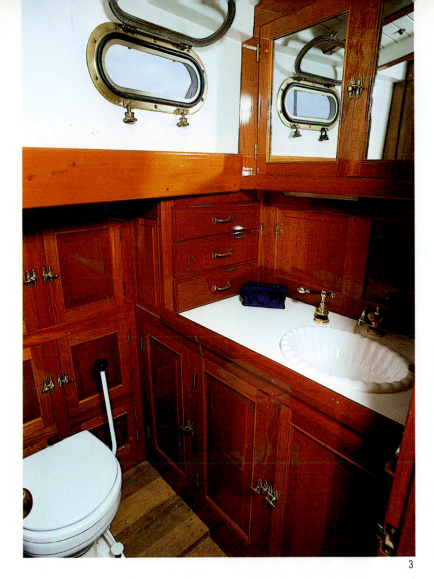

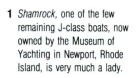

3

4

1 *Shamrock,* one of the few remaining J-class boats, now owned by the Museum of Yachting in Newport, Rhode Island, is very much a lady.

2 The French builder Beneteau is known for its bold, innovative styling. A large production builder of racer/cruiser sailboats, Beneteau used round shapes in the 35s5 head and adjacent shower stall, formed in fiberglass molds. The windows are narrow vertical strips.

3 The forward head of *Caroler* has raised mahogany paneling and six drawers built into the cabinet. The sink is handmade porcelain cast in a scallop-shell design. The simple but elegant Kohler fixtures are brass.

4 On most boats, there's no reason one can't be as comfortable as at home. Lighted mirrors in the head are an aid to grooming. Keeping colors light in small cabins helps allay claustrophobia and facilitates cleaning.

1

2

1 The flatter hull bottoms of
   powerboats create more usable
   sole space, as in the head of
   this small cruiser.

2 Even in a small head, the
   variety of materials is sometimes startling. This customized
   Thomas Gilmer ketch has
   caning on compartment doors,
   tiles on the sole, wood trim,
   plastic laminated countertops,
   a glass mirror, and stainless
   steel sink.

3 A contemporary sailboat head
   with plastic laminates on the
   sink structure for waterproofing,
   fiberglass pan in the sole for
   the shower drain, and teak trim
   for accent: standard construction
   practice.

4 Polished brass fixtures look
   almost as rich as gold, but at
   a fraction of the price.

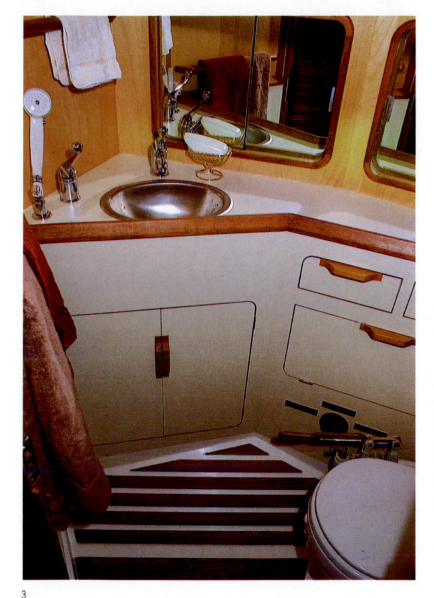

3

4

SHOWERS

The waterproof head compartment is ideal for installing a shower; few improvement jobs make as much impact in civilizing the boating experience.

To convert an existing head it is necessary to waterproof at least the floor and to drill a hole for a drain. The drain(s) should be located at the lowest point and connected to a hose that empties either into the bilge or into a sump fitted with a pump. If the sump is small, the pump should be electric and triggered by an automatic float switch. A grate is beneficial in that your feet won't slosh in standing water; it can be produced from strips of mortised teak or a Plexiglas panel with 1-inch holes drilled in it.

Telephone-type shower heads attached to a flexible hose are miserly with water and can be unhooked if you just want to wash your hair without getting the rest of your body wet.

Hot water may be obtained from a tank that is warmed by an electric coil or engine cooling water via a heat exhanger. This type of system requires AC electricity from a dock or generator, or running the engine. Another method of heating water is by means of an instantaneous propane heater that mounts on a bulkhead. A burner heats the cold water as it passes through a series of coils. These units are popular in some European homes because of their inherent economy—since there is no large tank, only the water used is heated.

Larger boats may be able to afford the luxury of a separate shower stall or minitub. Elaborate four-sided shower curtains aren't required, and a seat may be fitted for added convenience. Again, a one-piece fiberglass unit is best.

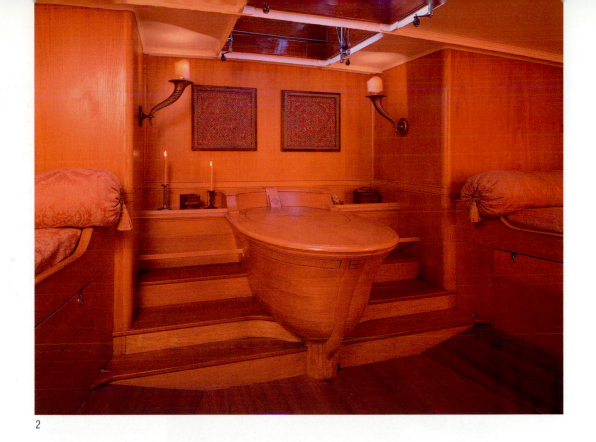

2

3

1 The opulent head aboard *P'zazz* is trimmed in olive-ash burlwood, with a solid onyx tub and 24-carat gold-plated fixtures. A backlit cut-glass mural separates the tub from the master bed.

2 The huge classic sloop *Astra* has an exceptionally beautiful and unusual tub perched like a christening bath between two berths.

3 Mirrors, mirrors, mirrors everywhere, plus gold curtains and fixtures make a bath in *Miss Marty* a truly hedonistic experience.

1

and replacement. Positive-action seacocks must be fitted to each hose exiting below the waterline.

Equally important is the type of toilet purchased. These range from fairly simple units with manual pumps to sophisticated electric units with chemical treatment and automatic valves. Perhaps the most foolproof—excepting the oak bucket—is the vacuum-type, whose only moving part is a bilge-type pump mounted separately from the toilet.

Plastic, porcelain (china), and teak seats are available for many models, allowing some freedom to please the finicky bottom as well as the discriminating eye.

BIDETS

Though seldom seen in the United States, some large European yachts feature bidets in the head. This assumes a hot-water source somewhat more sophisticated than water boiled on the stovetop, and a drain system with seacock and through-hull. There is certainly no reason why you can't have a bidet on your boat, given available space. But when sailing in the States with provincial male guests, do be sure they know what it's for!

SINKS

Not so many years ago a sink in the head of a small or midsize boat was considered a luxury. At best, fold-up aluminum or stainless steel sink units were mounted on a bulkhead for a low-profile wash basin. But with the wider beams prevalent today, a fixed sink of decent size is almost expected.

As in the galley, water may be supplied via pressure-triggered faucets, manual hand pumps, or foot pumps. The head sink won't suffer as much abuse as the galley sink, however, so fiberglass is a more acceptable material here. It is especially attractive if a decorator color is selected, which can be coordinated with fixtures and other trim or towels.

Only large yachts are likely to have space for two separate sinks, or for that matter room for two people to use the head at the same time. If there is room, though, there is no doubt that separate wash areas are luxurious.

TOILETS

While it may seem hard to justify spending hundreds of dollars on a toilet, it is money well spent. Cheap toilets with plastic internal parts break down more frequently and are more likely to clog.

A critical decision is whether to incorporate a holding tank or install a macerator and/or chemical toilet that treats the waste before dumping it overboard. This depends much on where you use your boat; in the Great Lakes, for instance, holding tanks are mandatory. On the oceans one would be wise to check with the appropriate mandating authorities (the U.S. Coast Guard and state regulatory agencies in the United States) to determine the latest requirements, which do change from time to time.

A large holding tank occupies a lot of space, and in many boats it will have to be fitted underneath a berth or settee. Though it may be watertight, some foul odors may escape, so give that some thought in choosing its location. Also, determine where the pump-out or discharge hose will be routed. It's nice to keep this hose out of sight yet accessible for inspection

STOWAGE

Medicine cabinets aren't particularly well suited to boats, as the rolling motion is sure to spill the contents. The underdeck area outboard of the toilet is an excellent place to build in shelves for toilet articles, suntan lotions, spare rolls of toilet paper, towels, and bed linens. Ventilation is important to prevent mildew, so the shelves can be left open-faced with net guards, fitted with high fiddles, or closed with louvered or caned doors.

Try to vary the size of shelf space so that small items such as aspirin bottles and prescription drugs can be kept neatly in place and separate from larger bins for towels and linen.

ACCESSORIES

As the architect Ludwig Mies van der Rohe said, "God lives in the details." Thoughtful additions such as generous towel racks, soap trays or dispensers, large mirrors, toothbrush holders, and good lighting are sure to make the head more of a pleasure to use. And what's particularly nice about these accessories is that they may be inexpensive plastic sundries purchased at a hardware store, elegant fixtures from top-notch department stores, or your own designs fashioned in wood or metal in a basement workshop. Whatever you choose,

make sure they are resistant to rust and corrosion, especially if situated below an opening portlight.

VENTILATION

Free-flowing air is important in the head to dry it after use, prevent mildew, and move out odors. One opening portlight will function as an exhaust when the boat is pointed into the wind. When this isn't the case, air may enter the portlight, making it an intake, so a second opening such as an overhead hatch or vent is necessary as the exhaust.

Unless the portlights are very small, privacy curtains will keep you from feeling spied upon at the marina dock. Avoid untreated cotton and other natural fibers in favor of mildew-resistant fabrics.

LIGHTING

Due to its typically small space and the overuse of teak in many boats, the head is at risk of becoming as dark and gloomy as a potato cellar. Consider lightening the bulkhead colors; well-deployed light fixtures can make all the difference. Small lamps mounted above the sink and around the mirror may be all that's necessary in a small head. Larger compartments might benefit from another source such

1 *Tiana*'s shower and minitub make the most of limited space.

2 *Rangga* is a familiar sight to charterers in the Virgin Islands. She is equipped with a sailboard stowed on davits, gas grill, teak decks, and all the amenities one could want in a vacation home, including a bidet in the head.

as an overhead light or downlights against the far bulkhead. Try to locate them where they won't get wet, and remember that metal shades are more likely to rust than plastic.

A PERSONAL TOUCH

Even though space is limited in a boat, the head should be a cabin that one can relax in. True, you aren't likely to languish for hours in a large tub with unlimited water supply, but you should be able to wash up, shave, and do your hair in relative peace and comfort. Consequently it is important that you be able to reach the things you need without stretching yourself into deep cabinets or contorting your body to reach shower controls. Consider the ergonomics of the space in planning your head.

A simple and worthwhile improvement is to build a seat that folds down over the toilet; it could be constructed of teak and used for a shower seat or padded and used for grooming. Try screwing in cleats to the bulkheads on either side and setting the seat on top; when not in use it can be hinged up or removed and stowed against one bulkhead. A mirror at the appropriate height would be desirable.

The head is also a good location for a knick-knack shelf with fiddles for placing the stuff in your pockets when you undress.

In such a small area it is difficult to execute a grand design scheme, but there is a host of small things you can do. How about painting the bulkheads a new color? Sewing new curtains for the windows? Buying a new bath mat or toilet seat cover? And how about that small piece of artwork—a framed print or wood sculpture screwed to the bulkhead—to distract the eye from all the highly utilitarian devices and gizmos?

1 *Obsession's* black sink with modern matching features contrasts with the blond wood trim to become the focal point, as well it should in the head.

2 This sink and cabinet slide forward over the electric head for use or back into the bulkhead for storage.

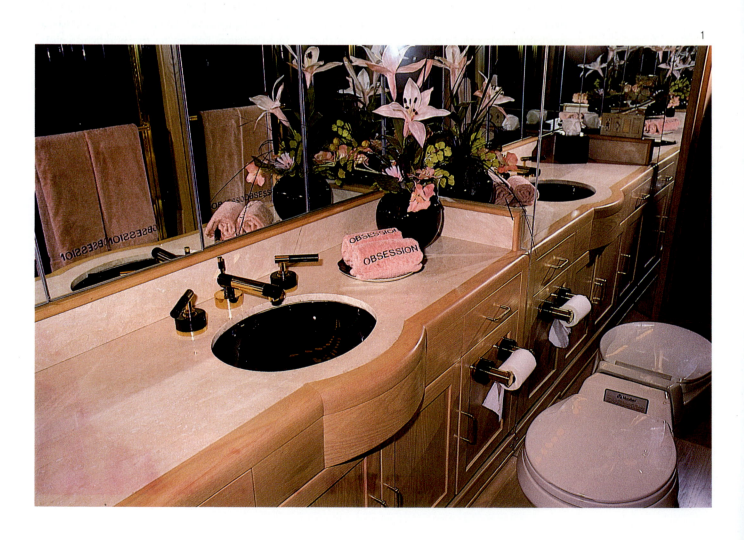

1

2

HEAD COMPARTMENT CHECKLIST

☐ How many toilets do you need?

☐ Do you need a sink? A shower? A tub? A bidet?

☐ What is the best location for the head, given the layout of the rest of your boat?

☐ Can the plumbing be routed to the sink and shower without major construction?

☐ Are there adequate drain systems?

☐ Can the toilet be used conveniently and safely by elderly people and children?

☐ Do you wish to separate the toilet and sink or shower in different compartments?

☐ Do you need 110-volt electrical service for shavers and hairdryers?

☐ Have you considered safety features such as handholds and nonskid floor surfaces?

☐ Are bulkhead surfaces and others water-proof?

☐ Is ventilation adequate?

☐ What lighting do you require?

CHAPTER TEN
Navigation Stations

nlike Dr. Seuss's backward-flying Who Bird, who only cared where he'd been, the yacht navigator must by necessity be forward-looking. He needs to know where he is at any given point in time, where he is going, and how he'll get there. Navigation charts, dividers, parallel rules, and other instruments are the tools he uses to make these calculations. While a separate, designated navigation area may be impossible in a small boat, it is certainly a desirable if not requisite feature on larger, ocean-traveling vessels.

People whose cognitive style is highly analytical obtain a great deal of satisfaction working out navigation problems. It is a science whose surface may be scratched or excavated, depending on how deeply the practitioner wants to "get into it." As with any good job, there is periodic feedback and reward. Even the person who hates math cannot help but feel a little smug when his guesstimates are verified by landfalls, electronic instrument backup, or communication with another vessel.

Regardless of your affinity for navigation, it is difficult to do good, accurate work on an icebox lid, dropleaf dinette table, or other makeshift surface where your posture is uncomfortable, the surface area doesn't fit the chart, and your pencil is likely to hit a crack and puncture the paper.

How you use your boat will be a factor in the space allocated to navigation. A daysailor won't have the same requirements as a long-range cruiser, but even a short coastal sail beset by fog or adverse conditions can quickly degenerate into a risky situation wherein accurate chartwork spells the difference between safety and disaster. When designing a new boat or planning the customization of your existing boat, give serious thought to the navigation function. Assume a worst-case scenario: It's dark, you can't see the harbor entrance, and the lights you had counted on to guide you in aren't visible. Do you want to tackle this problem sitting with a wet chart folded on your lap or sitting at a dry table with good light and all your charts, almanacs, and instruments ready at your fingertips?

LOCATION

Because of the close link between navigation and steering, the closer the chart table is to the helm, the better. In boats with wheelhouses it may in fact be possible for the helmsman to read charts and perform simple tasks even while steering. Unprotected flybridges and open cockpits aren't amenable to chartwork, because of wind, rain, and very often a lack of a flat surface. If there aren't adequate provisions at the steering station, chartwork is best performed in the security of a cabin belowdeck.

WHEELHOUSES

The best location for a chart table and navigation station depends on the wheelhouse configuration—helm, furniture, windows, and companionways. Some instruments should be accessible to the helmsman while on station, such as the VHF radio and radar. Others,

including the depthsounder, Loran, Decca, satellite navigation, log, barometer/barograph, water temperature, and wind speed may be mounted out of reach but still visible from the helm. If a companionway to a cabin below divides the wheelhouse dashboard into port and starboard sections, the chart table most likely will be located opposite the helm. Without such a companionway, the entire dash may be devoted to helm, engine and navigation instruments, and chart table, laid out in a sensible array that is convenient to both the helmsman and other crew who might be navigating.

In large wheelhouses with sufficient beam, the chart table might be located athwartship along one side of the house structure, thus providing perhaps a more comfortable orientation for standing or sitting if the boat rolls heavily.

Wheelhouse chart tables are generally constructed at a comfortable working height for someone in the standing position; to sit at the table a tall helmsman's seat is required.

HARDTOP COCKPITS

One of the most versatile and pleasant helm designs is a cockpit with a windshield, hardtop, and removable or roll-up canvas side and aft curtains. The hardtop should probably be made from the same material as the hull, though wood is a nice adornment on fiberglass and metal. It is a permanent, more effective alternative to the canvas dodger or navy top, but of course it cannot be taken down. Still, the area may be opened to the sun and wind during good weather, and buttoned up to protect against cold and rain. It is sometimes possible to use the part of the cabintop extending aft of the windshield as a chart surface, though this is probably best planned during the design phase so that the cabintop can be properly angled there for convenience. Failing that, some sort of wood chart table might be fashioned to fit that space. Either way you'll want a sizable fiddle at the bottom to keep charts from sliding off; a bin, pouch, or drawer for dividers and the like; and perhaps a hinged Plexiglas cover to keep the charts from flying about or getting damp.

Because *Nena VIII* is operated and maintained by a crew of just two, her bridge is equipped with a six-camera Panasonic monitoring system with pan and tilt features for remote security monitoring. Also: a fuel monitoring system, compact disk charting and plotting system, two King air-frequency radios, single-sideband radio, and Magnavox MX2400 satcom.

1

2

1 A trend in some singlehanded offshore racing boats, such as *UAP,* which competed in the 1986/87 around-the-world BOC Challenge, is chart tables built in the shape of a V so that when heeled, one side is nearly always horizontal.

2 The windshield and hardtop on *St. Kilda,* a Salar 40 motor-sailer, provides good shelter for the helmsman, who can also perform navigation chores if necessary.

3 The chart table in the wheelhouse of *Southern Cross* is convenient to the helm and navigation instruments.

4 *Trashman*'s canvas dodger, built by sailmaker Tom Clarke, protects the cockpit's fully instrumented navigation station and chart table.

3

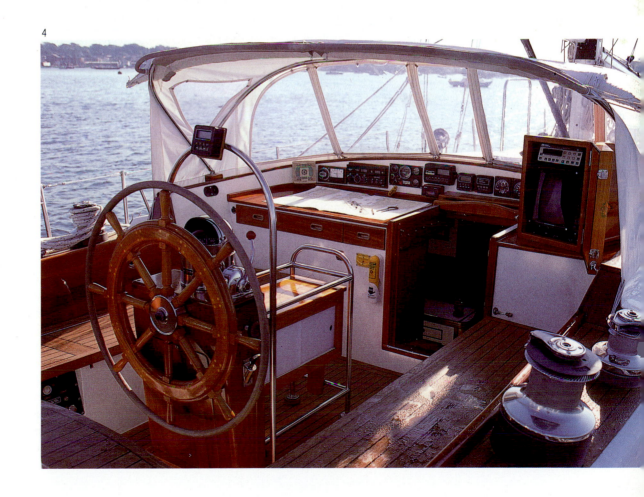

4

In smaller sailboats where space is at a premium, a workable chart table can be installed forward of the quarter berth so long as there is space left for the navigator's legs, as in the 36-foot John Holland sloop. In some designs, the table might drop to make a full-length berth.

SALOONS

The public demand for berths pressures the designer to sometimes forgo such amenities as the navigation station. Builders of low-end boats also find the extra cost of woodworking prohibitively expensive. More surprising are the expansive, opulent motoryachts in which no provision for old-fashioned hands-on navigation has been made; electronics, the buyer is led to believe, will do it all. But position coordinates are useless without a chart to plot them on.

A serviceable chart table is possible in many boats without major modifications. One of the simplest and least obtrusive solutions in a sailboat is either a permanent or fold-down table at the head of a quarter berth. This works best if there is a footwell between the berth and the partial bulkhead just forward of it that typically separates the berth from the galley or settee amidships; otherwise one must sit with one leg folded. The head of the berth may have a removable board to provide foot space; at night the table folds up and the insert board is fitted in place, a cushion placed on top, followed by sheets, pillow, and last but not least your happy little head.

As boat size increases, the quarter berth may be pushed aft and a separate seat fitted to face the navigation station. If fitted fore and aft, a small partial bulkhead separating the navigation station from the berth defines the space. If fitted athwartship, a custom-hinged stool seat that swings in to stow beneath the chart table saves space. Bench seats and swiveling armchairs with armrests are cushy and proper on larger yachts. In sailboats, an athwartship bench seat built with a concave top prevents the navigator from sliding inboard or off the seat altogether when heeled.

The sailboat navigation station should be kept near the companionway so that the navigator and helmsman can communicate easily. The motion is gentler here, too, than anywhere farther forward. At the same time, it should be offset sufficiently from the companionway hatch so that rain and spray won't hit the charts and electronic instruments.

Motoryacht arrangements differ in that the inside steering station is probably at the forward end of the saloon. Consequently, the navigation station should be handy to the helm, as in a wheelhouse. There is usually good space for charts and instruments behind the windshield and above the forward cabins.

DESIGN ELEMENTS

Even on large boats, the navigation station is a tight, compact area where the navigator can get lost in his own little world of plots, bearings, and star angles. In many respects it is more difficult to plan an economical space packed with gear than a large, more sparsely fitted area.

DIMENSIONS

The centerpiece of any navigation station is the chart table, which should be large enough to lay out full-size charts with a minimum of folds. On many boats, however, this will be impractical. Smaller tables require folding the charts so many times that the paper deteriorates prematurely. Also, the navigator may not be able to see both his position and destination on the same "page," making it difficult to plot courses. For coastal American cruising many people use spiral-bound chart kit books, the largest of which measure about 22 inches by 17 inches. Some chart kit companies sell custom boards specially designed to hold the book in place. In any case, consider the dimensions of the table surface with your charts in mind and remember that a large table will perform double duty as a writing, typing, or sewing desk.

The height of the tabletop above the sole should be about 2 feet 6 inches, and the chair height about 15 to 18 inches for comfortable seating. The tabletop can be angled down about 5 degrees or more if you find that more comfortable.

YACHT
PROFILE

Ilinga

Ilinga, a 1956 Huckins Fairform Flyer, Sportsman 40 model, cruises between 18 and 26 knots with a top speed of 34. She is powered by twin 340-horsepower Chrysler V-8 gasoline engines, burning just one gallon per nautical mile. A comparatively light displacement of 16,500 pounds contributes to her efficiency.

The bridge affords a good view forward and to each side; a chart surface with spring-loaded hold-downs is located to the right of the wheel.

Ilinga's home is Narragansett Bay.

A small desk in the saloon has a pull-out writing surface to save space.

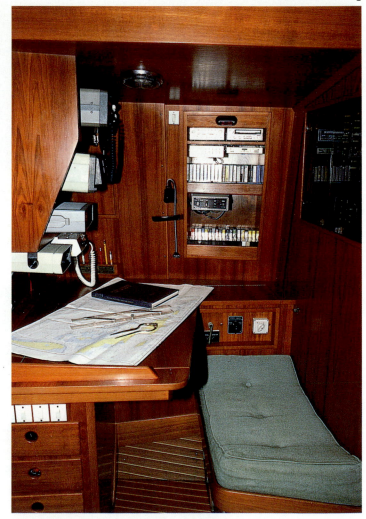

1 A pivoting stool on the Freedom 42 is a spacesaver; the desk also incorporates other good features to organize tools, instruments, charts, and files.

2 The navigator's seat in *Osprey*, a Baltic 51, is gently concave for comfort and security underway.

3 Real luxury is a cushioned swivel chair. It will be a sought-after seat for reading and lounging as well as nav work.

3

The Ideal Nav Station

A variety of elements combine to make a good navigation station. These include a large, smooth surface for chartwork, chart stowage drawers, a comfortable seat for the navigator, space for instruments within arm's reach, day and night lighting, and custom drawers and holders for the navigator's tools.

The seat, if fixed, should be mounted so that its forward face is aligned with, or slightly under, the front edge of the overhanging table. A backrest is nice for reading but not essential for chartwork, which generally has the navigator leaning over the table, supported by his elbows and forearms.

Instruments may be mounted flush in the surrounding paneling, which should be easily removable for service or accessing smoldering wires. The leads to the battery bank should be kept short to minimize voltage drop.

Adequate stowage for the all-important charts is often overlooked. It's difficult to work with charts that are rolled up for stowage, though overhead boards with circular holes are a convenient, out-of-the-way method. Drawers keep charts flat and well protected, though on small boats charts may have to be folded several times—the fewer the better.

LAYOUT

While almost any configuration of the chart table, stowage, and instrument array can be made serviceable, an L-shaped layout utilizing the side of the hull and a fore-and-aft-mounted table allows the navigator to have the accessories he needs at his side. With this layout it isn't necessary to reach over the table to operate the Decca, Loran, SatNav, radio, and other electronics, as they can be mounted in a board against the hull and beneath the side decks.

In a wheelhouse/saloon dashboard or other single-axis layout, try to mount some instruments in overheads above the table for easy access. Wooden boxes can be hung from the cabintop or under the side decks to hold electronics in a convenient position.

Think how the navigator will enter the area, especially if there is a fixed seat. There should be sufficient footroom both at the entrance and under the desk.

LIGHTS

The navigation station does not need general or atmospheric lighting, which makes electronic liquid crystal display (LCD) numbers faint and difficult to read. Such instruments

White and red lights over the chart table are important for accurate position fixes by day or night.

can be left in the dark. Small, bright, high-tensile spotlights with pivoting heads and flexible stems illuminate charts and notepads without wasting energy lighting the whole interior. There should be both white and red lights; a nifty light fixture is one with a pivoting red filter so that both colors can be had from one bulb. The red light is useful at night so that neither the navigator nor skipper's night vision is affected.

STOWAGE

The dramatic increase in chart prices in recent years makes them a substantial investment, and one well worth protecting. Folding shortens charts' lifespans, so the fewer folds the better. Here are a few stowage ideas:

• Inside desk—A small odds-and-ends compartment can be neatly fitted at the seat end of the desk to hold pencils, dividers, erasers, and the like.

• Drawers—A large, shallow drawer built in under the desk, berth or side deck provides dry, safe chart stowage.

• Overhead racks—An alternative to folding charts flat is to roll them up and slip them into a rack consisting of two parallel boards with 4-inch holes drilled in each. You'll need clips, weights, or some other device to hold them flat on the chart table. Also, to stow more than about half a dozen charts you'll have to roll up several together, making it annoying to find the one you want.

Chart kit books are generally protected by stiff cardboard covers, and thus can be stowed under bunk cushions if no other provisions are made.

You'll also want a bookshelf to hold cruising guides or pilots, almanacs, tide tables, light lists, and the many other publications the navigator refers to. Keep it handy to the chart table and seat, and oriented so the titles on the bindings can be read. Some sort of removable retaining bar or slat will keep them from falling out. Make sure there's enough space above the shelf to remove books.

A pencil rack can easily be fashioned from a piece of hardwood with spaced holes drilled in the top. This can also hold dividers. And include a shelf or an open-topped bin as a catchall for paper clips, rubberbands, erasers, magnifying glasses, rulers, and the clutter that invariably collects around any desk.

CONSTRUCTION

The basic structure of the navigation station in most cases will be wooden. This may include the chart table surface, but it must be a hardwood to resist gouges from pencil and divider points. A laminated plastic surface such as Formica is harder, more durable, easier to clean, but also slick.

The table, if unsupported on one corner (as is typical of many designs), must be constructed strongly. Assume that sooner or later someone will lean, sit, or fall on it.

When light weight is the goal, as in a multihull, the unit can be built with thin sheets of plywood properly stiffened with cleats and frames. Alternatively, a honeycomb-cored material can be used where greater strength is required, such as for supporting bulkheads, the desk foundations, and possibly even the top. For the table surface, choose a ply with a hardwood veneer (such as teak, mahogany, or birch) that works with the rest of the interior finish.

Because of the number of electronic instruments typically mounted there, the navigation area is a good place to locate the ship's electrical panel. A hinged board that provides quick access to circuit breakers, bus bars, and terminals will make adding instruments and troubleshooting easier. If the batteries are located nearby, there is the added benefit of keeping wire distances short, thereby minimizing voltage drop and enhancing performance.

1 The Sabre 42 navigation station has a handy tool drawer so that one needn't dig through lockers and heavy toolboxes when all that's needed is a simple screwdriver.

2 The Little Harbor 53 *Blue Star* has an under-the-berth chart bin; a shallow tray (shown) lifts out for access to charts in the deeper compartment below.

1

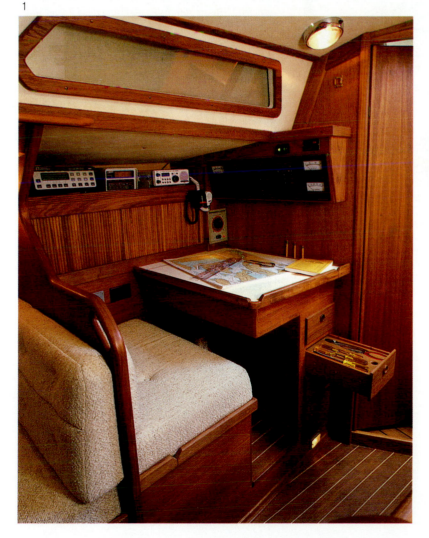

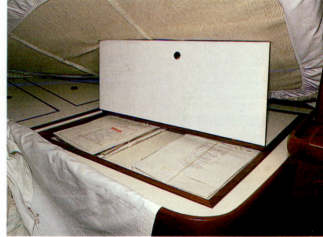

YACHT PROFILE

Rosalind

Rosalind is one of just two known surviving two-masted dipping luggers built in St. Ives, England. She was built by William Paynter and launched from the beach in 1903 as a commercial fishing vessel. Richard Griffiths, then a young art teacher, found her rotting in the mud at Shoreham Harbor, Sussex, in 1959, paid $300 for her, and commenced a long and arduous renovation. "She was half full of mud," he recounts, "and there were little trees growing out of her deck. She had been stripped of her engine, masts, cleats—everything! The anchor was the only piece of gear left." By scrounging around boatyards and nautical flea markets, he managed to resurrect *Rosalind*, and today she represents a stunning achievement in human tenacity and yacht history, not to mention beauty. Indeed, she was given the "Best Restoration" award during a classic boat rendezvous at the Mystic Seaport Museum. She measures 39 feet 11 inches on deck, 12 feet 6 inches beam, and 5 feet 4 inches draft.

Rosalind of St. Ives sails today as a private yacht along the East Coast of the United States. Now beautifully restored as a gaff-rigged schooner, she once sailed as part of the Cornish fishing fleet. In the 1890s, there were more than 90 double-ended commercial vessels like her fishing the Cornish coast.

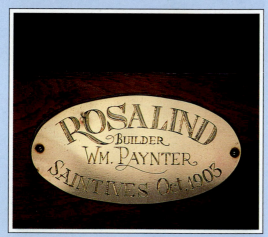

Originally christened *Susan*, the yacht was once a two-masted dipping lugger, meaning the mainsail and boom had to be "dipped" in order to tack. The type was also referred to as a "mackerel driver," for the species of fish the masters sought.

The chart table is located inside the companionway to starboard. The dividers are several hundred years old, traced to a Royal Navy warship of the 18th century.

Richard Griffiths, having owned and cared for *Rosalind* for more than 30 years, seems a part of her.

"First a fireplace, a leather seat and a Persian carpet, then comes the rest," says Richard Griffiths.

Once the fish hold, *Rosalind*'s saloon was restored with white oak frames and Sitka spruce deck beams, and finished with African mahogany paneling. Its warmth and distinctive personality are best enjoyed by the glow of her oil lamps and the flicker of her fireplace.

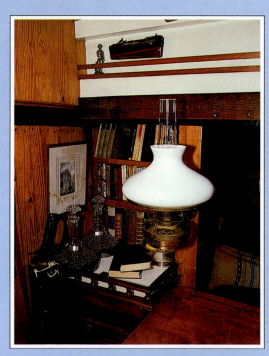

The "library" is a cozy corner full of great books and memorabilia, including a sword and scabbard.

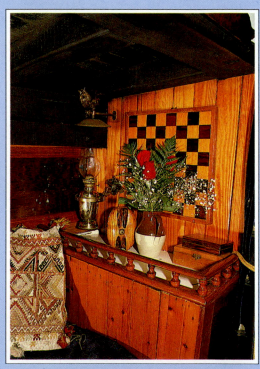

A hand-carved chessboard fits securely into fastenings on the saloon bulkhead, adding visual appeal to the yacht's still-life arrangement. A handmade Hungarian tapestry throw pillow and a large varnished block hint that this boat has cruised to many exotic ports.

CONVERSIONS

Though boat owners sometimes feel too much space is allocated to the navigation station, the opposite is more often the case. If a chart table is needed, first decide whether it must be permanent or if a portable or fold-up tabletop will suffice.

A portable chart board can be constructed of hardwood or top-quality hardwood-veneer plywood to hold a folded chart and stow in some preplanned space such as a quarter berth or locker, or against a bulkhead. The board can be held on the lap, laid on top of the galley or dinette, or snapped into temporary brackets installed above a settee or berth or on any sturdy structure such as the galley counter, dinette table, or bulkhead. Clevis or snap-apart hinges are good mounting fasteners. A fold-up leg may be necessary to support the near edge of the table.

If you're considering a fold-up chart table, look at bulkhead mounts first, as they provide a sturdy anchor for hinges as well as a flat surface to hold the table in the stowed position. Other locations could be the cabin or hull sides; if there isn't room for the table to fold, perhaps it can be made to slide on a set of wood or metal runners.

To install a permanent chart table in place of other furniture will involve more serious demolition and reconstruction. Sketch the new furniture piece and develop a construction plan before proceeding. Sometimes, however, you won't know everything involved until the old furniture is taken apart to reveal underlying supports. Carefully disassemble wood cabinets or berths piece by piece so as not to ruin adjacent veneers or supports that won't be removed, and check to see if any pieces can be reused, labeling them as you go; sometimes this is the best way to match wood grains or

other surface materials. Drill out bungs and unscrew fasteners rather than ripping pieces out by force. Use a cold chisel to break fiberglass tabs.

A sturdy table requires anchoring support pieces solidly in bulkheads with screws or bolts. If a bare fiberglass hull is to function as part of the structure, grind clean and glass in stringers that will serve as load bearers. The frames of a steel or aluminum hull can be drilled for through-bolting wood pieces.

Depending on the wood used, you may choose to paint, varnish, or oil it on completion. If using a laminated plastic surface, take care not to chip the edges, and bevel with a file for a neat, finished appearance.

NAV STATION CHECKLIST

- ☐ How many charts do you plan to carry aboard? Where will you stow them?

- ☐ What electronic instruments must be mounted in the nav station? At the helm?

- ☐ Do you want repeaters at the helm or nav station?

- ☐ Will you design the chart table for standing, sitting, or both?

- ☐ Do you require a permanent seat? Fixed, pivoting, or portable?

- ☐ Can the navigator communicate with the helmsman?

- ☐ Will you orient the chart table fore and aft or athwartship?

- ☐ Do you plan to use the chart table for writing, typing, or other activities?

- ☐ Should the tabletop be slanted or horizontal?

Forepeaks

owhere in a boat is space more restrictive than the forepeak. It is wide at the aft end and tapers to a virtual point at the bow. At deck level there is beaminess to work with, but at the waterline and below the hull fills in like the sides of a collapsing sandpit. The geometry of the forepeak is complex and confusing—except for the bulkhead, there is no plumb and no square, and there is no floor. Indeed, trying to use this space is like trying to build a ship's model inside the tailfin of a 1959 Cadillac.

Other considerations encumber the builder and designer. Weight must be kept at a minimum in the bow of the boat: In sailboats,

A piercing bow and long overhang, common in the 1930s, increase the yacht's waterline length when heeled, and thereby its speed, without incurring a penalty under the rating rule. Because J Class boats like *Shamrock* were only day sailed for the America's Cup, the wasted space inside the fo'c's'le was irrelevant.

excessive weight in the ends promotes hobby-horsing, and in a planing powerboat, weight in the bow interferes with control at high speeds. The forepeak space must also be accessible, which may require scooching on your belly across a V-berth, or an entrance from the deck, which is a sensitive area frequently doused by waves. Yet the dictum that says waste no space commands the designer and builder to make something useful of the forepeak. How well they succeed is a function of time, cost, and ingenuity, but there is no doubt that the rewards are considerable.

GROUND TACKLE

Because anchoring is done from the bow of a boat, it is necessary that anchors and rodes be stowed there. It is unthinkable to stow two or more chain or rope rodes and anchors on deck, so at least the rodes must go below. The shallow anchor lockers found on many modern boats may be satisfactory for racers, daysailers, and boats almost always docked, but there simply isn't room in them for stowing and organizing serious ground tackle. Furthermore, when the weight of ground tackle begins to exceed the weight of a crewmember, the deck-level anchor well is too high; better to place such weight lower and aft, closer to the boat's center of gravity.

Therefore, if the boat is to carry cruising ground tackle a large chain locker in the bow is indicated. It should extend aft of the overhanging bow so that heavy coils of chain do not adversely affect trim and performance. Chain or rope rodes can be fed through deck pipes and allowed to coil themselves on a flat board installed between the hull sides; without such a board multiple rodes will inevitably tangle in the V-shaped crease of the hull.

A door in the bulkhead separating the chain locker from accommodations aft will allow access not only to the rodes but also to electrical wiring and the nuts and backing plates of deck fittings such as running lights, cleats, and windlasses. Door louvers coupled with a deck vent will circulate air throughout the chain locker and help to reduce the smell of wet mud and seaweed. Anchor wells and chain lockers high above the waterline and sealed off from the rest of the boat's interior may have drainage holes in the hull; if the locker isn't sealed, a drainage hole in the floorboard and a large-diameter connecting hose to the bilge will help keep the area dry.

OTHER APPLICATIONS

The uniquely shaped space in the bow of a boat needn't be allocated just to ground tackle or the feet of people sleeping in V-berths. As boat length increases and adequate accommodations can be fitted elsewhere, the forepeak offers intriguing possibilities for other uses.

Sailboats carrying numerous bags of sails often utilize this area as a sail locker; a generous overhead hatch permits passing bags up or down without having to lug them through other cabins. They may be dumped on the floor to lean against the hull sides, stowed in canvas or net hammocks, or kept in wire or rope kennel cages for easy identification.

Few boats cannot profit by a workbench with vise where bent metal can be straightened, wires soldered, and small wood pieces screwed and painted. If there isn't space in the engine room for a workbench, the large walk-in forepeak is a good place for it.

Traditionally, crew slept in the fo'c's'le, located in the ship's bows because the motion made sleeping and living less comfortable than midships and aft, where of course the officers and guests slept. In today's midsize yacht, the large forepeak is frequently asked to accommodate the hired hands or junior crew. Fold-up canvas or root berths (see Chapter 7, "Staterooms") may be fitted to the hull sides, or hammocks hung from the deck. They are light and convertible and enjoy a high degree of privacy. If the boat is large enough, a separate companionway ladder provides private access from the deck, protected by a watertight hatch or booby hatch. A small sink and toilet may also be installed for the crew's convenience.

Even without separate crew quarters forward, the forepeak makes an excellent primary or secondary head; it is private, easily ventilated and frees up wider sections of the hull for living and sleeping space.

The forepeak can be customized for specialty jobs, too, including photographic darkrooms, drafting tables, computer work stations, and the like. True, they may be usable only at dockside or at anchor, but then it's unlikely one would attempt drawing or developing film on the boat while underway.

ACCESS

Occasionally you will see a boat with a forepeak accessible only from the deck, a full bulkhead separating it from the living space aft. One reason for this seeming oddity is to provide a watertight compartment in the bow, which is most vulnerable to collision and holing. This can be a wholly satisfactory arrangement in a large boat with a large hatch and companionway ladder leading from the deck to the sole. In such cases, the forepeak is essentially relegated to sails, ground tackle, deck scrubbing equipment, and other items needed on deck but not below.

Unless sail bags will be passed through the forward hatch or entry via a ladder is intended, the hatch needn't be large. Normally access to the forepeak is through a door in the forward bulkhead. The watertight integrity of the forepeak can be retained by installing a door similar to the type seen on submarines, with a thick rubber gasket and some sort of positive mechanism to compress the door against it. Such extreme measures needn't preclude use of the forepeak for berths, extra toilet, workbench, or stowage.

1

2

FOREPEAK CHECKLIST

☐ Can you afford to sacrifice living space for a large forepeak?

☐ Will you need to berth crew there in a pinch?

☐ Is drainage to the bilge required?

☐ Are deck fittings, wiring, and other systems accessible?

☐ Are anchor rodes accessible?

☐ On sailboats, how many sail bags will be carried? Where will they be stowed? How will you move them on deck?

☐ Is there adequate ventilation?

☐ Can the forepeak be made watertight?

☐ Have you included electric lighting in your plan?

☐ Can you plug a hole in the event of collision?

3

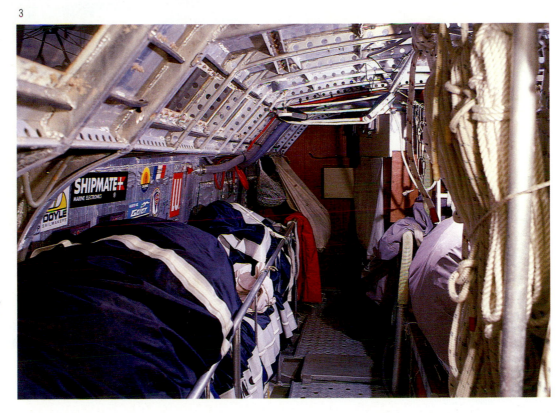

1 *Weatherly*'s forepeak "basket" berths, with thick mattresses fitted in aluminum frames, prove that temporary berths need not sacrifice comfort. They fold up against the hull when not in use.

2 *Karin,* a 50-foot wooden yawl built in Germany before World War Two, has a large forepeak for sail and line stowage in addition to the chain locker. She is owned by Mike and Bev Muessel, co-owners of Oldport Launch Service in Newport, Rhode Island.

3 A large sail inventory is a key ingredient to competitive sailing in events such as the BOC Challenge. *Biscuits Lu,* skippered by Guy Bernadin, has a kennel to hold and organize sail bags.

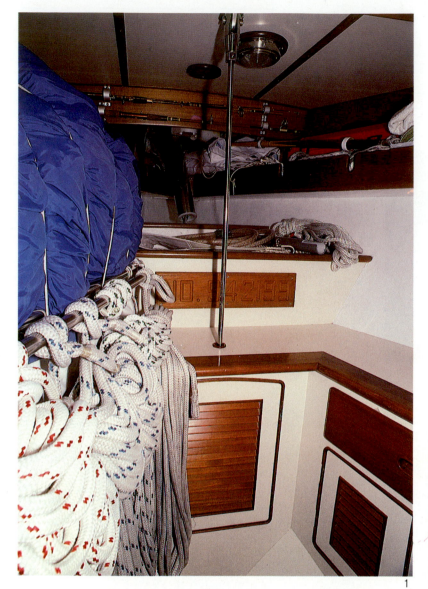

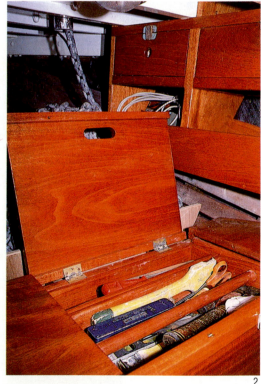

1 Without V-berths, the forepeak has room for sail bags, lines, and miscellaneous gear. The tube forward is the chain pipe and the tie rod in the middle takes the load of the inner forestay.

2 The schooner *Sophia Christina*'s forepeak is not wasted space. Builder David Jackson incorporated shelves and bins to hold the many tools and equipment needed aboard a cruising boat.

CHAPTER TWELVE
Wheelhouses

The wheelhouse may be the most satisfying cabin on a boat. It is Command Central, the Nerve Center, Hub of the Universe, where one can steer, navigate, sleep (if there is a pilot's berth tucked away somewhere), or just hang out on a damp day with a cup of coffee to watch the rain come down. It is light, airy, dry, and warm, yet by virtue of its elevation and wraparound view, it seems part of the world it surveys, not some dreary burrow sunk in a dark chasm. A wheelhouse should feel like your private pleasure dome; if it doesn't, it needs help.

The bridge of Peter Taggares's classic Chris-Craft *Teco II* is bright and airy, with a guest bench behind the helmsman's chair.

1

1 Color can play an important role in demarcating different levels and reducing the apparent height of super-structures such as wheelhouses. A dark-green hull and orange handrail draw attention from the soft cream of this tug yacht's wheelhouse. So does the bright lavender exhaust stack, not visible in the photo!

2 *Aquel II*'s tinted, wraparound, swept-back windows are essential elements in its fast, contemporary style.

3 Traditional wheelhouse appointments generally include three to five forward-facing windows. Side doors provide easy access to the deck. A nice feature of *Francis Marion* is the "Portuguese deck" forward of the wheelhouse, which may have its own seat and enables convenient access to the foredeck or to the cabins below via a booby hatch.

4 The superb metalwork on *Antipodean* adopts a variety of unexpectedly gentle shapes and angles. The traditional wheelhouse visor is discarded in favor of a sleek, "bald" appearance.

2

3

4

FUNCTION

HELM

By definition, the wheelhouse contains an inside steering station—a wheel—and that is its primary purpose. Also commonly referred to as a pilothouse, it may enclose the sole steering station aboard or serve as a foul-weather backup to a flybridge station, from which the commanding view of the bow and stern makes docking maneuvers easier. In either case, the helm should have full engine and navigation instrumentation or at least repeaters, a comfortable seat for the helmsman, and a chart table or navigation station nearby (see Chapter 10, "Navigation Stations").

VISIBILITY AND VENTILATION

Good visibility over the bow is critical, yet even in the best designs there may be blind spots. The side view through large windows is generally good. The view aft depends on the cabin design and window configuration, but some provision for seeing what lies astern should be made. Wipers and a rain wheel mounted on the windshield in front of the helm will aid visibility in stormy weather.

Opening windows forward and on the sides provide excellent ventilation. Where no flybridge exists, an opening hatch—a sunroof or T-top if you will—above the helm is an added source of fresh air. An electric fan that can be adjusted to cool the helmsman or defog the windshield is a sensible idea.

The size of windows is a safety concern, especially on boats that venture offshore. Breaking seas can blow out large panes and let in enough water to render a vessel unstable and in extreme cases even sink it. (In many documented knockdowns and sinkings, it is the leeward windows—broken by the force of the cabin slamming into the water—and not the windward windows being struck by waves that precipitates disaster.) Windows are larger

1

on midsize motoryachts than sailboats, since they are less likely to go offshore and since the wheelhouse is generally higher and therefore less vulnerable. Still, on ocean-cruising sailboats and motoryachts alike, installing fittings for storm shutters is the prudent thing to do. Smaller windows or portlights are obviously safer, but their restricted visibility poses other problems, most notably during maneuvers in crowded harbors. On sailboats, the helmsman should be able to see the sails, and this requires exact placement of windows and overhead hatches or clear panels.

DESIGN

On all but the largest yachts, the wheelhouse is a prominent design feature. This is due mostly to its height above deck, height that is needed for the helmsman to see over the bow. Also, its house line is often distinct from and higher

2

1 *Record*'s wheelhouse is a great place for pooches as well as people to kick back and check out the view. The mechanical linkages for the throttle (left) and variable-pitch prop (right) can be seen running through the floor to the engine room below.

2 *Ilinga*'s uncluttered helm station is painted a cool blue.

than the line of the cabins forward or aft. Consequently, great care should be given in its design to keep the superstructure from looking like a bunch of toy building blocks randomly plopped atop a mismatched hull.

Wheelhouses may be located just about anywhere and still look good. Commercial ships, working fishboats, and some traditional cruisers look salty and purposeful with the wheelhouse/bridge located far aft or forward; a dead-center location tends to make the hull look as though it's bowing up at the ends from the midships weight. As mentioned, height of the helm is critical to visibility. This calculation will have a lot to do with the design; standing headroom is presumed.

In profile, the wheelhouse may have a vertical face for a workboat or turn-of-the-century yacht look; a face raked forward to protect the windshield from rain, deflect the force of breaking waves, and increase deck space; or a swept-back face for a sleek, modern appearance. If the angle is extreme, this last arrangement can make visibility difficult; it is most often seen on low-profile pilothouse sailboats where aerodynamics are a consideration, and on megayachts for which the illusion of speed is integral to the overall design.

Variations in the thwartships plane of the wheelhouse face might include a gentle radius, a flat surface across, or three to five angled sections, depending on the number of windows. Each will impart a distinctive stylistic effect and should be in keeping with the hull and other superstructures so that these components look like parts of the same whole. A swept-back wheelhouse face and a plumb bow would look incongruous. But as soon as you utter such pedantry, some designer will prove you wrong by successfully combining these seemingly incompatible elements, so perhaps it is best to just say "whatever works."

A short, overhanging coachroof or visor often looks better than a coachroof terminated forward at the windshield. In fact, the coachroof may overhang on all four sides, partly for looks (to create a shadow line, for example, that reduces the apparent height of the house), but also to reduce window glare and provide foul-weather protection on the side decks.

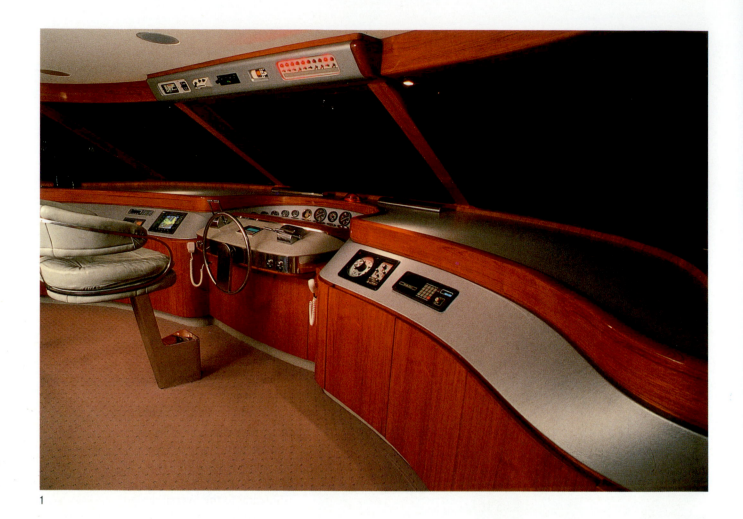

1

1 Futuristic styling describes the bridge of *Numero Uno* with its angled stainless steel helm seat pedestal and silver, wrap-around accent band running the length of the dashboard.

2 The catamaran *Popeye's* is a superboat-class offshore racing powerboat driven by Al Copeland and sponsored by his Popeye's chain of fast-food restaurants.

3 The bridge of *Crystal*, the largest sportfishing boat in the world, has plush, adjustable upholstered seats in which a captain might almost lie back with electrodes strapped to his temples and "think" port and starboard to steer the yacht.

2

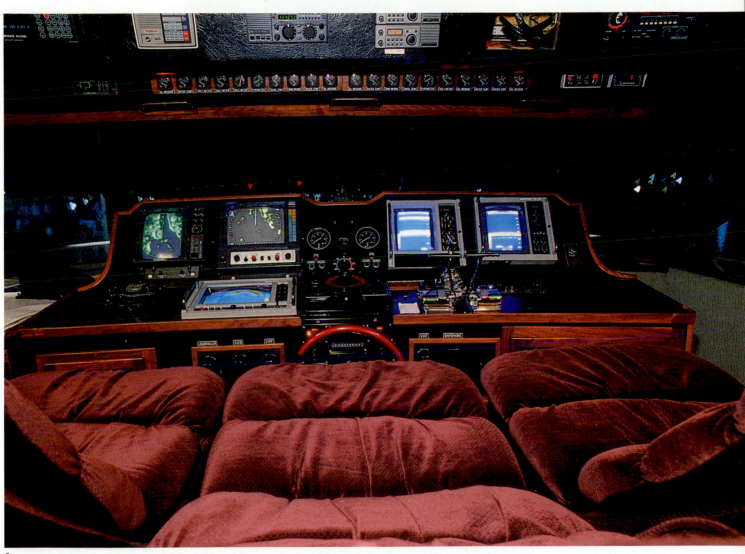

3

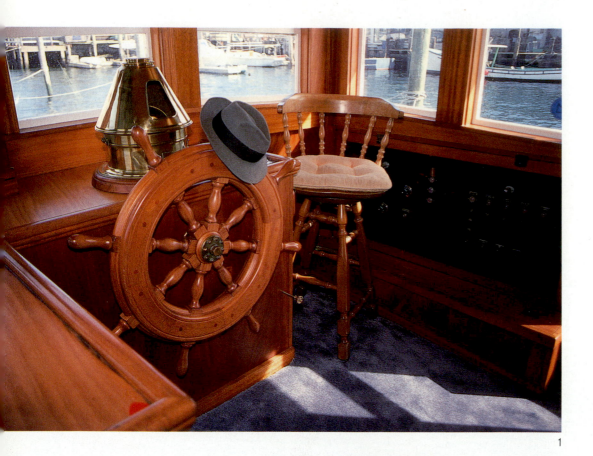

1

2

1 The massive brass compass binnacle and wooden wheel in *Southern Cross* convey a strength and purpose befitting her U.S. Navy lineage.

2 Even sailboats can have snug, enclosed wheelhouses with inside steering stations for use in foul weather.

3 The antique compass binnacle and throttle controls on *Red Witch* are so beautiful that one would want to display them even if they didn't work.

4 *Jolly Dolphin* was custom-built for an experienced yachtsman who wanted to cruise Canada's Maritime Provinces without unnecessary exposure to the elements. The forward-leaning wheelhouse face is a frequently seen feature of commercial fishing boats.

3

4

WINDOWS

Naval architect Chuck Neville says, "One of the most prominent parts of a boat are the damn windows. They should call attention to themselves, their style, and what line they follow. Typically they should follow the housetop line, but sometimes they'll follow any number of things. The bottom of steamer windows may follow nothing, while the top of sailboat windows might follow some feature line."

Windows are without doubt a key element in the success or failure of a wheelhouse. Consider their shape, size, and number. Accepted ratios of length to width are tried and true, but any shape is possible, and if your boat is going to break rules elsewhere you might get away with unorthodox proportions—skinny rectangles, rhomboids, circles, or ovals on end perhaps. And you might consider tinted glass to cut down glare and increase privacy.

Even with tinting, you'll probably want some sort of blinds or curtains inside to control light and privacy. A traditional wheelhouse treatment is captain's lace, which looks right on the right boat and quite wrong on anything else. Today there are many types and colors of adjustable blinds available, and curtain style is limited only by the method of hanging and the selection of fabric, which is practically infinite.

For more information on window treatments see Chapter 5, "Light, Air, and Color," and Chapter 18, "Soft Coverings."

Cheap frames such as extruded aluminum channels and rubber gaskets can do a good boat a grave injustice; more appealing are stainless steel and chrome-plated bronze. Or hide the frames inside the cabin walls for a really clean look.

LAYOUT

It's nice to keep the wheelhouse sole fairly open so you can ramble about when anxiously navigating in the fog, pretending like Walter Mitty that you sail in harm's way as captain of a potent destroyer, and to permit other crew to be "backseat drivers."

The helmsman's seat, if permanently fitted, may be of the folding type to permit standing, though if it is placed correctly, with enough space between its legs and the wheel, this should not be necessary. A double-wide bench or another seat on the other side of the wheelhouse enables a companion to keep you company. Large motoryachts are often fitted with a large, elevated bench seat behind the helm, so that others may see where they're going without being in the helmsman's way. This could conceivably double as an off-watch pilot's berth, though its thwartships orientation might dump the occupant during a particularly steep plunge.

A better berth would run fore and aft against one side of the wheelhouse; depending on the configuration of the saloon and other cabins aft, the foot might "disappear" through the aft cabin bulkhead—as in a quarter berth—so that only part of the berth intrudes upon the wheelhouse.

The navigation station should be somewhat handy to the helm, either forward against the windshield or beside or behind the seat, so that minimum hassle is experienced darting from the wheel to the charts. As discussed in Chapter 10, "Navigation Stations," some instruments should be immediately within reach of the helmsman, while others can be mounted at the navigation station.

If space permits, folding captain's chairs can be set up for extra visitors to the wheelhouse. Like the kitchen at home, the wheelhouse has

1

2

1 This pretty little motorsailer at
the Port Townsend Wooden
Boat Festival in Washington
has a door in the front of the
wheelhouse. Notice the lovely
camber of the house roof.

2 *Aardvark*'s lines are those of a
North Sea trawler. The elevation
of the helm requires a step
outside the door and a guard-
rail for security.

3 The exquisite joinerwork on
Kiyi shows several nice details,
including the visor, which is
both functional and decorative.

3

1

a way of becoming the center of activity aboard. Indeed, in some designs small dinette tables are incorporated into the layout, as well as side tables, wet bars—you name it. But there is something to be said for restricting this work area to business purposes, namely steering and navigation. You know what they say about too many cooks in the kitchen!

ENTRY

Access to the wheelhouse may be from the deck or another cabin. Port and starboard doors leading from the side decks are desirable, though in some designs where interior furniture is given priority, only one door is possible. These are generally sliding types, as there often isn't space inside to secure the door open, and if the door opened outward someone inside might belt an unwary deck stroller over the side. The problem with sliding doors, however, is the difficulty in making them watertight and airtight. Perhaps someone will invent a van-type door on articulated hinges.

Depending on their location forward or aft of the wheelhouse and the arrangement of other cabins, steps from the wheelhouse may lead down to the forward cabin or the saloon; since the whole purpose of a wheelhouse is to provide all-weather protection for the helm, it doesn't make sense to have to go outside to get to it. Check headroom carefully and mark low overheads with a bright color to protect foreheads.

1 A bench behind the helm is a wonderful place to sit and observe the world passing by while the helmsman does all the work.

2 Behind the helm in *Executive Sweet*'s wheelhouse is a cushy L-shaped settee trimmed in whitewashed oak. Can you see yourself playing a hand of poker at 20 knots, with four aces in one hand and a mint julep in the other?

DECOR

One of the nicest things about a wheelhouse is the ease of decorating; more than most cabins, the wheelhouse possesses certain attributes that give the owner a freer hand. For one, the typical wheelhouse is essentially a small room, a box with vertical sides and horizontal bottom and top so that there are fewer tricky angles and space problems than in, say, a V-shaped forward cabin. The windows are large, the headroom more than average, and the floor spacious, which opens up broad avenues of approach.

The wheelhouses of classic wooden boats are frequently paneled with an attractive hardwood—mahogany, cedar, ash, or tongue-and-groove teak for instance—and moldings are used extensively to trim, accent, and hide the wall-to-overhead joint, window, and panel-section seams. The sole might be oiled or varnished wood, or perhaps some recent owner has remodeled with plush carpeting. On clean wall surfaces there may be a brass clock and barometer here, a small print there, elsewhere perhaps a wall-mounted stainless steel vase that holds a dried flower arrangement. Off-white curtains are tied back. The space is at once warm and cheery. Can you imagine yourself some chilly fall morning chugging along through the salt marshes of South Carolina's Low Country, the angled shafts of sunlight warming your face as you gaze out the window, one hand on the wheel, the other absently feeling for your teacup on the dashboard?

Inside the pilothouse of a 35-foot sailboat you might find a tall, padded swivel chair with armrests, mounted on an adjustable, solid stainless steel column. None of the windows open, and visibility is somewhat restricted because the designer wanted to keep the house low. Because the panes are smoked Lexan to keep the interior cool and to make seeing inside from the outside difficult, at least there are no curtains to get in your way. Most of the time you steer from the cockpit, but when it's cold and blustery you retreat to the pilothouse, shed your foul-weather gear and take the stainless steel destroyer wheel (you disdained an ornate wooden wheel in favor of a clean, functional look). Under sail, you find it more comfortable to turn the seat sideways a bit so you can brace one foot against the cabin side (smudges on the coordinated vinyl hull and cabin liner will easily wipe clean once you've made port). The other crew have preceded you inside and are stretched out on the dinette and upholstered swivel chairs opposite, trying to play a game of whist (you don't worry that they've soaked the cushions, because these are covered with an emerald-green textured woven fabric treated with a water-resistant spray). Through the hatch above your head you notice the mainsail needs trimming, and turning to the crew with a smug look on your face, you try to decide who you'll order topside. Rank does have its privileges!

As always, your chosen style revolves around the central concept of the boat—race or cruise, work or pleasure, trendy or functional. Do you see vinyl-covered panel boards for a contemporary padded effect, or lacquered hardwoods inspired by the Renaissance? Windows covered by lavender miniblinds or pearl-white muslin curtains? Cushions upholstered in muted jewel tones or splashy primary colors? Recessed lighting, as in contemporary offices, or brass table lamps that might have adorned the lounge of a gentleman's hunting lodge? A print of the yacht *America* hanging on the wall, an original watercolor by your daughter, some abstract wire sculpture fashioned by a neighbor, or heaven forbid, a fuzzy photograph of your own boat waddling through mewling seas? Hang the photograph in your office. After all, why would you need to look at a picture of your boat when you're on it?

2

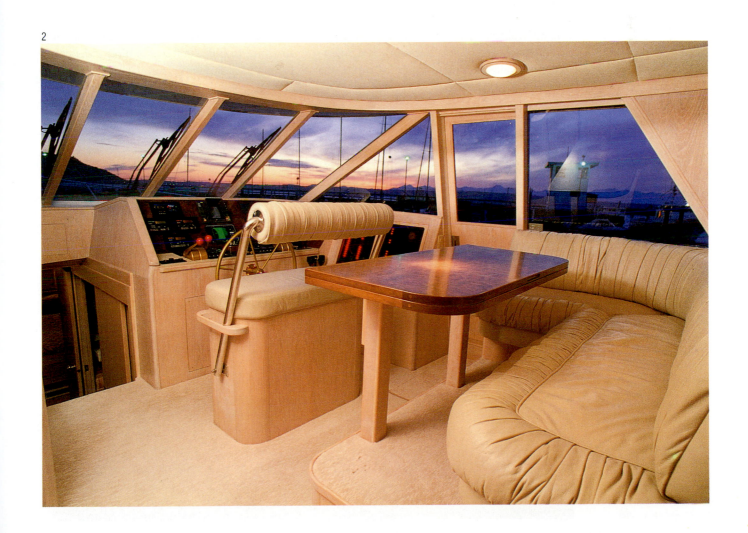

ADDING A WHEELHOUSE

Constructing a wheelhouse where none has existed is a major project and requires advanced skills. Yet it may be the intelligent course if you've bought a bare hull—fiberglass, metal, or old wood—and wish to design your own cabins and superstructure. Of course it must be structurally sound, and this will require familiarity with the materials of choice.

Aluminum is often used for tall above-deck structures on steel yachts to save weight; some sort of insulating gasket between aluminum and steel is necessary to prevent corrosion. For the person lacking aluminum welding skills and equipment, wood may be the wiser course.

An all-fiberglass wheelhouse indicates a series of rather complicated molds that probably won't be cost-effective on a one-off, custom basis. A wooden structure covered with fiberglass can achieve outstanding results if the worker takes the time to finish it properly—that is, fill the weave pattern with a resin and powder mixture, and sand and fair carefully.

A telltale sign of amateur work is a superstructure built absolutely square. Despite the earlier statement that wheelhouses are essentially boxes, careful study of boat cabins and wheelhouses reveals that this isn't quite the case. The top should be given some camber for shedding water as well as for strength and beauty. Laminated deck beams covered with layers of thin plywood and fiberglass cloth work well. The wheelhouse sides might be vertical but in most cases should have some tumblehome so that they lean in at the top for a superior look (see Chapter 2, "Attention to Style"). The wheelhouse face might have a better appearance if raked forward or aft. Careful calculations will be required to achieve good results and to build the structure according to plans.

Work out the overall dimensions with the entire boat in mind; don't start here and figure out the rest of the cabin plans later. A scale cardboard mock-up may reveal unsightly errors—too high, too short, too narrow, too long. The wheelhouse is too dominating a structure to hide its flaws behind a veneer of paint and ornamental trim.

1 *Truant's* helm is at the forward end of the deckhouse, which incorporates a dinette and galley in the same open area.

2 Multiple horns can very nearly play a tune, and are certainly capable of blowing ragbeaters out of the water when sneaking up from astern.

3 A powerful searchlight, operated from inside the wheelhouse, is a valuable aid at night in searching for navigation marks or open space in a crowded anchorage.

4 *Pandora's* small wheelhouse has a bench seat for guests; on a cold, windy day you won't care that there are no sculpted arm and backrests to support your weary limbs.

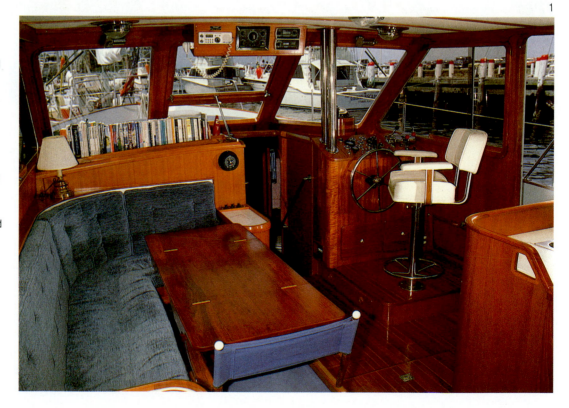

1

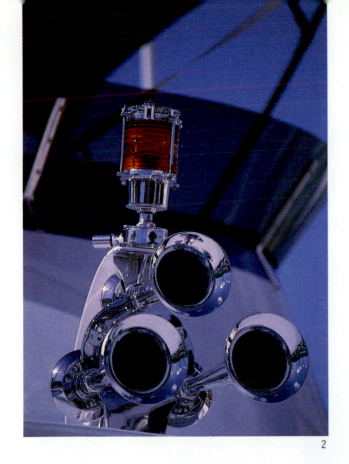

2

3

4

YACHT PROFILE

Thunderbird

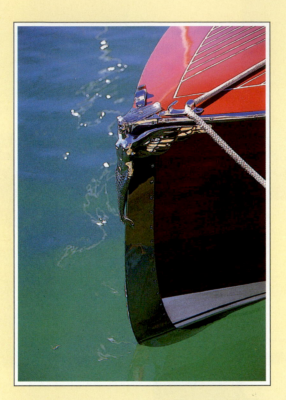

Thunderbird is an immaculate 55-foot lake yacht designed by John Hacker in 1939, and still the queen of Lake Tahoe. She is built of Honduras mahogany and powered by twin 1000-horsepower V-12 Ellison engines used in World War II P-38 airplanes. Top speed is 70 mph.

The small figurehead is a stainless steel casting of a mermaid.

Bill Harrah, owner of the famous Reno casino bearing his name, owned her for a time.

All of *Thunderbird*'s parts, including her full array of instruments, are original.

Cabintop details, including searchlights, horns, and rows of fasteners over the stainless steel sheeting, glisten in the sunlight.

☐ How many steering stations will there be?

☐ Where will you mount navigation and engine instruments? Do you require repeaters?

☐ What type of helm seat do you prefer? Bench? Upholstered chair? Folding?

☐ How much seating for crew do you want? What type?

☐ Is the wheelhouse a primary or secondary gathering spot?

☐ How many entrances from the decks? From the cabins?

☐ Hard or soft floors?

☐ What kind of windows? Frames? How many should be opening?

☐ Have you determined a traffic pattern through the wheelhouse?

CHAPTER THIRTEEN

Engine Rooms

nobody likes to spend a lot of time in the engine room; it is dark, greasy, and smells of petroleum. One enters with caution, generally induced by some signal of trouble or malfunction—a little red light glaring from the instrument array, black exhaust smoke, an unfamiliar smell, or perhaps something amiss in the feel of the throttle: a hesitation, a miss, sometimes no response at all. Even when one enters simply to check the dipstick, the task is counted an unpleasant one, best completed quickly before that monster slung over the bilge awakens.

First-time boat buyers seldom pay attention to the nuances of engine room design, preferring to test the backrest angles of the settees, check headroom in the staterooms, and measure the lengths of berths. But the experienced yachtsman knows that the union of boat and owner is a marriage with stepchildren included. Like it or not, the engine is part of the package. Like it or not, the engine requires periodic service and repair. And even if you prefer to pay your yard to perform maintenance, the day will dawn when you are called upon to enter that peculiar Hades. Soon you'll

1

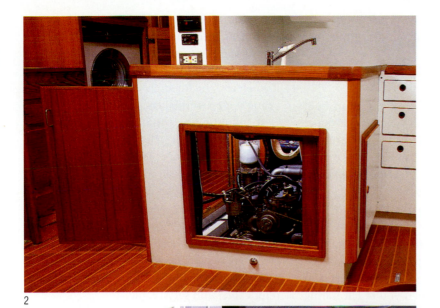

2

1 It takes a lot of horsepower—4,000 from twin MTU diesels with KaMeWa waterjets—to drive *Lady Frances,* a Trident 105 motoryacht built by Derektor Shipyard.

2 The auxiliary engine in the Freedom 42 is located under part of the galley counter.

3

3 In *Hawkeye III*'s engine room all moving parts, including small pumps and large generators, are installed on antivibration mounts and roll-out tracks for easy access.

4 Access to *Crazy Horse*'s engine room is through a hidden, hydraulically controlled hatch/stairs in the cockpit.

4

appreciate a well-planned engine room, and thank the designer and the builder. Either that or curse them.

ACCESSIBILITY

Engine rooms are as varied as the boats built around them. And often that is how it is done: The engine is bolted to its beds in a bare hull before the furniture is installed and the deck fastened. If this is the only way your engine can be removed, you're in trouble.

Ask yourself these two questions: How easy is the engine to service? How easy is it to remove altogether? In some boats the engine is mounted under the cockpit, accessible only by disassembling seats, galley counters, stairs, and god knows what else. Then you're left staring at the flywheel, face to face with a beast you have no way of evicting. Like an animal leering from its tight burrow, it leaves no opening even to feel the hoses, screws, and handles, let alone view whole sections of the engine, transmission, and drive train (i.e., couplings, propeller shaft, and stern gland).

In other, perhaps larger boats, the engine room is so spacious you might be tempted to assign it as quarters to your teenage daughter and her giggly friends. There is actually a door on the entryway, and though you might have to duck to get through, it is at least possible. And you might have to perform a short Russian steppe dance down the ladder or over the sill, but once inside there is headroom to stand or at least sit, an overhead lightbulb in a wire cage that ingeniously illuminates this otherwise dark and shadowy space, and enough elbowroom that you can lay your hands on all parts of the engine or even rub it for good luck if you feel so inclined. In short, there is room to swing the proverbial cat. What a pleasure!

It should be said that engine rooms house more than engines. The list of guests might include an auxiliary generator, a hot-water heater, an air-conditioning unit, a water-maker, a fuel tank, an electrical panel, pumps, alarms, a fire extinguisher, an air compressor, a refrigeration compressor, various filters, and certainly yards of hose and wire. It is no small challenge to plan an engine room with all these items in mind so that each is easily identifiable, removable, and serviceable.

CONSTRUCTION

In many boats you'll be dealing with at least two kinds of materials—the hull of the vessel itself, which might be fiberglass, metal, or wood, and the essential box structure over the engine, which is probably plywood covered with veneers on the outside (at least where it abuts the accommodations) and left bare or covered with pegboard on the inside.

Since mounting equipment directly to the hull is frowned upon, expect to fiberglass, weld, or glue (depending on hull material) wood blocks that will serve as mounts and anchors for all the gear to follow. Wood is an excellent material to screw into or bolt through—especially hardwoods, which can

1

2

give a thread good bite and withstand compressive loads.

Plywood walls make the spaced clamping of hoses and wires fairly simple; a couple of small screws and the appropriate hanger secure hoses and wire, prevent abrasive wear from vibration, and facilitate organization. Indeed, adhesive labels, printed with the names of the various items (for example, "HOT WATER TO GALLEY SINK," "POSITIVE TO #2 BATTERY," "HYDRAULIC RETURN FROM BOW THRUSTER"), save time every time maintenance is required.

Unless weight is an important consideration, use ³/₄-inch plywood for the basic structure. If saving weight is desirable, honeycomb-cored panels may be used instead; they are light and possess some insulating ability. However, their compressive characteristics may be poor if the wood sides of the sandwich are thin, so you'll want to anticipate where they might require through-bolting or serve as anchors for large screws. You might need to replace the core in those spots with solid wood.

Fiberglass-to-wood joints should be taped for added strength, waterproofing, and sound insulation. End grain may be sealed with epoxy or the joint glued. Rather than screw plywood directly to plywood, add hardwood cleats to furnish sound bases for joints. Paint all bare wood following application of the proper primer; a clean, smooth, light-colored surface catches less dirt, is quicker to clean, and makes spotting leaks easier.

SOUND INSULATION

Plywood by itself doesn't possess sufficient sound-deadening characteristics to contain the din of an internal combustion engine. In fact, the hull acts to capture the sound waves and redirect them upward. While plywood mutes the noise to some extent, more can be done to enhance the pleasure and audio comfort of crew in the cabins and on deck.

Over the years, all manner of materials have been glued to the interior walls of the engine room to silence the thrum of the valves and pistons. Even carpeting! Nowadays, however, specialized products are manufactured specifically for this purpose. Most comprise a sandwich incorporating foam cores, thin sheets of lead, and Mylar or aluminum foil sheathing.

3

The foam removes low-frequency sounds, and the lead does its best to cut down high-frequency sounds. Together with the protective foil covering, they form a flexible liner that is available in thicknesses to more than an inch. Obviously, the thicker the liner, the better the soundproofing.

Contact cement is generally the stipulated adhesive, but be sure to follow manufacturer's instructions. And remember that once a section of liner comes into contact with another surface, it's damn hard to remove. Find a helping pair of hands, measure and cut carefully, and maneuver in place with care and trepidation.

Sound will escape wherever it finds a path, and an oft-neglected avenue is the area directly behind the engine. Propeller shafts are prone to getting in the way of cockpit-to-hull barriers, as is much of the other equipment mounted in the engine room. But a partial cover is better than none. A "curtain," as it's called in the business, may be fixed to any suitable overhead, including the underside of the cockpit floor, and extended downward as far as feasible. Line this too with sound-insulating foam.

It may seem that the perfect engine room is a padded cell. Yet engines must breathe air to function. Diesels in particular have tremendous lungpower and have been known to "swallow" practically anything, including their own oil, in their mad thirst for sustenance. This

1 Engines mounted underneath the wheelhouse sole are generally easy to service, especially if there is space for the mechanic to climb down.

2 The Yanmar diesel in Peter Rachtman's South Pacific 42 is easily serviced from the starboard side by removing the inboard side of the galley counter, but what about the port side?

3 The durable Sabb diesel in *Quintus* is capable of being hand-started, a certain comfort on a boat with small battery capacity.

is why many boats with large power plants have large ducts leading from the engine room to simple shells or decorative scoops mounted high on the cabin sides to ensure adequate air supply. Small engines usually find enough air entering through chinks in the sound-deadening armor to perform just fine. If an outward-opening compartment door is hard to open when the engine is running, it signifies insufficient free air supply, resulting in low pressure in the engine room.

DESIGN FOR MAINTENANCE

In the ideal world, the engine room would have comfortable seating all around. But that is seldom the case, and it is not uncommon to find oneself laid over the top of the engine, struggling to loosen an unseen nut, with some lever pressing square against one's solar plexus. If you have the luxury of planning your boat from scratch, give serious thought to the space around the engine. Room to kneel is better than an awkward sprawl.

Oil changing systems. Considering all of the technological advances found on modern gasoline and diesel engines, it is surprising that few manufacturers have developed simple, efficient oil exchange systems. Occasionally you will find one with a hand-operated oil sump pump, but they are generally small and time-consuming. Unfortunately, the dearth of internal oil exchange systems may be more a matter of trying to keep costs low than it is an engineering conundrum.

Before you buy an engine, ask how the oil is retrieved. Many models have no provision other than sticking a tiny rubber hose attached to a hand pump into the dipstick tube. The engine must be run beforehand to warm and thereby reduce the viscosity of the oil in order for it to flow through the small-diameter hose. But this may make the pump too hot to hold without wrapping rags around it.

A minor improvement on the dipstick method is a larger hose built into the oil pan; there is a removable cap into which one can insert, say, a half-inch pump hose. Same system, just bigger. Even when the tube is intended to discharge the pan by gravity, often there's no space or access below the engine to hold a bucket.

Numerous gadgets on the market make extraordinary claims about how easily they work. Some use small electric motors to suck out the oil, but few perform as well as billed. The answer, it seems, lies with the engine manufacturers, and until they address the problem, owners are left with a messy, laborious job on their hands.

So, make sure that the dipstick tube or whatever orifice you use to retrieve oil is conveniently situated in relation to the engine box. You might build in some sort of drip pan under it to catch oil, and you'll want a source of rags or special oil-absorbent cloths (which don't pick up water) handy to clean up spills. A paper towel dispenser in the engine room isn't as crazy as it sounds.

Workbenches. On large boats there may be room to install a workbench in the engine room. Considering the type of emergency work that sometimes needs to be performed aboard—cleaning spark plugs and filters, soldering loose electrical connectors, drilling and sawing wood—even a small workbench is a lot handier than a seat in the cockpit. It is the perfect home for a vise, an assortment of tools, and a drawer of spare parts. Heavy toolboxes might be stored underneath, held in place by restraining boards or straps.

If a fixed workbench is out of the question, perhaps you can build a portable workbench that mounts beside or over the engine and stows against a bulkhead when not in use. And as long as you're at it, a simple stool or bench seat may as well be constructed, too.

Lighting. Tedious work demands good lighting, which is sadly lacking in many boats. One or more overhead bulbs in wire cages (to prevent breakage) will provide general lighting, but you'll still need spot lighting for specific jobs. This need might be satisfied by a trouble light on a short cord that is easily coiled and hung on a hook in a convenient place, or you might invest in one of the various headlamps that strap around your forehead like a miner's light or are fitted to eyeglass frames so

YACHT
PROFILE

A Modern, Flashy Skiboat

The sleek and sexy little Ski Challenger built by Bayliner has bright color bands wrapping around the cockpit and across the seats and engine cover.

The padded helmsman's seat offers security and is located within arm's reach of the towing post.

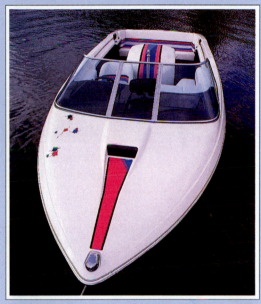

A splash of "spilled" paint is a good joke on passersby.

The 351-cubic inch inboard/outboard engine is concealed beneath a custom fiberglass cover with accent stripes. It is lined with a reflective cooling blanket and soundproofing.

YACHT PROFILE

Record

Record is a 61-foot Norwegian packet owned by Ron Ackman, co-owner of Oldport Launch Service in Newport, Rhode Island. She was built in 1934 of 3-inch fir planking trunnel-fastened to 8-inch by 8-inch fir frames on 12-inch centers. She was licensed to carry freight and 96 passengers and operated commercially until 1976.

Record's steadying sails help minimize roll in beam seas. Draft is 7½ feet.

The saloon and study are paneled with painted tongue-and-groove.

The two-cylinder, two-cycle semi-diesel's bearings are externally lubricated. It uses compressed air to start. The 90-horsepower Brunvoll engine swings a 44-inch variable-pitch prop.

The owner's tools are neatly organized on a board in the engine room.

that the light beam follows your line of sight. They look silly but work surprisingly well. Last, a flashlight with a permanent mount near the entrance to the engine room will always be of service.

Safety. Because of the inherent nature of internal combustion engines, there exists a greater possibility of calamity in the engine room than perhaps any other place on board. Fire, explosion (mostly from gasoline engines or generators), electrical shock, lacerations, and broken bones are possibilities that must be safeguarded against.

While good installation and maintenance procedures are the best defense against damage and injury, other precautions are indicated. Foremost is the mounting of a fire extinguisher convenient to the engine. Commercial passenger vessels are required to install automatic Halon fire extinguishing systems in the engine room, and this is a sensible practice on all large boats with complicated systems.

Moving parts, such as belts and pulleys, should not come in contact with any part of the engine box. Furthermore, they might be isolated behind fabricated metal guards to keep shirt cuffs or jewelry from catching, or perhaps painted a bright color to draw attention.

Batteries emit explosive vapors when charging, and so should be kept in acidproof boxes with tiedowns. Gas engines must have flame arrestors installed on the carburetor to prevent sparks from igniting a leaky fuel line or vapors

☐ *How much space can you "sacrifice" for the engine room?*

☐ *How much space will there be on all sides of the engine(s)?*

☐ *What is involved in removing the engine from the boat?*

☐ *Is there provision for sitting down?*

☐ *What other equipment must be installed in the engine room?*

☐ *What space is there for tools?*

☐ *Does fire control consist of fire extinguishers or an automatic system?*

☐ *Is there a workbench?*

☐ *How many lights are there? What type are they? Where are they mounted?*

☐ *Are all government safety requirements satisfied?*

in the bilge. Separate and clearly mark 110-volt AC and 12-volt DC wiring.

Engine maintenance and repairs are not the sorts of things we like to think about when we go boating. But the fact is the engine is the heart and soul of most boats; our comfort and our safety depends on it. Consequently, engines and the surrounding equipment and fittings are of vital importance, meriting close attention in both the design and construction phases.

Cockpits, Companionways, and Flybridges

*n*o part of a boat is used more than the cockpit or flybridge, for it is here that underway activity is focused—steering, navigating, line handling, socializing, even falling asleep. And at anchor or dockside the cockpit is the most comfortable outdoor place to plant yourself and enjoy the sun and wind. Indeed, there is something therapeutic about reading a book with the sun on your back, conversing with friends, or simply staring at nothing at all. Dockside, pride of ownership wells as passersby sneak looks at your boat; worries about jobs and futures seem far away, and the biggest problem in your life is how to refill your drink without getting up.

LAYOUT

The common on-deck gathering point varies from boat to boat according to its type. On a sailboat, it's the bench seats of the cockpit. On a motoryacht, it's the bridge and aft cockpit or after deck, and on a sportfisherman it's the flybridge and fighting chair, which makes a most regal throne even when there are no lines over the side. Because so much time is spent on deck, these on-deck gathering points deserve plenty of attention with regard to their location, layout, and appointments.

Sail. The basic cockpit configurations for sailboats are aft and center, with minor variations such as windscreens, hardtops, and the effects of great cabins and pilothouses, which may slightly alter cockpit location and size. There are advantages and disadvantages to each, and the choice boils down eventually to personal preference.

Aft cockpits are lower and hence less exposed to wind and spray than center cockpits. For the same reason, roll is minimized and self-steering wind vanes are easier to install; and due to lower freeboard, boarding may be more convenient. Aft cockpits are more traditional and are for some purists the only arrangement that seems "right."

Center cockpits provide some protection from following seas, and their height above the water makes up in part for their more forward location in terms of taking spray. This arrangement presumes an aft cabin, which is a highly personal choice based on need for privacy, how the boat is used, and aesthetics. Passageways between the saloon and aft cabin tend to increase the height of the cockpit seats and eliminate some stowage space. Consequently, under-deck passageways imply a trade-off: In

1

2

3

4

1 In good weather, life aboard a boat centers on deck.

2 *Anadarko*'s windshield and hardtop provide shelter from wind, rain, and sun. Removable side curtains enable the crew to tailor the enclosure to the weather.

3 *Lively*'s all-weather cockpit enclosure extends over just the forward sections, so that in good weather crew can move aft to take in the sun and feel the breeze on their cheeks. Eight windows ensure good visibility.

4 A sleek wooden sloop reaches in a brisk breeze while competing in the annual Classic Yacht Regatta in Newport, Rhode Island. The new cockpit cushions look comfy, though backrests are minimal—higher coamings would destroy the fine lines of the hull and cabin.

return for the convenience of moving about belowdeck in bad weather, without having to go topside, one accepts the ungainly appearance of a "layer cake" deck/cockpit plan. On some designs, the cockpit coaming looks like a gondola strapped to the back of a lurching elephant. Above about 50 feet, the hull lines can absorb the visual impact of a center cockpit more graciously.

The choice between wheel and tiller steering has a big effect on cockpit design, with the latter generally impossible on center cockpit designs, though an emergency tiller on the afterdeck, or wherever access to the rudderstock is possible, can and should be incorporated. Center cockpits may also be difficult to fit with pedestal-and-cable steering systems and may be limited to hydraulic or pull-pull systems. In brief, steering options are greater in aft cockpit designs, which is a factor to consider if you have strong biases about feel of the helm, maintenance, and so forth.

Pilothouse models with inside steering invariably rob space from the cockpit, and on small boats leave nothing but a vestigial area with short bench seats, poor visibility, and limited comfort at the helm, though it certainly needn't be that way. Some motorsailer designs with flush afterdecks avoid this problem by installing the outside steering wheel against the aft face of the pilothouse so the helmsman can see over it. Seating then may take the form of benches or deck boxes bolted to the deck.

In a very few boats, such as the Tartan Tock ketch, a great cabin aft pushes the center cockpit farther forward than the conventional two-thirds of the distance aft. A truly central cockpit is more exposed to spray and a high cockpit to rolling motion, and hence probably works best on larger boats.

Power. Flybridges are almost universal on modern motoryachts and certainly on sportfishermen, where the height advantage is requisite for spotting weedlines, birds, and the other telltale signs of fish. Of course there is the added benefit of being able to see all ends and sides of the boat during docking maneuvers.

Most often reached by a ladder from the afterdeck or cockpit, the flybridge commands a wonderful view and enjoys unobstructed sunshine. Canvas biminis and side curtains provide protection during inclement weather, as does the windshield. Seating may take the form of padded benches or swivel chairs. Instruments, charts, and glass holders may be mounted on the dashboard. And there should be storage under the seats and dash for life jackets and miscellaneous lightweight gear.

1 A small sportfisherman trolls the California coast, outriggers and fighting chair at the ready. The boat has two steering stations, one inside and another on the flybridge. The bimini is furled in temperate weather.

2 *Crazy Horse*'s stylized tuna tower has a secure enclosure, padded seat, and all the controls necessary to drive the boat hard to the fishing grounds.

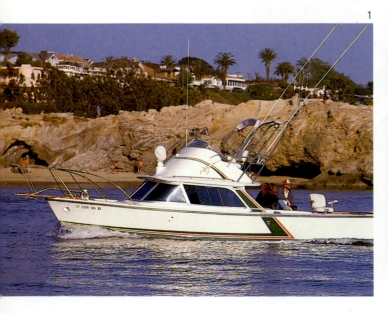

1

2

3

4

5

6

3 A quality fighting chair is not only a piece of functional equipment but a thing of beauty in its own right. A chair crafted with careful joinerwork, stainless steel welding, and decorative detailing can cost several thousand dollars.

4 *Crystal* is ready for just about any kind of fishing with all sizes of rods and an alloy, 200-scoop, four-compartment baitwell equipped with lights and flow-through filtration.

5 A fisherman is only as good as his gear, and a Penn International reel is one of the best.

6 Dual fighting chairs are for optimists.

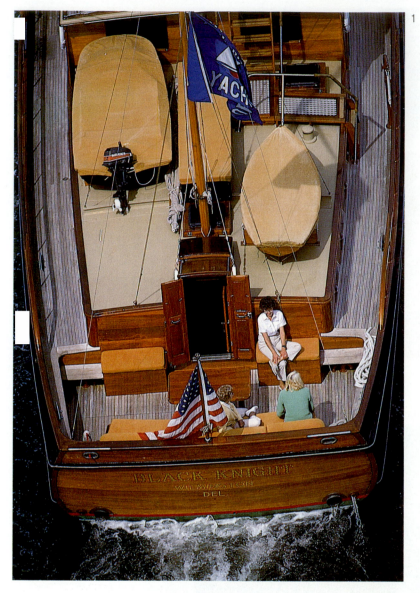

1

3

2

218

Sportfishermen don't sacrifice cockpit space simply because the helm is in the clouds; after all, the fishing action takes place at the transom. It's a different matter with trawlers and motoryachts. The so-called cockpit model again incorporates a somewhat vestigial stern cockpit that is not much used except for boarding, fishing, watersports, or as a spillover seating area, perhaps equipped with folding captain's chairs for that purpose. Depending on size, tri-cabin designs may utilize the deck of the aft cabin as a gathering point, especially if the aft cabin extends to the full width of the boat.

ERGONOMICS

Critical to cockpit comfort are the dimensions and proportions of seats or benches, helm height, and other design elements that make moving about comfortable and convenient. There's nothing worse than a seat that's too tall or a backrest too straight when you're spending hours in one place.

Though the term *traffic flow* may sound pretentious and inappropriate for cockpits and flybridges, it pays to visualize how people will move about, especially underway, so that the helmsman isn't interfered with and the legs of other crew aren't trampled by the "gofer."

A critical dimension for sailboats is the distance between the seatback and foothold, since when the boat is heeled, the athwartships-facing crew will be least strained with their feet braced and legs straight. An error in this measurement can make it virtually impossible for crew to keep from sliding to leeward.

Backrests should be angled 5 to 10 degrees for comfort. Those built of wood or molded fiberglass may also have some curvature to support the shoulders and a firm, proud spot to support the sacroiliac, which is of tremendous value in reducing back strain. Many of the more expensive automobiles now feature adjustable back braces for the same reason, and as one is likely to spend as much time seated in the cockpit of a boat as in a car, attention to this detail will save a chiropractor's fee.

The relationship between the steering wheel and helmsman's seat is equally critical. The same principles discussed in Chapter 12,

"Wheelhouses," apply here: Too close and you can't stand up to steer without the backs of your legs hitting the seat, too far away and when seated you have to lean forward to reach the wheel, thereby straining the back.

A popular avant-garde postcard a few years ago was captioned, "Anytime can be naptime—Get horizontal!" Four photos showed a small, frumpy man curled up in the oddest places—a garden, a bar counter, and the like. Certainly napping is a favorite pastime of crew during a sea journey. And therein lies the value of bench seats that are more than 6 feet long. Falling asleep in a cockpit chair isn't any easier than sleeping on an airline or bus; it just ain't the same as stretching out with a pillow under your head, putting your back against the coaming, bending the knees, and catching some real hard-core Z's!

The sportboats do it best with padded sun decks, where—the brochures promise—beautiful bikini-clad girls languish seductively as they tan.

WEATHER PROTECTION

Without inside steering, life in the cockpit can turn quickly sour when the weather grows foul. Dodgers over the forward end of sailboat cockpits shield crew from spray and wind, and in hot, sunny weather a bimini gives much-wanted shade. A combination of the two, perhaps in conjunction with snap-on side curtains, gives all-around protection. The only caveat is making some provision for visibility in all directions and for the handling of sail controls.

Flybridges present many of the same problems, frequently more so since there is no cabin in front of the seats and helm to knock down wind. A windshield is a basic feature, as is the convertible bimini that can be folded up when not needed for sun protection. It is not uncommon to spend several thousand dollars for fancy side and aft curtains with zippered windows and doors to achieve a real greenhouse effect. In cold temperatures it can make all the difference between pressing on and turning back, or between fun and hardship.

Vinyl glass windows are easily scratched, and care must be taken when folding them not

1 *Black Knight*, once the New York Yacht Club's committee boat for America's Cup races, is an early version of what today is called a "cockpit" model motoryacht. Out of the wind and far removed from the activity on the bridge, the only drawback to such a cockpit is engine fumes when running downwind.

2 This shot of *Octopussy* shows both sheltered and open seating on the boat deck, and a young woman enjoying the exhilarating ride on the afterdeck. Even on a large yacht, the designer is challenged to create a variety of gathering places, each with unique qualities.

3 The upper deck of *Crazy Horse*, built by Admiral Marine, has a large L-shaped seating area, wet bar, and easy access to the flybridge.

to crease them sharply. Exposure to the ultraviolet rays of the sun will eventually make them brittle and foggy. In cold weather, the material can shatter. Ideally, vinyl glass windows should never be folded, but that is unrealistic on most boats.

Canvas is something of a misnomer, as most exterior marine fabrics today are acrylic. Supported as they are by a network of aluminum or stainless steel tubing, these fabrics can fully tax a skillful seamster to create a handsome, tight-fitting structure. Colors, though somewhat limited, can usually be coordinated with the hull, cabin, and other key elements. See Chapter 3, "Decked Out," and Chapter 18, "Soft Coverings," for more information.

1 The Sand Hen is a shoal-draft ketch with centerboard for trailering and beaching. In the Florida heat, a bimini is essential, especially if you're bald!

2 The Black Watch 30's bimini is a good design in part because it is the same color as the boat, and insofar as possible its lines follow critical lines of the boat.

3 The twin dodgers on Esquipoise, a Mason 53, protect the main companionway and the aft stateroom companionway. The smaller dodger forward keeps light rain and sun from the saloon entrance, and the larger one aft extends to the mizzenmast, partially shielding the cockpit. For tropical climates a bimini affords shelter for the remainder of the cockpit.

4 The booby hatch or doghouse protecting Moondrift's aft companionway is unobtrusive but doesn't lend itself well to the fitting of canvas for cockpit shelter.

5 The Gatsby 39's outside steering station is located on the flush afterdeck. Bench seats double as useful stowage lockers.

6 A watertight companionway such as this one on Spirit of Sydney, a BOC Challenge entrant, offers the ultimate security against leaks and boarding waves.

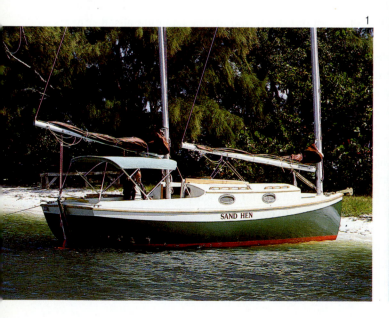

COMPANIONWAYS

Essential to the cockpit traffic pattern is the companionway. It must be shielded from the weather, convenient to the cockpit, and easy to negotiate in all conditions. On a sailboat it may be a simple, small sliding hatch with removable washboards or swinging doors. On a motor-yacht it may be a sliding patio-type door. Obviously the design of the boat and its intended use will determine the appropriate entryway.

For offshore cruising, the smaller the companionway the better. A bridge deck not only shrinks the opening but reduces cockpit volume as well, thereby minimizing the amount of water it can hold and that which must be expelled by scuppers and drains after a boarding sea. Furthermore, it provides additional space inside. Though there should always be at least a low sill between the cockpit and interior, companionways without bridge decks are certainly easier for children and elderly folks.

Large Plexiglas, Lexan, or safety glass doors add immeasurably to the amount of light inside, but care must be taken that they aren't exposed to waves (mostly by steering the boat away from boarding seas). Storm covers are a sensible safety feature for offshore work. All doors must be sturdy enough that no one will crash through during a sudden lurch, and it goes without saying that all entrances should have positive locking mechanisms, key or combination locks, and even alarms where security is a concern.

4

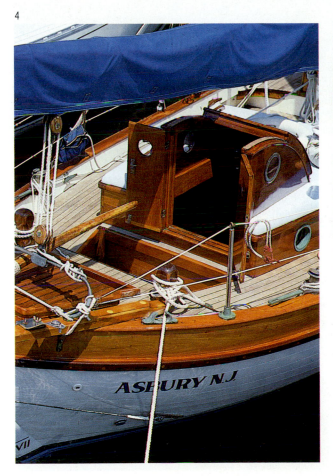

5

6

EVERYDAY PLEASURES

Steering and sitting idly are hardly the only activities centered in the cockpit. In good weather, it's a fine place to eat. Permanently fixed, hinged, and removable tables accommodate everything from cocktails and hors d'oeuvres to full-scale lunches and dinners.

Swimming ladders and boarding gates encourage diving over the side if it's relatively easy to get back aboard. Cockpit showers are seen more frequently nowadays and are especially appreciated if hot water is available.

Dinghy excursions are part and parcel of cruising fun. Davits and under-the-cockpit "garages" eliminate towing, which is hazardous in big seas. Sometimes a garage door folds down to form a swim platform as well.

Cockpits with floor space right to the edge make standing near the rail easier than kneeling on bench seats. Fishing and children's water games such as towing toys are among the activities encouraged by such a design.

1

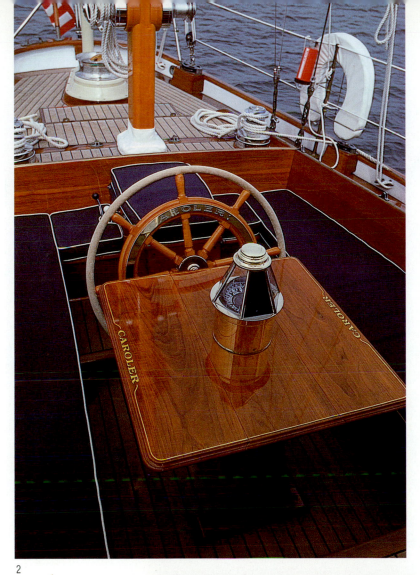

1 *Margin Call*'s spacious cockpit is a fine place for alfresco dining in warm weather.

2 *Caroler*'s cockpit is varnished teak with a dropleaf table built around the compass binnacle. The lettering is inlaid gold leaf. Chris Page, who built *Caroler* in a wing of his house on Cape Cod, first built a mock-up of the cockpit. In it he actually entertained friends and family until he felt he had refined the design to his liking.

3 The fiberglass cockpit table in the Beneateau Oceanis 500 is colder and more utilitarian than varnished teak but requires virtually no maintenance.

1

2

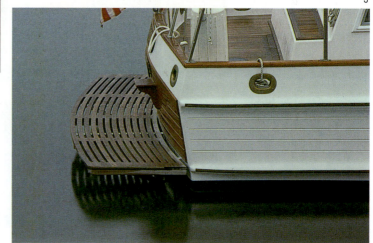

3

4

1 *Lotus*'s afterdeck is well equipped for watching the sunset in Charlotte Amalie, U.S. Virgin Islands. Folding deck chairs with removable cushions complement built-in seats and a triangular table.

2 A fold-down swim platform in the transom of the Cabo Rico 38 incorporates a ladder and shower.

3 The teak swim platform on the Grand Banks trawler is a handsome, useful addition.

4 *Kiyi*'s fantail transom with wicker chairs, round wicker table, and a planter full of roses makes one feel as though he were relaxing at a garden social.

5 Captain's chairs with canvas seats and backs are handy, light, and good-looking. *Ilinga*'s owner also keeps two small folding tables for drinks and hors d'oeuvres.

5

SAFETY

The cockpit, flybridge, and other on-deck gathering points should be designed to keep crew on board and free of injury. Lifelines and rails should be securely through-bolted, tall enough to brace your legs above the knee, and periodically inspected for corrosion. Handholds at the companionway, on the cabin where crew exit the cockpit or the side decks, and at other key locations help guard against accidental falls. Nonskid deck and cockpit floors provide traction; while fiberglass requires waxing to prevent the gelcoat from deteriorating under the sun's ultraviolet rays, wax should never be applied to any surface that is walked on. Throwable life rings, life jackets, emergency strobes, and man-overboard poles should be mounted in or handy to the cockpit. And try to avoid unnecessary obstructions on deck and floors that could trip a person; certainly vents, cleats, and the like are required fittings, but their intelligent placement will minimize accidents.

The cockpit and flybridge involve complex shapes and numerous fittings that should be worked out well in advance of construction or customization. As is often the case, you may not know what works best until you've lived with your boat for a few years. Once problems surface, you'll gain a better understanding of your requirements and possible solutions. It may be that moving a seat, cleat, or stanchion is all that's needed. Or you may decide to construct a hard top, windshield, adjustable helm seat, or cockpit table, or change steering systems, or make any number of modifications that will enhance your pleasure afloat. Develop a plan with sketches, a bill of materials, and cost estimates, and try to anticipate the effect of your changes on other systems.

☐ *How much seating is required?*

☐ *Are traffic patterns to the helm and companionway unobstructed?*

☐ *Are there lifelines and handholds to prevent you or your crew from falling overboard?*

☐ *Is there adequate protection from heat, cold, and rain?*

☐ *Is there sufficient stowage space for lines, fenders, horns, life jackets, and other gear?*

☐ *Do you want cushions on all seats? If so, what type of foam and fabric?*

☐ *Is access to the foredeck from the cockpit convenient and safe?*

1 *Astra*'s comparatively low pedestal is flanked by engine controls labeled in Italian; the helmsman's seat doubles as a deck box and is protected by canvas.

2 The forward-facing rack-and-pinion wheel in this catboat's cockpit creates unusual seating situations. The helmsman may sit on the box aft of the wheel or to either side, depending on conditions.

3 A slatted teak box over the helmsman's seat provides reasonably comfortable, level seating at different angles of heel. Underneath, the tillerhead on the rudderstock is exposed for quickly mounting an emergency tiller.

4 *Sumurun*'s helmsman's seat is removable to permit sitting or standing.

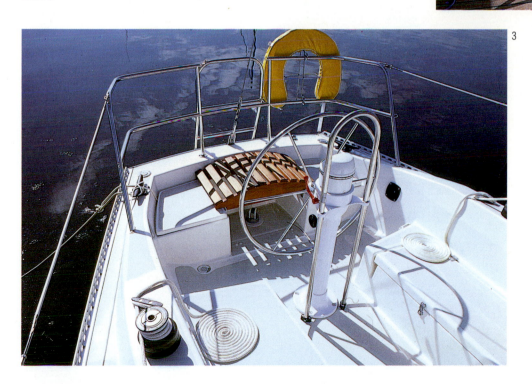

4

3

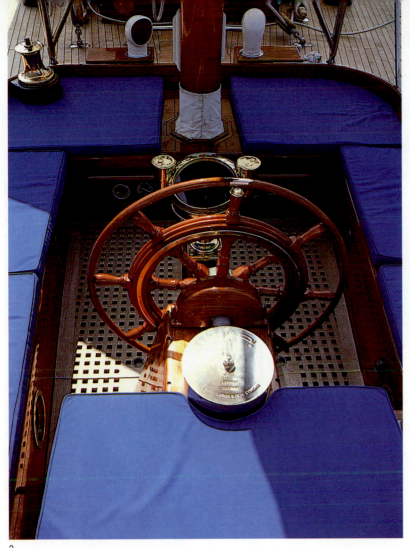

2

3

1 A custom wooden pedestal is the centerpiece of *Anadarko*'s large U-shaped cockpit.

2 The gleaming brass binnacle in the cockpit of *Belle Aventure* is just one of the fine details that won this 95-foot Fife the "Best Of Show" award at the 1981 Newport Wooden Boat Show. The cockpit sole is teak, and a varnished, raised coaming surrounds the cockpit for back support.

3 Forward of *Sumurun*'s pedestal is a lovely curved console for instruments and engine controls.

1

2

3

1 The helm of this small wooden powerboat built in Maine by the Landing School is appropriately simple.

2 The styling of the Fountain muscleboat is bold, sexy, and sleek, colored red for passion and black for *baaad*. Ample padding around the helm is part styling and part necessity—at 60 mph the ride can be bone-jarring.

3 The Towerhouse 40 is a custom all-out sportfisherman. Though there is a small cabin forward, most of the area is given to the cockpit and a sheltered seating and stowage area around the helm. The pedestal is a unique structure of wood and fiberglass.

CHAPTER FIFTEEN
One-Cabin Layouts

he enclosed, womblike coziness of boat cabins is perhaps strongest in the one-cabin layout, partly because of its small size and partly because of its efficiency: The stateroom, saloon, galley, and head must all occupy the same essential space, so that from one seat it may be possible to cook, navigate, and sleep without really moving. While the space may be tight, there is also a certain paradoxical feeling of openness that is missing in larger, highly compartmentalized boats. Whether by neces-

sity or design, the one-cabin interior is a unique challenge to plan and fit out.

One-cabin interiors are best suited to solo cruising or the small, well-acquainted family. Otherwise you may find yourself cruising with a friend, and perhaps a friend of your friend, who is really no friend of yours at all. Suddenly the shortcomings of your little pleasure dome are bared: You and the stranger knock knees at dinner, he leaves his clothes strewn about his berth, and worse, at night you can actually

The interior of the Pacific Seacraft 31 is a seeming paradox—cozy yet open. Partial bulkheads and privacy curtains open up the space visually as well as psychologically. A fiberglass pan provides furniture foundations, but teak conceals much of the plastic.

The Division of Space · **ONE-CABIN LAYOUTS**   *231*

hear him *breathe!* You can hear his jowls flap, and you can almost see his pale flesh quivering. Forget that somewhere some dear woman loves this man; to you he's an uncouth barbarian, an intruder. If you'd met at a bar or dinner party, you might have actually liked the guy, but here on *your* boat, he's . . . he's . . . he's . . . *disgusting!*

You consider your options: Sleep in the cockpit; ask him to sleep in the cockpit and keep his duffel in the seat locker; bide your time, since after all, it's just two more nights; or give the guy an accidental "tap" that sends him falling over the side when your mutual friend isn't looking. "Harry? You mean he's not down below?"

The secret to successful one-cabin living is to be selective about who shares your sacred space. And if your boat is very small, like the owner of a two-seater sportscar you won't have to worry whether some jerk is flicking his cigarette ashes in the backseat—because there isn't one. It's a decided advantage of moving further *down* in size.

DOUBLE-DUTY FURNITURE

The challenge of designing a one-cabin interior lies in the planning of accommodations for (1) sleeping, (2) eating, (3) cooking, (4) navigating, and (5) toiletry, all in a limited space.

Sleeping bunks must also be comfortable for sitting; tables have to function as dining surfaces, chart tables, and food preparation counters, and they might also be asked to lower to increase berth size; toilets may have to be positioned under berths or other furniture; sinks and stoves might have to "disappear" when not in use. There is no end to the ingenuity required.

1

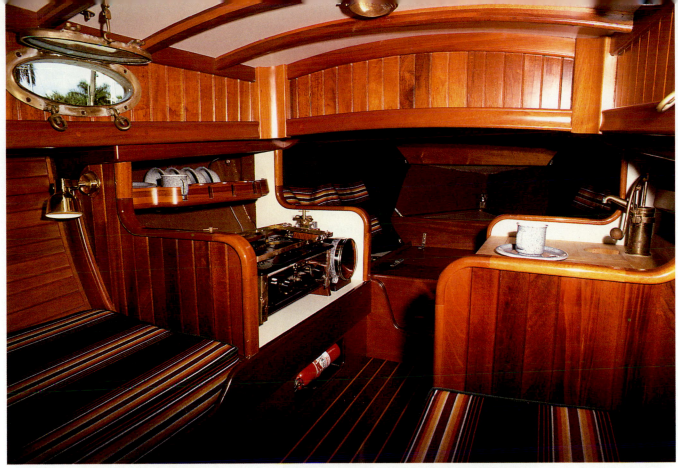

2

3

1 The Pearson 28 cabin plan is similar to the Pacific Seacraft 31, with partial bulkheads and head and galley aft.

2 The charming little *Glimmer* is a Prudence 23 built by Parkins Marine in Florida. The concealed toilet is forward of the bipartite galley. Soft fabric pouches slung against the hull give light, space-efficient stowage.

3 Olga Lundin shares the 15-foot *Bris*'s tiny cabin with husband Sven, who likes to build his unusual boats in church lofts and trailer them behind bicycles. The Swede rounded Cape Horn in a similar boat.

Berths/Settees. Give careful thought to the width of berths that double as settees; if are too wide, the edge may not allow you to sit comfortably, catching the backs of your legs, or the backrest may not support your back. Pillows or custom wedge-shaped cushions propped against the side of the hull can help. If there is cabinetwork outboard of the berth, angle it outboard at the top to make leaning against it more comfortable.

Slide-out berth extensions increase width, possibly to that of a double, while allowing the fore-and-aft passageway to remain unobstructed during the daytime. The cushion insert can be used as a backrest for the settee/berth when not being slept on. Snaps or Velcro tabs will keep it in place.

The Concordia convertible berth (see Chapter 7, "Staterooms"), which incorporates a mattress and covers in a fold-down backrest, is an excellent means of stowing pillows and bedding out of sight and out of the way without having to dismantle the berth each morning.

Short V-berths might be extended aft over the settees, assuming there are no partial bulkheads to obstruct installation of a removable or fold-down extension board. Advantages of partial bulkheads, besides adding strength to the hull and decks, are that they provide places for mounting reading lights and function as backrests so one can sit up in bed.

Additional seating might take the form of folding chairs or stools, swing-out stools as are sometimes seen installed in compact navigation stations, or portable seats that mount between settees or in place of the companionway ladder.

1

2

1 *Miriam Elizabeth*, a Knudsen 25 built in 1937, calls Lake Memphremagog, Vermont, home waters. Al Briere restored her, and successfully races her in local events.

2 There is only sitting headroom in *Miriam Elizabeth*, but as designer Uffa Fox said, "If you have to stand, go on deck."

YACHT
PROFILE

A Classic Chris-Craft

Bill Miller, of Portland, Maine, restored this 1959 27-foot Chris-Craft and keeps her on the Royal River in Yarmouth, just a few minutes from Casco Bay. Twin 235-horsepower Chrysler V-8s might push her up to 30 knots if Bill were ever to throw the throttles wide open, which he won't. Fifteen knots suits him fine, and he figures it suits the venerable wooden hull, too.

Her dinette converts to a double berth, augmenting the V-berths forward. The overhead makes a good rack for stowing fishing rods, and a hinged shelf on the forward side of the dinette backrest makes a commanding perch for the television when Bill stays at the marina and watches the Wimbledon or U.S. Open singles play.

The pretty little cabin cruiser promenades for the photographer, ignoring just for a moment the marina's no-wake rule. At Fay's Boatyard on Lake Winnipesaukee, an hour or two's driving time westward, one can see a half dozen or more Chris-Craft of 1950s vintage, ranging in length up to 50 feet overall, but none perkier than this.

In this view from the wheelhouse into the cabin, dark mahogany contrasts sharply with a white painted overhead.

YACHT PROFILE

Brazen

Danny Greene, a graduate of Webb Institute, designed the 34-foot steel Brazen *for world cruising. The hull was built by the Gladding-Hearn Shipbuilding Company in Somerset, Massachusetts; the deck, interior, rig, and sails were built by Danny. She was completed in about a year after Danny's previous fiberglass boat sank following a collision with an unidentified object.*

The peculiar hard dodger protects the companionway and has a removable top window for ventilation in the tropics. The sails are fully battened and the mizzenmast is unstayed. Both spars are built of spruce and epoxy with Herreshoff box sections.

Danny planned *Brazen*'s saloon so that the settees could be converted to one large playpen for lounging and comfortable sleeping in any weather.

Brazen has a completely modular interior constructed of plywood and taped with fiberglass. Each component was designed to be removed through the main hatch for painting or modification. The entire interior came together in a few months. A fine handcrafted traditional interior would have taken years to build, and Danny decided he'd rather be sailing.

This detail of *Brazen*'s interior shows the modular bookshelf, a wooden manikin Danny uses in design projects, and the racing oars he uses for exercise and sport in one of his custom three-part dinghies.

Tables/Countertops. There is seldom enough counter or table space on small boats. Even if there isn't room for a permanently mounted table, it may be possible to install a small, removable tabletop secured by bulkhead hinges, a removable pedestal in the sole, or snap-apart hinges fixed to some other foundation such as the companionway coaming, galley, or bunk face. One clever table type mounts on an offset pedestal and revolves from a centerline position to an off-centerline position, depending on its function of the moment.

Try to make the table at least large enough to hold a folded navigation chart. Fiddles, while useful in keeping plates from sliding off, get in the way of chartwork; for this reason removable fiddles make sense. Be sure to keep the table surface smooth and free of holes and fittings that would cause the charts to puncture from pencil leads and dividers.

Counter extensions are easy to make, perhaps consisting simply of Formica-covered plywood surfaces that stow under berth cushions when not in use and mount on the sides of furniture foundations when needed. They might also be permanently mounted with piano hinges and latched securely in the down position, assuming they do not obstruct access to drawers or other stowage compartments.

Galleys. The complexity of the galley is largely a function of the elegance of meals desired. Expectations are necessarily more modest in small boats, yet with a few pots and pans and an improvisational cook there is no reason why the elementary galley cannot produce fine cuisine. In lieu of permanent galley units, a molded camp-style sink with integral tank may suffice for dishwashing. And certainly there are many portable stoves that can be set up on a table, counter, or even in the cockpit for meal preparation. Water, of course, can be kept in jugs with handy spouts or pumps if there is no permanent tank. Portable coolers furnish basic refrigeration during daytrips and short cruises.

A compromise between a space-hogging permanent galley and individual campground components stowed separately is a compact galley unit that slides on tracks mounted under

1

V-berth, and one gains access by removing insert boards and cushions. Another possibility, providing a more prominent situation for the throne of leisure, is to build a removable seat over the toilet with a backrest and cushion; in this configuration the toilet doubles as a comfortable cabin seat and is disguised for propriety's sake if not for aesthetic reasons.

PRIVACY

Make no mistake: The one-cabin interior plan is lacking in privacy, and one would be well advised not to crew aboard such a boat for extended periods if he is timid about undressing, urinating, or snoring in the presence of others. Unlike a house, wherein room dividers and the rearrangement of furniture can isolate certain areas, a boat interior must take shape within highly restrictive parameters. An easy and flexible material is fabric: Privacy curtains can be set up just about anywhere to conceal the toilet area and to separate sleeping areas. Tracks screwed to the overhead or screw eyes connected by string facilitate the hanging and drawing of curtains. Coupled with partial bulkheads or bulkheads with "windows," curtains can divide the interior into two cabins at night; use tiebacks to hold them out of the way during the day. A more substantial alternative is sliding or folding doors, but visual, not audio, privacy is the best that can be expected in small-boat interiors.

STOWAGE

The need for tidiness is undeniable when living in a single cabin. It helps to be anal about picking things up, but no amount of compulsiveness will do any good if adequate stowage compartments are lacking.

Make a list of all the gear and supplies that must be carried, then design stowage areas to accommodate them. Will you carry charts? How many? Books? Paperbacks or large hardcovers? Tools? Pots and pans? Where will you stow clothes? Is a hanging locker required? Try to be economical; the less you carry, the easier it will be to keep the cabin clean.

Underberth bins utilize otherwise wasted space, but they aren't very convenient, especially when someone or sundry somethings are

1 The Freedom 28 has a nifty table that folds flush against the hull and an insert cushion to provide full-length sleeping berths.

2 Within the confines of a small cruising sailboat, every space-saving innovation counts. The Contessa 26 has a galley counter extension that provides valuable extra space for food preparation.

the cockpit seats, side deck, or cockpit sole. The unit might contain a sink and stove with perhaps a single drawer for utensils. One can be custom made from hardwood and plywood, painted or varnished to suit. If the water supply is separate, a detachable pump hose works fine.

Toilets. For many, a through-hull toilet or self-contained porta-potty is a minimum requirement for civilized living aboard. When there isn't space enough for a head compartment, the toilet generally ends up under the

sitting on top. They are also harder to keep clean and dry. Compartments built under the side decks are good for small books, flashlights, dishware, and personal effects; however they may restrict sitting headroom over the berths, so check normal seating areas first. It may be possible to hang shallow clothing bins on the forward or aft face of a partial bulkhead, if one is present; even dress shirts and skirts can be kept wrinklefree by carefully rolling them up and stacking them. Hammock nets and soft pouches may be slung over V-berths, against the hull, for additional clothing stowage.

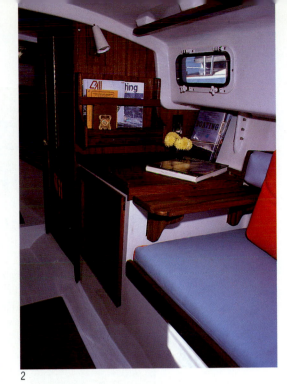

2

OPENING UP SPACE

The same design principles that help create a sense of spaciousness in larger boats work just as well in pocket cruisers. A two-cabin plan might work better as a one-cabin layout with cut-down bulkheads or windows cut out to let air, light, and vision flow from one end of the boat to the other. In a hull of small interior volume, full bulkheads sometimes trade off more in ventilation and sense of spaciousness than they give back in privacy and as mounting surfaces for lights. Here are some other ways to open up space:

- Mirrors—A strategically placed mirror reflects the image of the area before it and seemingly doubles the amount of open space; you'll want a mirror for shaving and makeup anyway.

- Color—Use light colors—white, beige and soft yellow for example—to keep corners from becoming lost in darkness. Stay with a simple color scheme.

- Texture—When using textured fabrics on the hull ceiling or overhead, avoid strong, bold patterns and thick naps that bring too much attention to themselves. Similarly, the overuse of oiled or varnished teak is oppressive; keep it to a minimum or experiment with blond and other light woods. It's okay to use holly, beech, cedar, and even some softwoods such as spruce. The effect is distinctive, original (it once was much more common—everything comes full circle in time), and more spirited than dark woods.

- Fabric—Curtains, again, open up space when pulled back, and the right choice of fabric and color can lend a highly decorative touch to the interior. But don't try to employ too many different materials, colors, and patterns, because the result will be a busy mishmash that overwhelms the eye. Better to keep the furnishings simple, with a few accent items such as throw pillows and curtains to highlight certain areas. Consider using one material to cover all berth cushions, and another for curtains, area dividers, and soft stowage pouches.

- Barriers—Remove unnecessary barriers, such as nonstructural bulkheads and partitions. The area under the cockpit is frequently wasted space, though more and more builders of small production boats are beginning to incorporate double athwartship berths here; this assumes of course that there is no engine in the way and makes a good case for inboard/outboard or outboard power for small boats. Some ocean voyagers eliminate the cockpit footwell altogether to prevent a dangerously large volume of water from weighing down the stern, and also to increase space below; with access from the main cabin, this aft area becomes almost a "garage" or "basement," ideal for stowage, placement of the head or workshops, and numerous other uses that might not otherwise be possible.

YACHT PROFILE

Itatae

Itatae is a 27-foot cat schooner designed by William Garden and built by Paul Luke in 1954. Justin McGuire and Barbara Lieberwitz have owned her since 1984. "As I began to write," Justin recounts, *"it sounded like an ad for Freedom Yachts . . . unstayed masts, everything led to the cockpit, simple rig, lazyjacks, no muss, no fuss! But then that's* Itatae; *a boat whose time came back. She's a simple boat really, no teak-and-holly sole here. Just gray paint. In fact, she's mostly painted, with just enough brightwork to drive us crazy."*

Itatae (pronounced Ee-Tah-Tee and named for the pilot boat in James N. Hall's book, *Far Lands*), measures 27 feet LOA, 9 feet 8 inches beam, and 4 feet draft. The pretty wooden double-ender sails now from her home port of Barrington, Rhode Island.

Curved bulkheads open into *Itatae* 's tasteful saloon, where two opposing settees double as berths. The forepeak is used for stowage of lines, foul weather gear, and miscellaneous equipment.

The cook's seat collapses against the mast when not in use. The down position places it in front of the coal stove, where on a cold night a pot of bean soup is the perfect curative.

Though she is a small double-ender, *Itatae* has a roomy cockpit with a high, staved coaming providing a comfortable backrest. Stem to stern, she is a jewel.

The dropleaf saloon table stows in the galley at night; the legs fit into reinforced holes in the sole.

It is sometimes strange how many people, on first glimpsing the interior of a one-cabin boat, shake their heads and mutter words to the effect that it must be awfully hard to live in such a small and public space: "My, it is small," they say, perhaps adding, "Better you than me."

Equally strange is how many people adapt quite easily to one-cabin living. Invariably they are better ventilated, which is an important attribute in the tropics or in any humid climate. Maximum spaciousness is achieved for a given boat length, and layouts are not limited by the placement of bulkheads. In fact, many experienced yachtsmen prefer simple cabin plans; their response to skeptics is, "If you want privacy, stay home." Or take a passenger liner!

Part III

Details ∎

Woodwork

Many builders today have eliminated all or most wood from the decks of their boats in an effort to reduce maintenance: aluminum toerails, stainless steel handholds, and cockpit coamings integral with the deck mold have all but replaced their earlier, wooden counterparts. This trend typifies modern mass-production boats attempting to cut costs and to achieve a look different from the traditional style (born of necessity) that emphasizes teak decks, wood houses, and Bristol brightwork.

The interior, however, is a different story. While some of these same builders have made dramatic moves toward synthetics belowdecks too, wood remains the material of choice for most builders, even when hidden behind plastic laminates and veneers. The reasons are simple: Wood possesses qualities that simply cannot be duplicated by metals, plastic, and other synthetics; wood is easy to work, pleasing to the eye and touch, warm feeling, and readily available in a wide variety of species (teak, oak, mahogany, spruce, pine, etc.), sizes (plank thickness, width, and length), and forms (solid planks, plywood sheets, veneers).

Despite price increases, wood still costs less by weight than fiberglass, aluminum, stainless steel, Kevlar, and carbon fiber composites. And it possesses very attractive engineering properties, including good tensile strength, spring-back (depending on construction methods, this is sometimes desirable, sometimes not), and

1

1 John Helpenstall won "Best of
   Show" at the 1989 Land and
   Sea Classics rendezvous in
   Port Ludlow, Washington, with
   his 17-foot Fairliner Torpedo,
   pulled by a 1948
   candied-apple red Packard
   Victoria Super Eight.

2 Shipbuilder Bob Derektor built
   Grey Goose II for personal use
   at his Mamaroneck, New York,
   yard. The centerpiece of the
   saloon is a table of mahogany
   with a rosewood top, built over
   the 140-horsepower engine.
   The bulkheads are oak, the
   overhead is UltraSuede, and
   the settees are covered with
   blue leather.

workability. Some species, such as cedar, are so pleasantly aromatic that they are used to line clothes closets. Others, such as teak and iroko, resist rotting to a great degree and thus are popular choices for use on deck.

All these reasons aside, there is yet another quality of wood that no other material can match: magic. Deep in our genes we carry some primal affinity for wood, perhaps because it has figured so significantly in man's technological development—making fire, constructing dwellings, fashioning weapons and tools—not to mention the importance of trees in manufacturing life-giving oxygen. The message is: Wood is good.

Conventional plank-on-frame construction of new boats has dwindled since the advent of fiberglass, yet there exist pockets of resistance along the coasts of Maine, Washington, and elsewhere, where this building method is still revered, and the training of apprentices to perpetuate the art and craft is a near-sacred if anachronistic institution.

Wood-epoxy hull molding, especially as developed by the Gougeon Brothers of Bay City, Michigan, has done much to perpetuate wood as a hull material, as it offers an attractive blending of natural wood and modern chemistry. By taking advantage of wood's inherently excellent structural properties, then saturating it with epoxy resin on all sides, strong, durable hulls can be produced that resist rot and splitting yet retain sensory appeal. These cold-molding techniques work not only for entire hulls but for other structures, including interior woodworking.

Wood figures to be an important boatbuilding material as long as it is cost-effective. (How well the world's forests are managed in the next century will be telling.) Today, almost all boat interiors, fiberglass and metal boats included, are to some degree finished in wood. From floor members, bulkheads, bunks, and drawers to ornamental trailboards and figureheads, even as coring in hulls and decks, wood in one form or another is used in vast quanti-

1

ties, to the point that some sources, such as Burmese teak forests, have become seriously depleted.

Whether you plan to do the woodworking on your boat or employ a professional boat carpenter, the style and quality of woodwork says a lot about you and your boat.

JOINERWORK

Joinerwork is essentially the nautical equivalent of cabinetwork and derives from "join" and "joinery." It is the craft of joining separate pieces of wood in a manner that is both strong and attractive. In fact, some joints, if properly executed, are stronger than the wood itself. On boats, joints are almost always glued or epoxied, though sometimes they may also be secured with mechanical fasteners such as screws or bolts.

The common butt and miter joints are ubiquitous in house construction, but while you may see appropriate applications for these joints in yacht interior and deck carpentry, there are other, more complex alternatives that offer better strength and appearance and hence are kept in the boat carpenter's repertoire like arrows in a quiver. Each is different from the next and has its own preferred applications.

1 The traditional skylight is constructed with pretty dovetails joining the sides.

2 The oak sheer clamp in *Karin* is made of several pieces joined by locked scarfs.

3 The corner of this window frame is a miter joint, and the casing a simple butt joint.

4 A corner block is an attractive way to finish the corner of a piece of cabinetry or furniture; the alternative is a butt joint with the endgrain of one piece showing.

3

2

4

1

2

3

4

5

1 Larry Pardey used splines to join the planks in *Talesin*'s companionway hatch. Had he terminated the splines before the end of the plank they would be called "blind splines," which are generally considered more clever since the joints are hidden, but showing off is part of the appeal of top-shelf carpentry.

2 The simple lap joint fastening the horizontal and vertical pieces of a companionway door provides greater surface area for gluing.

3 The teak cockpit grate in *Miriam Elizabeth* was constructed by cutting a series of interlocking dadoes.

4 The spokes in *All Is Best*'s wheel are mortised into the rim.

5 *Sumurun*'s proud builder's plaque is nicely set off by the varnished tongue-and-groove planking behind.

Scarfs. When joining two pieces of wood end to end to make one longer piece, a scarf joint is used. Because an end-to-end or butt joint lacks the necessary strength, each of the two pieces is planed or cut to a fine-edged wedge shape (with a length-to-depth ratio of, say, ten to one), then the two surfaces are mated and glued. There are numerous variations on the standard flat scarf. Some are notched to form a mechanical bond, some are keyed with a small third piece of wood at right angles to the others, and some are stylized for purely aesthetic reasons. Typical applications are wooden spars, whisker poles, and cap, rub, and toerails.

Tongue-and-groove and splined joints. Because wide planks tend to shrink and split as they age, and because they are increasingly difficult to find in any case (diminishing supply of mature trees), special joints are required to join narrower planks edge to edge. Tongue and groove is a joining method familiar from the knotty pine planking in family rooms and basement conversions. The tongues and the grooves can be made by rabbet planes, table saws, routers, or shapers, depending on the precision required. Dowels can be driven through the joints to increase strength and to resist warping—a sure sign of a carpenter who cares about the lasting value of his work.

Normally, tongue-and-groove planks are all the same width, but should you want to vary widths to avoid a repetitious effect, use a random sequence; otherwise, your intended inconsistency will end up as a consistency of another sort.

The splined joint is similar; here, however, both joining edges are grooved to receive a thin third piece, the spline, which thus interlocks the two planks. If the grooves do not extend to the ends of the planks the spline cannot be seen after assembly and is said to be "blind." Splines can also be used to strengthen conventional mitered joints (two boards joined at 90-degree angles, with each end cut at a 45-degree angle). The spline not only increases the surface area to be glued but also functions as a mechanical lock to prevent failure. This is essentially the same method used to "key" or "butterfly" a scarf joint.

These joints are commonly used to fashion tabletops built of hardwoods (unfortunately, many today are plywood covered with plastic or wood veneers), and to panel bulkheads and cockpit coamings on traditionally styled yachts.

Mortise and tenon. This is a difficult joint to make, though very strong, as it consists of a square or rectangular hole (mortise) cut in one piece and a matching peg or tenon cut from the other; the fit must be precise, and a fair degree of skill with tools is required. Mortise-and-tenon joints are a common feature of fine furniture; on yachts you might see them in galley tables (where horizontal supports join the vertical legs) and furniture foundations.

Dovetail. Regularly used in hardwood drawer construction because of its strength and beauty, the dovetailed corner is a series of wedges or sockets cut into one piece and matched with corresponding pins in the other to form an interlocking joint. This attractive joint is also suitable for deck boxes and other furniture-type pieces.

Lap. Two boards whose ends are to be joined at a right angle may be secured with a lap joint. Half the width is cut from the end of each board—one from the top and one from the bottom—so that when assembled the two notches lap one another. The result isn't as strong as the mortise-and-tenon joint and not as pretty, but certainly suitable for some applications such as floor timbers and bunk supports.

Block corner. While dovetailed and box joints look good for small corners such as drawers, they are too time-consuming and busy-looking for larger pieces, such as the vertical corners of galleys and dressers. A block corner incorporates a narrow, rabbeted length of wood to join two large surfaces at right angles. One seam is replaced by two, equidistant from the corner, which in turn can be rounded without fear of splitting. This is a handsome, furniture-quality joint.

Moldings. Moldings and trim pieces are used to hide seams; their purpose is usually more decorative than structural. Just as in stock home carpentry, molding can be cut to an almost infinite variety of shapes. Because the frequent use of plastic laminates and wood veneers covers unwanted seams, molding is less commonly seen on boats today. It remains, however, a distinctive way to finish the edges and corners of cabinets, bulkheads, and furniture, as it hides end grain, may function as a fiddle if cut to stand proud of a horizontal surface, and can incorporate handholds for personal security.

Bungs. Bungs or plugs are round pieces of wood that hide screw and bolt heads, which of course must be countersunk. They can be purchased in quantity from chandleries in teak and mahogany, or cut with a plug cutter from the same material as the piece being fastened to make a perfect match. Alternatively, they may be cut from a wood of contrasting color. In either case, the grain of the bung should be aligned with the surrounding grain. A spot of glue secures a bung and prevents the ingress of moisture.

Bungs are generally cut from the same species of wood into which they will be set, and aligned with the grains running parallel. The bung at left shows the effect of contrasting colors and grains. Precut teak and mahogany bungs or plugs are available in chandleries.

RECOGNIZING QUALITY

The instant you step aboard a boat, you gain an intuitive sense of how well it's constructed. There are all sorts of tipoffs: the quality of fabric, the tasteful use of colors, textures, and patterns, the feel of solidity underfoot, and perhaps most of all, the general appearance of the joinerwork. It isn't at all difficult to recognize poor and mediocre work, or for that matter, top-shelf carpentry.

Expert workmanship mandates sharp saws, chisels, and plane irons, for no amount of skill can completely overcome a dull or ragged-edged tool. Joint seams should be fine, thin lines, the less perceptible the better in most cases. Run your finger over the seam; you won't feel a bump if it's good work. On many production boats you can detect the use of filler materials—sawdust or powders mixed with resin or glue—to fill gaps between pieces. There's a good chance that such pieces were precut in the builder's woodshop according to a pattern, making it difficult if not impossible to get a tight fit on board. The best boatyards cut and test the fit of wood pieces *on* the boat—cut and check, cut and check until it's right. There is a price to be paid for such labor-intensive craftsmanship, and not everyone wants or can afford to pay it.

Professional joinerwork assumes a beauty all its own, and you might prefer to have a box or dovetail joint readily visible, even highlighted, rather than hidden by the carpenter's art. Joints can be especially decorative when the two adjoining wood pieces are of different species with contrasting grains and color.

This level of joinerwork is seldom left unfinished; oil or varnish is the accepted way to protect the wood and facilitate maintenance. Brightwork is a subject worthy of a book-length discussion in itself, but at the least one should be able to distinguish smooth, clear, hand-rubbed finishes from hazy, quickly applied, rough-feeling "alligator" surfaces.

VENEERS

Wood veneers are commonly used in boat interiors. It is possible to buy plywood with a veneer of teak, mahogany, or birch, for example, already glued to one side. This practice is cheaper than using solid hardwood stock. You may also purchase more exotic hardwood veneers and affix them to surfaces yourself. Of the two types of veneer—rotary cut and slice cut—the slice cut is more attractive, more stable, and of course more expensive.

LAMINATING

It is odd that some of the mainstay joints of good joinerwork have all but disappeared from many yards, while laminated door frames, tillers, and beams are almost standard fare in medium-priced boats.

Woodwork laminated on a form over which thin strips or veneers of wood are bent, epoxied, and clamped until cured is attractive, strong, and shapely. Today, a technique called vacuum-bagging is often used in place of clamps to ensure uniform pressure on all surfaces; this involves covering the entire structure with a plastic bag and drawing the air out with a pump. The entire hulls of cold-molded boats are sometimes built this way. The end product is extremely strong—stronger than one solid piece of wood of the same thickness, which may not have survived steam bending to the same radius anyway.

Contrasting colors of strips and veneers, as seen in tiller construction—mahogany and ash for example—can add to the stylishness of the finished product. Choose your subject (e.g., tiller, door frame) woods carefully, however, lest the effect backfire. Boatbuilder and designer Tom Colvin says that all too often the member " . . . will look more like a bent barber pole than a work of art."

INLAYS

A mark of exquisite craftsmanship is the use of decorative inlays in tabletops, deck hatches, and other suitably flat surfaces. They have no utilitarian function and are created to accent an otherwise dull expanse of wood or simply to show off skill. The design might be anything—a ship, a seascape, a sunrise, a unicorn or other animal, or a simple radiating pattern. Inlays are made by cutting out the shapes with sharp knives and chisels and filling the shallow "grave" with thin wood pieces of different and contrasting color. The result is an elaborate jigsaw puzzle made with hand tools.

Historically, furniture decorated with highly stylized inlays of cherry, rosewood, and other beautifully exotic hardwoods was considered the height of fashion. Some styles would seem too ornate today; however, the judicious use of inlays—perhaps an abstract design in the center of the saloon table, or stars inlaid in the corners of deck hatches—can add a custom touch that is sure to draw praise.

1 *Golden Eagle*'s interior is finished in bird's-eye maple veneer with mahogany trim.

2 Wooden boatbuilder and teacher Joe Trumbly of Gig Harbor, Washington, installs a beautiful laminated knee in his personal boat. The boat is a blend of Port Orford cedar, oak, and Alaskan yellow cedar.

3 The diamond inlay in the coaming top of this Rybovich sportfisherman adds interest to the cockpit detailing.

4 Painted inlays in paddles made by North River Boatworks are decorative but must be well sealed to prevent the glue from dissolving.

1

2

3

4

1

1 Wood decks can be arranged in a variety of patterns. *Wahoma*'s planks run parallel to the rail and terminate in a nibbed kingplank. Curving the planks at the bow to this degree is difficult. The 50-foot bridgedeck cruiser was built in 1939 by Lakewood.

2 The kingplanks on *Karin*'s deck are varnished for accent; varnishing more than this would result in a dangerously slippery surface.

3 Teak planks are frequently nibbed at the covering boards, but nibbing at a margin plank at the house sides is unusual.

4 The teak decks of *Independence,* an Irwin 52, are oiled to a warm brown color. If the kingplank was omitted and the converging planks overlapped, the design would be called a herringbone.

2

TEAK DECKS

Teak decks provide inherent nonskid footing and certainly set off a boat from others in the same marina. It is an expensive option from those builders who offer it. Teak can be allowed to weather and turn silver, or it can be oiled to retain its pretty, original light-brown color.

Most teak decks are made from quarter-sawn planks about ⅝-inch thick, bedded in polysulfide adhesive sealant and screwed to the deck. The seams are filled with a polysulfide adhesive sealant such as Thiokol. Screw-holes must be bunged.

An alternative method, particularly well suited to retrofitting old boats, is laying down thin (⅛- to 3/16-inch) strips of teak (you may have to add plywood first). Use epoxy for an adhesive, and fill the seams with epoxy thickened with black graphite powder. Staples are used to hold the strips down until the resin cures. This method eliminates troublesome bungs, which, if allowed to dry out, may pop out and let water into the deck core via the screws.

Various standard patterns have been developed over the years: The planks may run parallel with the centerline or may follow the curve of the rail; where planks meet on the foredeck they may be herringboned or join a king plank; joints in planks may be staggered, nibbed, and scarfed—the possibilities are just about endless. Although varnish robs teak of its nonskid properties, sometimes the covering boards adjacent to the rail or house can be varnished just to set them off.

We may think of teak decks as a traditional treatment, but many contemporary designs, such as those from Swan and Baltic, Van Lent, and Denison, incorporate teak decks to good effect. The decision is a highly personal one, generally based on aesthetic as well as practical considerations.

3

4

CABIN SOLES

Wood in the bilge has always caused problems, namely rot. So it is not surprising that many fiberglass boatbuilders either cover wood structural members with fiberglass or construct structural members such as hat sections from foam and fiberglass. At the least, bare wood can be coated with epoxy.

Production builders have turned increasingly to fiberglass inner liners and pans to speed up construction and reduce costs, but this is a cold and noisy solution. The all-teak or teak and holly sole is both attractive and a good nonskid surface, assuming it is left unvarnished, which it frequently isn't on high-priced yachts. The planks are generally laid on top of plywood, bedded, screwed, and bunged. If done properly, an all-wood sole should last the lifetime of the boat.

The subject of carpeting is a controversial one (see Chapter 18, "Soft Coverings"); suffice it to say that if there is wood below the sole it should be allowed to breathe. This means no "wall-to-wall" carpeting; throw rugs are a better option.

CARVINGS

The all-teak interiors that for many years characterized boats built in Taiwan were often showcases for Chinese carpenters who felt they possessed underutilized sculpturing skills (the results often suggested otherwise). The bas-relief carvings of poppy flowers and serpentine dragons on stateroom doors and bulkheads were at first highly prized, but after a few years they became almost caricatures of themselves and began to disappear when they became the butt of jokes.

Nevertheless, carving has a place on some vessels, perhaps the most appropriate being the figureheads and trailboards of clipper-bowed sailing yachts. These are usually painted to clearly depict the subject: an eagle or a mermaid, for instance. Carvings won't work on just any boat, but on some old schooners the more conspicuous error might be their omission.

1 The dragon is a symbol for number one—everything strong, rich, and good—in Chinese culture, and is a common subject of craftsmen in traditional boatbuilding.

2 The figurehead is a time-honored ornament on the bows of sailing ships. Though a duck is a far cry from the busty figurehead of a maiden calming angry seas, it nevertheless adds interest to the design.

3 Clipper bows are traditionally decorated with trailboards, usually carved and painted, often with gold leaf.

1

2

3

1

2

3

1 *Whitehawk*'s carved eagle
befits her stately lines.

2 The knurled end of this
wooden bow rail provides a
decorative terminus to a
graceful curve.

3 The Dutch are fond of clever
carvings atop outboard
rudders.

FINISHES

A raw wood interior will eventually fade and stain to the point that a massive restoration effort is required. The wood must be finished, but a yacht-quality finish involves more than a quick sanding and the application of oil or varnish. A first-rate boatbuilder likely employs one man whose job is only to varnish exterior and interior trim. Production builders may speed up the process by having him spray certain pieces in a specially equipped and ventilated room, then install the pieces in the boat when they are dry. A trained eye can tell the difference between sprayed and brushed varnish.

As in a home paint job, a good measure of the work is in preparation, not in application. All surfaces must be smooth and dust-free. A natural oil sealer such as Tung oil increases the life of a varnish finish; avoid synthetic oils beneath the varnish, as the ingress of moisture will cause delamination. The first varnish coats may be thinned with solvents to enhance penetration and adhesion. Subsequent coats must be applied at proper intervals for good adhesion to previous coats, and depending on the type of oil or varnish used, may even be hand-rubbed to prevent a milky, rough look. This becomes more critical as coats build up thickness; it is not uncommon to apply six or more coats. Exterior trim requires more to combat the sun's ultraviolet rays; special ultraviolet-resistant additives in exterior varnish help to prevent degradation.

Let us not forget the old standby, paint. Marine enamels are still popular choices belowdeck, though they require repainting every few years (more often if applied to high-use surfaces). More expensive epoxy and polyurethane paints give durable, high-gloss, almost lacquer-like finishes that are also easy to clean and retain their brilliance for a long time. One- and two-part types are good choices for bulkheads and furniture foundations. As with any high-gloss paint, nicks and blemishes will show up grievously, so the careful filling and sanding of surfaces is a must.

Surface finishes say a lot about your boat. Good surface preparation is the key, and takes more time than actually applying the paint or varnish. If you value your time at all, it simply doesn't make sense to do a shoddy job that will offend the eye and will soon chip and peel, requiring more work after one or two seasons.

1

2

1 Wooden block cheeks are at home on a wooden vessel.

2 Teak-and-holly cabin soles are common, but the combination looks equally classy in the hatch construction of *Miriam Elizabeth*.

BEFORE YOU BUY OR BUILD . . .

Consider carefully the amount of exposed wood you want; too little may be plain, too much could end up a nightmare. There is no question that wood is beautiful, but it requires a lot of work to keep looking good. Do you have the time and skill? Can you afford to pay the yard to do it for you? These are bigger questions than you might think. The world is full of boats with once-beautiful brightwork, now checked, yellowing, and peeling due to neglect. Those owners might have been better off without the varnished teak caprails, cockpit coamings, and hatches. But if you are up to the task of preserving your wood trim, buy a good book on the subject and roll up your sleeves. You may despise the work, but the stunning appearance of Bristol brightwork and the increased resale value of your boat will be ample reward.

Color Coordination with Wood

All woods have a natural color or hue that distinguishes them; indeed, their warm colors are a major appeal. Consider the color of the wood you want at the same time you look at fabrics for upholstery, carpeting, and curtains, as well as the color and texture of other surface materials such as tiles and plastic laminates.

The best woods for the interior are teak; Honduras, African, and Philippine mahoganies; rosewood; silver bali; butternut; oak; black walnut; cherry; and yellow cypress. The best woods for the exterior are teak, silver bali, delmari, Honduras mahogany, dense Douglas fir, and longleaf yellow pine.

Species	Coordinating Colors
Reddish Woods	
Ash	White, black, and yellow
Basswood	
Birch	
Cherry	
Elm	
Honey locust	
Maple	
Red cedar	
Redwood	
Bluish and Purplish Woods	
Magnolia	White and yellow
Black walnut	
Yellow poplar	
Pine	
Greenish Woods	
Black locust	Black, white and yellow
Magnolia	
Yellow poplar	
Gold and Light-Brown Woods	
Aspen	White, black, brown, blue, purple, and pink
Birch	
Black locust	
Cypress	
Cedar	
Pine	

Source: Tom Colvin

CHAPTER SEVENTEEN

Alternative Materials

espite the appeal and advantages of the all-wood yacht interior (see Chapter 16, "Woodwork"), wood is not the only material suitable for deck and interior structures, cabinetry, fascias, and trim. Indeed, advances in metallurgy and chemistry have produced numerous new materials that possess superior characteristics, and some of the products made from these materials are ideal for use in the marine environment. This is not to say that wood is obsolete; just that there are alternatives which can in many cases do the job better, are sometimes cheaper, and sometimes simply provide a different look. When deciding on materials for specific purposes, the owner should consider, among other properties, the materials' respective strengths, maintenance requirements, weights, lifespans, and appearance.

METALS

Before the last half of this century, boatbuilders were restricted in the metals that could be honestly installed in seagoing yachts. Iron, steel, and bronze were their mainstays, and often wood seemed a safer choice. Corrosion was and is the nemesis of metals in a saltwater and salt air environment. In recent decades, however, the development of new alloys has produced metal products that are greatly if not totally resistant to galvanic, electrolytic, pitting, and crevice corrosion. There is usually a price to be paid in tensile, sheer, and compressive strength, in fatigue failure, and in expense. Still, the modern yacht is fitted with all manner of metal parts and hardware, some better suited to their jobs than others.

Stainless steel. It would be difficult to find a boat today without stainless steel on it, for it is the preferred material for stanchions, mast rigging, outriggers, tuna towers, and such hardware as sail tracks, sheaves, cleats, and horns. Contrary to its name, stainless steel is not totally resistant to staining or corrosion. Common types such as 304 and 316 stainless steel are alloys of iron, carbon, chromium, nickel, and sometimes small amounts of

1

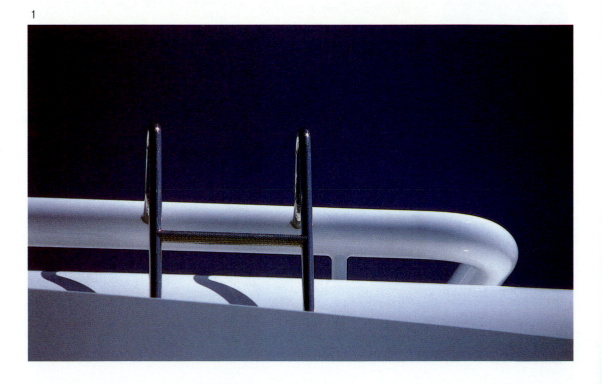

1 The stainless steel and aluminum metalwork on *Antipodean* is exceptionally clean, possessing a highly sculpted look that elevates the welder's craft to a near artform.

2 *Grey Goose II* is a 72-foot high-performance, long-distance cruising machine built by Bob Derektor. The aluminum sloop has a 3,100-square-foot fully battened mainsail, a lifting bulb keel that adjusts draft between 8 and 16 feet, and an articulated pendulum rudder that stays perpendicular to the water.

2

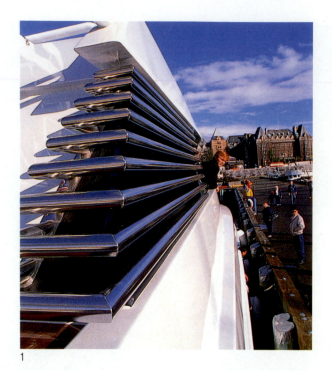

1

molybdenum. While the addition of some metals increases corrosion resistance, adding too much can seriously weaken the final product, so metallurgists are constantly experimenting to achieve the best compromises in physical properties.

What might be called a breakthrough product in recent years is Nitronic 50, which is an alloy containing carbon, manganese, phosphorus, sulfur, chromium, nickel, molybdenum, nitrogen, niobium, and vanadium. It has many industrial uses and is most often seen on yachts in the form of solid rod rigging made by Navtec, Inc. Principal advantages include improved resistance to corrosion, minimal stretch, reduced weight, and greater strength than same-size wire rope (1 × 19). Of course its cost is also greater than conventional stainless steel types, which explains why Nitronic 50 hasn't replaced the others in less stressful applications.

In any case, stainless steel toerails, handholds, pulpits, and rails are just a few of the on-deck applications for which metal has supplanted wood on many production boats. It isn't maintenance-free, though an occasional wipe-down and polish is about all that's required. A more likely problem is staining caused by "stainless" through-bolts that, as you learn only too late, aren't austenitic at all and rust. A pox on the purveyors of fraudulent disguised ferritic and martensitic fasteners!

Belowdecks, stainless steel sheeting makes an excellent galley counter—waterproof, virtually scratchproof, durable, and easy to clean. Of course the sinks are most likely stainless steel too, but then you expect that. Sheeting screwed to bulkheads and overhead surfaces also works well as a heat shield for stoves, fireplaces, and cabin heaters. Tiles might be prettier but are not always as practical, since stainless sheeting can be bent to conform to radiused corners. (Note: stainless steel is more easily sheared than cut with a saw.) It is also suitable for compression posts, table legs, and fiddles, all of which might have been made of wood.

Quite apart from the excellent physical properties of stainless, a good reason to choose this highly polished metal is to achieve a decidedly contemporary decor. While some might consider it hard and cold, that is precisely the effect some designers are after (consider the 1950s' modernist architecture of glass-and-steel buildings). It's anything but warm and cozy. Coupled with smoked Plexiglas hatches and cabinet doors, synthetic-lined bulkheads and overheads, and metallic-colored synthetic materials, stainless steel helps to create a sharp, modern theme.

Copper, brass, and bronze alloys. Copper is a soft metal once used as an antifouling sheathing on ship bottoms; in fact, in the 1980s several enterprising (not to mention optimistic) persons have attempted to replace copper and tin bottom paint with copper sheathing on fiberglass boats. But because of the difficulty and dubiousness of using mechanical fasteners such as screws in fiberglass, the sheathers have had to rely on adhesives and to date haven't been able to find one that can stand the test of sea and time—eventually they've all delaminated. Elsewhere, copper's use on boats has been pretty much limited to electrical wiring and fuel lines, though today flexible gas lines frequently replace copper in this application as well.

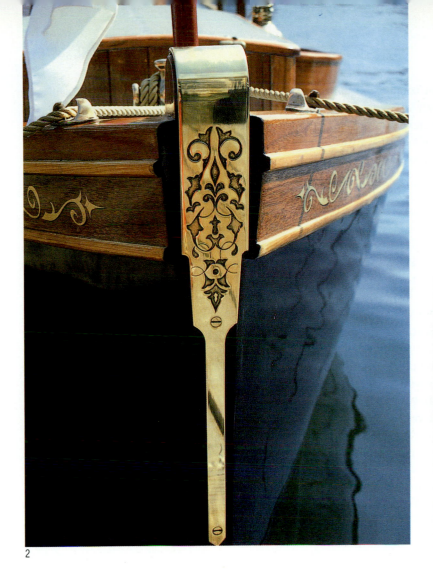

2

3

4

1 The engine vents on *P'zazz,* designed by stylist Glade Johnson, are a series of stainless steel tubes that become a significant element in the yacht's exterior styling.

2 Decorative brasswork on the stem of this traditional sailboat requires regular polishing but certainly sets her apart from the crowd.

3 The brass clock and barometer are nicely integrated with glass lamps to form an interesting cluster on the bulkhead.

4 Opening bronze portlights are a good choice on the right boat, and need not be limited to the cabin sides. This portlight provides a light source through the aft face of the cabin.

Brass is an alloy of copper and zinc, and because the zinc quickly disappears in a salty environment, brass is mostly found in clocks and barometers and other fancy instruments protected belowdecks. Manganese bronze is a type of brass (nearly 60/40 copper and zinc, with a small percentage of manganese) and therefore shouldn't be used underwater and seldom on deck.

Zinc-free copper alloys using tin, aluminum, silicon, and nickel are true bronzes and much more corrosion-resistant than brass. Much deck hardware is made from bronze, sometimes chromed for easy maintenance and a more polished appearance (bronze turns green as it oxidizes). Over time, however, chrome tends to pit and ultimately to peel, so chroming bronze is always a trade-off between maintenance and finish. When peeling begins, some owners strip the rest of the chrome to see if they like the "new" bronze look. If not, you can remove the hardware and have it rechromed.

Copper-nickel alloys such as Monel (a proprietary name for a 70/30 mix) are highly corrosion-resistant and an excellent choice for fuel tanks and propeller shafts. Occasionally one reads of a boat whose entire hull was constructed of Monel or some other copper-nickel alloy, but high cost is a major drawback.

Aluminum. Marine-grade aluminum alloys using magnesium, manganese, and silicon to help resist corrosion are widely used on boats. However, the white film of oxidation that forms in salt air prevents them from retaining a smooth, polished finish. Aluminum is a versatile metal in that it may be cast, rolled, extruded, and wrought according to the needs of a given product. Perhaps aluminum's greatest triumph over wood has been in the making of masts, booms, poles, and other columnar structures. These may be anodized and left bare or may be chemically etched and painted with polyurethanes to obtain the high-gloss finish so highly prized on yachts.

The French in particular are fond of building entire boats of aluminum, and the constructors of steel megayachts often use aluminum for the superstructure to save weight. Unlike steel, however, aluminum does not weep the telltale stains of rust to warn of impending failure; in

1 Lapis lazuli is a semiprecious stone used for decorative accents. The wood moldings follow the arc of the handle's throw.

2 Ordinary fixtures such as handles and locks may be coordinated with the rest of the interior design plan. Gleaming brass doorknobs have a rich look.

3 A bonus of buying an old boat for restoration is the discovery of fixtures and hardware no longer commercially available. The keyhole and lever handle are distinctive.

4 French cruising sailors are partial to unpainted aluminum-alloy hulls for their strength and easy maintenance.

addition to a vigilant eye, the owner of a metal boat will sleep easier with an electronic surveillance system that detects stray electrical currents.

Steel and iron. Iron ore is the raw material dug from the ground and processed to produce both iron and (with a small percentage of carbon added) steel. Cor-Ten steel, which has a bit of copper and chromium added, has been used with considerable success for building steel-hulled yachts. With chemical etching and the application of durable primers and polyurethane paint systems, steel hulls are virtually resistant to corrosion and offer the ultimate protection against damage caused by grounding or collision.

The galvanizing of anchors, shackles, and other hardware is a process that involves dipping the piece in molten zinc; however, its surface finish is dull and rough, and its lifespan is limited. Consequently galvanized steel has given way to stainless steel, bronze, and aluminum in many marine products.

PLASTIC

Perhaps of more interest in the finishing of boats is the development of new plastics that possess outstanding physical properties and are increasingly used in the manufacture of products traditionally made of metal and wood. For example, on a given boat you might find a plastic spacer between the engine transmission and propeller shaft, plastic seacocks, laminated tabletops, pumps, deck cleats—in short, it's everywhere. Indeed, fiberglass boats *are* plastic (its proper name is FRP—fiberglass-reinforced plastic).

Plastic simply means that the raw material is a combination of chemicals that, when heated (by adding a catalyst to polyester resins or by mixing two chemicals to form epoxy), participates in a chemical reaction whereby small molecules permanently link to form larger molecules. The process has undergone years of intensive research and development, so that today plastic has to a great extent shed its reputation of being cheap and easily breakable. A Marelon seacock or cleat is incredibly strong and cannot be marred or damaged even when repeatedly struck with a heavy hammer; and because these products cannot corrode or become electrolytically active, they are ideal for use on steel boats.

3

4

1

2

1 Because round-bilge steel boats are very expensive to build, most have hard or radiused chines, the latter being a compromise between hard chines and rolled plates. *Rosemary Ruth* is a 36-foot Tom Colvin–designed pinky schooner built in 1976 by Fred McConnell.

2 A well-built steel hull properly painted with modern coatings is difficult to distinguish from fiberglass.

3 *Popeye's* Lexan windshield is very strong and stylish. Lexan is the famed bulletproof material used in the windows of presidential limousines.

4 These sandwich sections are samples of coring materials such as PVC used to achieve strong, lightweight hulls.

Delrin bushings in pumps and Duratron ball bearings in mainsheet travelers are durable, low-friction, noncorroding substitutes for machined steel.

Synthetic fabrics made of acrylic, nylon, olefin, polyester, rayon, and vinyl make up a high percentage of curtains, upholstery, and carpets used both in the home and in boats, not to mention the clothes we wear. Many of these fabrics are blends that far exceed 100-percent natural materials such as cotton and wool in terms of waterproofing, durability, mildew resistance, and colorfastness.

Plastic laminates such as Formica are used as veneers to cover plywood bulkheads, countertops, and furniture foundations. They are available in a wide variety of colors and patterns; are easy to cut, install and maintain; and resist scratching, fading, chipping, and mildew. Some builders have run wild with wood grain and marbleized laminates, intended to impart the feel of real wood or marble. They seldom do. The pattern is actually a "photograph" of the real material, transferred to the outer laminate by offset printing. In most instances, real wood veneers or marble (if you can handle the weight) are better-looking choices.

Wood countertops are a traditional treatment, but must be kept scrupulously clean, especially after cutting meats on them, to prevent salmonella poisoning. Stainless steel, as mentioned, makes a practical, attractive (if cold) surface. A nice alternative is tile, available in ceramic, vinyl, rubber, and fiberglass. Be sure to use a waterproof grout for easy maintenance and to prevent delamination.

It might seem from the above examples that an entire boat could be built of plastic, and that is almost true. Spars and rudderstocks can be constructed of fiberglass, resin, and carbon fiber; the hull and deck can be molded of fiberglass and Kevlar; interior furniture can be molded of fiberglass; cushions can be made of synthetic foam and covered with synthetic fabric; lights and other fixtures can be made from plastic; windows can be made of Plexiglas or Lexan. You see how it goes. About the only things that still must be made of metal are engine blocks and electrical wiring, though fiber optics are fast replacing copper wire in the telecommunications industry and it is probably just a matter of time before superconductive plastics revolutionize the electrical industry as well. In the 21st century some company will no doubt develop a strong, heat-absorbing plastic that can be used for engine blocks and high-speed parts such as pistons, cranks, and camshafts as well. Ceramic pistons are already in use. Corrosion will then be a thing of the past, though new problems, like the osmotic blistering of fiberglass hulls, will creep forward to replace them in our nightmares.

1

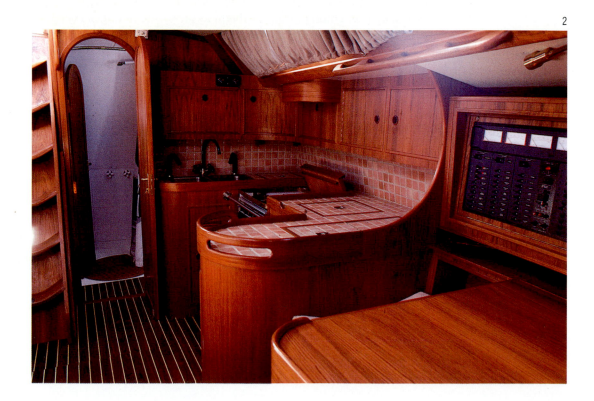

2

3

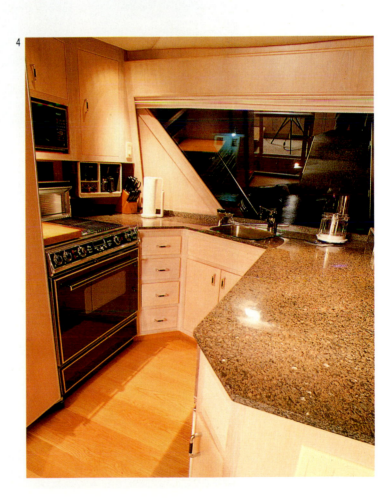

4

1 *Palmyra*'s stainless steel countertop around the galley sink is highly durable and guarantees there won't be water leaks to cause rot or delamination of the underlying wood.

2 Plastic laminate countertops such as Formica are utilitarian, inexpensive, and available in a wide variety of colors and patterns, but other materials are also suitable and more distinctive. The pink tiles in *Obsessed* are washable and attractive, though comparatively heavy. Epoxy grout prevents mildew.

3 The galley on *Island Spirit*, a 66-foot Cheoy Lee Long Range Motoryacht, has a Corian marble countertop. The window blinds are wood, and the 22-cubic-foot refrigerator/ freezer has an ice dispenser in the door.

4 Genuine granite countertops are indeed beautiful but only practical where weight isn't a concern, such as in the galley of *Executive Sweet*.

Mylar (clear) and Kevlar (brown) are space-age materials commonly used in sails for their strength and low-stretch characteristics. These boats are competing in the St. Francis Yacht Club's Big Boat Series on San Francisco Bay.

MAKING CHOICES

Much of the challenge of designing, buying, and fitting out boats lies in the making of choices: What shape of hull, material, color, layout, and types of equipment do we want? If there were no choices it wouldn't be much fun. The sea, as it turns out, is not easily mastered. One can continue learning throughout one's lifetime the nuances of navigation, the secrets of meteorology and oceanography, and the tactics of seamanship. But it all begins with the boat itself.

For several millennia boats were built solely of natural materials—trees, plants, and animal skins. Not until the 19th century did the first iron-hulled ships appear, and it was only in the late 1940s that fiberglass reared its moldable head and announced itself as a material to be reckoned with. Oddly, it seems almost a traditional material compared with the so-called exotics now available, so rapid is progress.

Fortunately, one doesn't need to join the high-tech bandwagon unless one wants to. It is still possible to commission the building of a wood-hulled sailing vessel or motorboat, sew cotton sails and skip the engine altogether, defecate in an oak bucket, and carry water in animal-skin pouches from nearby streams. Few would quarrel with the purist's right to pursue his own philosophy in boats, but most of us are looking for compromises between tradition and advanced technology that at the same time satisfy our desire for hassle-free leisure and nurture our deeper spiritual needs.

The typical midsize modern yacht is a good example of blending new and old materials to form an efficient, strong, and attractive package. The hull is probably fiberglass, largely laminated from polyester resin over a variety of woven fibers. The fibers are designed to distribute loads according to stress analyses calculating likely spots for impact and fatigue failure. Some boats are built entirely of epoxy resin, which is stronger and has better adhesive properties, and others are using vinylester in the gelcoat and first laminations to minimize the chances of osmotic blistering. The hull may be solid or cored with end-grain balsa or foam to achieve greater stiffness as well as lesser weight. The deck is also fiberglass, cored with end-grain balsa to prevent oilcanning.

Alternative Materials Guide

Here is a list of basic boat components and the common materials from which they can be constructed and commercially purchased. Studying this list can help you become aware of the options available.

Component	Materials
Hull	FRP (fiberglass), steel, aluminum, Monel, wood, ferrocement
Bulkheads	Plywood, honeycomb sandwich, FRP
Furniture	Plywood, hardwood, softwood, FRP
Spars	Aluminum, wood, FRP, carbon fiber, steel
Engine	Iron, aluminum
Cleats	Wood, bronze, stainless steel, plastic, aluminum
Seacocks	Stainless steel, plastic, bronze
Rope	Manila, Dacron, nylon, Kevlar, Spectra
Hose/Piping	Plastic, rubber, copper, stainless steel
Anchors	Stainless steel, galvanized steel, aluminum
Sails	Dacron, nylon, Spectra, Mylar, cotton, Kevlar
Cushions	Foam, cotton
Upholstery	Synthetics, cotton, wool, leather
Soles	Wood, FRP, steel, aluminum
Windlass	Iron, stainless steel, aluminum, bronze
Windows	Glass, Plexiglas, Lexan
Frames	Plastic, bronze, stainless steel, steel, aluminum
Tanks	FRP, wood, aluminum, Monel, steel, rubberized fabric
Rudderstocks	Steel, Monel, FRP, carbon fiber, titanium
Rudders	Wood, FRP, steel, aluminum
Propellers	Bronze, stainless steel, plastic
Sinks	Wood, FRP, stainless steel, plastic
Tuna towers	Stainless steel, wood

Spars are aluminum extrusions painted with two-part polyurethane for a smooth, high-gloss finish. Hatches are bulletproof Lexan set in stainless steel or aluminum frames. Handholds may be wood, if a natural accent is desired, or stainless steel. Windows are glass, Plexiglas, or Lexan set in plastic, bronze, or stainless steel frames.

The cabin sole is supported by fiberglass and foam beams, then covered with plywood over which teak and holly strips are laid. Furniture foundations are built of plywood covered with plastic or wood veneers, as are bulkheads. Cushions are made of open- or closed-cell foam and covered with fabrics chosen by designers or owners.

Fixtures such as lights, switches, pumps, fans, and sinks may be plastic, stainless steel, or any number of combinations.

In truth, the modern yacht contains a great variety of materials carefully chosen for long life, appearance, and aesthetic appeal. In the standardized production yacht, these choices have for the most part been made for you, but as you begin customizing features you regain the right to choose the materials used. Wood mast or aluminum? Cotton duck cushion covers or polyester? Wood veneer bulkheads or Formica? Glass windows or Plexiglas? Aluminum anchor or galvanized steel?

A case can be made for any of the above materials. Much depends on the type of boat, how it will be used, your skill and availability for maintenance, and last but not least, your values. The choice of boatbuilding materials reflects one's individual beliefs. The wooden boat lover wouldn't be caught dead in a fiberglass boat that looks like a refrigerator inside; likewise, a performance boat fanatic would no sooner consider a traditional plank-on-frame wooden boat than he would a goatskin coracle. Fortunately the world is big enough to supply man with a great variety of materials, and man himself is visionary and diverse enough in his character to keep making original choices.

1 Glass etchings in mirrors have become popular in recent years, showing a variety of original artistic concepts. How well the fashion wears in coming years remains to be seen.

2 Stained glass accents used with discretion add a dash of brightness and interest to an otherwise ordinary surface.

CHAPTER EIGHTEEN

Soft Coverings

efore the yacht interior is decorated with upholstery, curtains, hull liners, and carpeting, it is a world of hard surfaces—wood, metal, and fiberglass—that is somehow incomplete, unfit for human habitation. Comfort and beauty rely to a great extent upon cushions and mattresses; the color, texture, pattern, and feel of fabrics used for upholstery or slip covers; the sewing style used; how they support the human body in all positions of work and relaxation; and how they meet the eye. Soft coverings are critical finishings to any customizing or restoration job.

Built by Eric Goetz Custom Sailboats, *Whisper VII*'s saloon is simple, relying on blue-and-white striped upholstery with a teak-and-holly sole to reinforce the theme.

SEATS AND MATTRESSES

In any cabin a large percentage of the surfaces are occupied by upholstered cushions: settees, navigation seats, berths, and backrests. Thus it is no small wonder that first impressions are highly influenced by the fabrics and how they work with the paint, varnish, and veneers used on bulkheads, hull liners, furniture foundations, joinerwork, and cabin soles. Bold patterns or busy? Primary colors, pastels, desert or jewel tones? Leather, cotton, wool, or synthetics? And how do they coordinate with varnished teak moldings, synthetic marble

Fabric Guide

Fiber Types	Characteristics
Natural Fibers	
Cotton	Soft. Dyes well. Fair resistance to wear and ultraviolet. Stains and is flammable unless treated. Wrinkles and shrinks.
Wool	Resilient. Dyes well. Breathes. Naturally flame-retardant. Shrinks. Poor abrasion and ultraviolet resistance. Pills.
Linen	Strong. Moderate resistance to ultraviolet. Pleasing texture. Wrinkles. Shrinks. Requires special cleaning; poor colorfastness.
Synthetic Fibers	
Acrylic	Soft. Durable. High resistance to ultraviolet. Dyes well. Flame-resistant. Plush, woollike look. May shrink and pill. Moderate abrasion resistance.
Nylon	Strong. Good resistance to abrasion and staining. Blends well with other fibers. Cool and soft. Easily cleaned. May pill; melts at high temperatures. May appear shiny.
Olefin	Good resistance to mildew and abrasion. Strong. Heat-sensitive; flammable unless treated.
Polyester	Resists wrinkling and mildew. Cottonlike appearance. Easy to clean. Ultraviolet-sensitive. Does not take color well.
Rayon	Soft. Blends well. Fair abrasion and ultraviolet resistance. Weak. Shrinks. Flammable.

countertops, plain Formica foundations, Levolor window blinds? It is of course a big puzzle, and each piece plays its special role.

Foam. Excepting the megayacht with its home-style chairs and beds, the vast majority of small and midsize yachts are well served by foam cushions on settees, seats, and berths. Medium-firm (about 1.8 to 2.5 pounds per cubic foot) open-cell polyurethane foam is the most commonly used type; its resilience varies according to quality. (Check compression ratings: Foam that is too soft may bottom out; foam that is too firm may be uncomfortable to sit or lie on for long periods.) Some foams are fire retardant, which is an important safety consideration; however, many so labeled will still burn and emit dangerous gases. Check specifications carefully.

Besides polyurethane foam, other types include latex and Airex, the latter being *closed-cell*, which means it is buoyant in water and oftentimes uncomfortably firm. Closed-cell foam is generally used for relatively small cushions (because of its tendency to shrink and expand according to temperature) and is best suited to on-deck use, where it is firm underfoot and won't become waterlogged when wet.

A 4-inch thickness is considered a minimum standard, though 5 or 6 inches is decidedly more comfortable, especially for berth cushions. Backrest cushions won't be subject to the same amount of compression, and therefore needn't be as thick.

Fabric. The manufacture of upholstery fabric is big business, with numerous companies continually developing new products they hope will gain them a few points of market share. Even the boatbuilding business merits its own trade journal, *Marine Textiles*, wherein one can find glossy, expensive ads from such industry giants as Phillips Fibers Corporation and Uniroyal Coated Fabrics. These plus dozens of smaller original equipment manufacturer (OEM) companies vie for the attention of boatbuilders, many of whom, such as Bayliner and Wellcraft, rely heavily on chic, state-of-the-art fabrics to distinguish boats in their new model year from those of years past. Trade names come and go, but some, including UltraSuede, Naugahyde, Scotchgard, and Herculon, are household words. Lesser-known names such as Sunbrella, Finesse, and Nova Suede still represent substantial research-and-development and advertising investments on the part of their manufacturers.

And fabric represents just part of the marine textile business; there is a host of companies, each marketing its own particular specialty item, including threads, snap fasteners, hardware, grommets, webbing, and so on.

With this in mind, if you are planning to select and purchase your own cushion covers, there are tough decisions ahead. By hiring a marine interior designer to help plan and execute your new boat or restoration project, you'll be benefiting from someone else's knowledge of products. Much of course depends on who uses the boat, and how and where. The cushion fabric for a family cruiser that will carry kids with dirty feet must be more durable than the fabric chosen for a corporate yacht whose guests are well-behaved adults dressed more for a champagne reception than a day at the beach.

Climate is a factor, too, as the right fabric for the damp and drizzly Pacific Northwest or Irish Sea just won't perform as well in the tropics. And vice versa. Appropriate colors vary with geography as well, though the well-traveled cruiser needs an interior that can adapt to its surroundings.

Standard cushion fabrics include the families of acrylic, vinyl, synthetic leather, wool-and-nylon blends, olefin, and polyester. Each has its advantages and disadvantages. Leather, for example, is durable and rich-looking, yet must be kept dry. Acrylics are colorfast, water repellent, and mildew resistant, but may pill, shrink, and absorb oily stains. Herculon and rayon are durable, lightweight, and resilient, but are subject to shrinkage and degradation in the sun. Vinyl is very rugged, easy to clean, and waterproof, but it doesn't breathe well and feels clammy to the touch. Costs vary significantly, from cotton at the low end to leather at the high.

Fabric protection. While many synthetic fibers have water and stain repellents "built in," you may find it wise to add your own measure of protection. A number of spray-on repellents are available, including Scotchgard, Fibre-Seal, and Stainmaster. Follow the manufacturer's instructions, which will probably call for several applications with follow-up after cleaning and at the end of each season.

Keep in mind, too, that many synthetic fabrics pill when laundered, and many should be steam-cleaned on the boat rather than dry-cleaned. Again, note manufacturer's instructions.

All Is Best's saloon settees are leather. The chessboard is inlaid on a rosewood table. The 70-foot charter boat, built of fiberglass by Camper and Nicholson, takes its name from a line by 17th-century bard John Milton: "All is best, though we oft doubt."

1

2

3

4

1 *Pandora*'s aft cabin might be too dark were it not for the red floral chintz.

2 *Executive Sweet*'s U-shaped lounge relies on neutral coverings in UltraSuede with contrasting colors in the throw pillows for interest.

3 The subtle colors of a flame-stitch upholstery weave in *Numero Uno*'s wheelhouse keep the pattern from becoming overly busy.

4 The Gatsby 39's tufted red velour dinette coverings in combination with brass shelf rails recreate a 1920s parlor, consistent with the design of this classically styled motor cruiser.

Choosing a theme. If possible, cushion fabrics should be selected when the rest of the interior is planned; if not, you'll have to work with what exists, and the color and pattern of the fabric you like just might not work with a heavy all-teak interior, or a perforated vinyl overhead, or a blond wood hull ceiling.

It is often best to stick with a single scheme of one or two fabrics in small boats, where the cushions in all cabins are likely visible from any vantage point; mixing patterns, textures, or colors between the saloon and forward cabin can create an assault on the optic nerves despite bulkheads, whereas using one fabric on cushions and a coordinating fabric on pillows in both areas is very unifying. On larger boats, in which cabins are separated by long passageways, levels, or decks, there is the possibility of distinguishing the children's or owner's cabin from the rest of the boat and from one another. Still, most designers like to conceive of the yacht as a whole, and strive to maintain continuity from cabin to cabin, figuring that even if the eye cannot see inside two cabins at once, the memory will.

Where bulkheads, soles, and hull liners are kept simple, as in the traditional Down East interior with white painted bulkheads and varnished mahogany trim, bolder fabric patterns are possible. On the other hand, an all-natural wood interior showing lots of highly defined grain might benefit from plainer fabrics that don't fight one another for attention. Many production builders today seem fond of cushion fabric with small repeating patterns—white or gold designs on navy blue, for example—but beware that the motion of the boat can make such patterns seem to "float," increasing the likelihood of queasiness and seasickness.

Some designers suggest choosing a neutral color for most surfaces, including fabrics, then using stronger colors or patterns for selected accents such as throw pillows, curtains, spreads, and the like.

Dark colors may impart a warm, snug feel, or a dreary one if the color is off a little. Strong colors require good lighting to be fully appreciated, as they can suffer in dark corners or at night. Light colors are cooler and impart a greater sense of spaciousness, but may not be

as cozy. Be aware that fluorescent and incandescent lights treat colors differently, and test accordingly.

Monochromatic color schemes have become popular in high-performance sportboats, some custom-decorated motoryachts, and a few contemporary sailboats. Black, in particular, has enjoyed a resurgence of interest, as have silvers and golds. Fabrics with pearlized or metallic finishes seem to fit the monochromatic theme well.

Determine your objectives and priorities early in the fabric selection process. Do you want a cool- or cozy-feeling interior? Elegant or casual? Do you want to make the cabin feel wider or narrower than it really is? Longer or shorter? Adjust from darker colors at foot level to lighter shades at eye level, or stay the same? Emphasize practicality or sensuousness? The choice is yours, but then again, you're the one who has to make it work.

Just as you would at home, obtain swatches of the fabrics that interest you and try them on board before buying. The cost of material and labor is high enough that you won't want to make a mistake.

1

1 The numerous pillows in *Sargasso*'s saloon give it an overstuffed look.

2 *Awesome*'s monochromatic color scheme is typical of many sportboats.

3 The hand-painted pastels in *Lady Frances*'s sky lounge are an example of color as theme, especially since there is no real style to the furniture.

2

3

1 Pattern is the accent in *Mary J*'s dining area. The wood is white oak, countertops are Avonite, and faucets are gold-plated. Tungsten, halogen, and incandescent lights are mixed throughout the boat.

2 Ralph Jordan commissioned Jack Sarin to design *Mary J* and Cooper Yachts of Vancouver, British Columbia to build her. Built of Airex-cored fiberglass and measuring 91 feet overall, she frequently cruises the "inside passage" to Princess Louisa Inlet and Chatterbox Falls.

3 Pattern becomes theme in *Obsessed*'s guest cabin, where the spread fabric is carried to the bulkheads with a foam backing. The painting struggles to save it from ultimate boredom.

2

3

1

2

3

4

1 The "black" stateroom in *P'zazz* features 24-carat gold-plated fixtures and coverings of black leather and satin mixed with gold threads.

2 Symmetry and balance are key in *Golden Delicious*'s saloon, with matching coffee tables and with settees and overstuffed chairs all covered in UltraSuede.

3 Pink suede and bright-green suede trim juxtaposed against bird's-eye maple veneer set apart this made-for-charter motorsailer, *Fantaseas*.

4 Where auditory privacy is either impossible or unimportant, "soft doors" are an intelligent alternative. *Calypte*'s saloon and forward cabin are separated by an attractive cotton door hung on string.

1

2

Cushion construction. Unless you're a skilled seamster, you'll probably have your cushions professionally covered. First you must decide whether to have them upholstered or simply have slipcovers made. This depends to an extent on the size of your boat, the fabric, and how the fabric will be used. For many owners, slipcovers make sense, since they can be removed for cleaning, and make fitting replacements easier. Lightweight cotton pillow covers, for example, can't be expected to last more than a few seasons anyway.

Cushions can be covered in one of several styles. Boxed cushions, with square corners, are simple and traditional. Piping is an optional accent, sometimes made with a contrasting color. Bull-nose cushions, built up under the knees, provide support and a more sculpted look. Pleating, quilting, and midcushion cording create a sumptuous, overstuffed appearance that invites lounging.

Designer Anne Brengle suggests keeping the detail work plain if the fabric has a busy pattern. Conversely, for plain or unpatterned fabric, she gives the okay to finish as elaborately as desired—pleated or button-and-tufted. Piping, she notes, lends a more tailored appearance to the edges of slip covers.

Because of potential corrosion problems, cushions should be assembled without metal fasteners such as staples and tacks. Nylon zippers are almost universally used, though they too can become difficult to use after time.

The bottoms of berth and settee cushions can be covered with canvas to save expense and help the foam hold its shape; this especially makes sense with any cushion that cannot, because of its shape or for some other reason, be reversed.

WINDOWS, PORTLIGHTS, AND HATCHES

Covering small portlights with curtains is sometimes more trouble than it's worth. If the portlights are frequently open, the salt air is likely to attack the fabric anyway. Large fixed windows are another matter. The ability to control light and protect interior furnishing from ultraviolet attack, as well as adding another design element, are good reasons to consider curtains, blinds, or shades.

Cotton, polyester, and acrylic fabrics are good choices for curtains. On most boats, especially sailboats, they will be fastened to tracks top and bottom to prevent swinging when the boat is heeled and to make a neat appearance. Tiebacks perhaps work best on large motoryachts.

Several fire-resistant fabrics such as Glen Raven Mills' Firesist and Millerton Industries' Visa are ideally suited to windows located near and above stovetops.

Pull-down shades, perhaps in conjunction with curtains, have gained tremendous popularity in recent years. Hunter Douglas's Duette shades are made with a honeycomb construction to improve insulating qualities, and were developed originally for the solar housing market. Horizontal pleated shades such as those manufactured by Verasol have a clean, near-translucent look that is well suited to large motoryacht windows. They represent yet another variation of this state-of-the-art window treatment, and are available in a wide variety of colors and fabrics. A unique quality of these materials is the ability to trim them to the odd shapes often found in yacht windows. Other manufacturers offer shades made of tinted Lexan and Mylar to cut glare and ultraviolet rays.

Last, miniblinds such as those made by Levolor have found their way from land-based residences to the dock and are now frequently seen on motoryachts and larger sailboats.

When studying your options in window treatments, pay particular attention to the hardware used to hold them in place. Some have an annoying tendency to rattle, and others are difficult to slide. However, there has been a lot of improvement in recent years, so if you look long enough you should be able to find a system that pleases you as well as the idiosyncrasies of your boat.

Overhead hatches, especially those above berths, admit enough light to be bothersome at times (such as during the morning hangover). Sliding shade panels, with their tracks hidden between the deck and liner, are a much-appreciated luxury.

3

1 Piping adds interest to the navigator's seat in the Nautor-built *Calypte*.

2 Sculpted settee cushions support the back and legs and add visual interest.

3 French lace, imported by Rue de France of Newport, Rhode Island, is a lovely alternative to the traditional captain's lace hung in the wheelhouse windows of Victorian ships and yachts.

CARPETS

For years, wood has been the traditional cabin sole material, and it still is the recommended finish for wooden yachts and others with wooden structural support members. Breathing is critical to avoid dry rot. Small throw rugs often are just the right accent, providing an interesting detail without hiding the beauty of the wood around it. Care should be taken to prevent such rugs from slipping on varnished soles; using a nonskid rubber pad or perhaps Velcro tabs works well.

In many power and motoryachts, however, fully carpeted interiors are standard. As with cushion fabric, specially treated carpet fibers have been developed for the marine industry. Today most are nylon, olefin, acrylic, and wool, the latter being used only rarely. The other three can all be solution-dyed, a process in which color pigments and ultraviolet inhibitors are added to a molten polymer solution before the fibers are extruded. In construction each may be tufted, woven, knitted, or needle-punched. Many companies offer specialized lines for decks and interiors. Marine carpeting should always have a synthetic backing material.

In selecting a carpet, consider its chances of getting wet or dirty, how exposed it is to the sun, and the frequency with which it will have to be lifted to gain access to engines, plumbing, or other systems beneath the sole.

HULL LINERS AND OVERHEADS

Just as the cabin soles of wooden boats must be allowed to breathe, so must the hull planks. This means using a spaced ceiling of slats rather than an airtight barrier. Many fiberglass boats have wood ceilings that look quite nice.

However, many powerboat and a number of midpriced-sailboat builders find it easy and attractive to glue vinyl, synthetic suede, or other fabric to the hull. This eliminates the need for a fiberglass inner liner or expensive wood finish. Foam-backed fabric gives a soft, plush feel, and the foam acts as an insulating barrier to reduce noise, retain heat, and keep out cold. The inquisitive buyer might also investigate the fabric suppliers of the van-conversion industry for innovative products.

Similarly, soft overheads represent an alternative way of finishing off the underside of the deck. Synthetic suede, Naugahyde, and vinyl liners, perhaps perforated for ventilation and again mated to a thin layer of foam, can be a swank, sexy treatment of an otherwise unnoticed surface.

CHAPTER NINETEEN
Cabin Soles

*T*he lexicon of yachting never hesitates to advance obscure, archaic words and terms for otherwise simply identified and understood boat parts and boat-handling maneuvers. Just for the record, the floor of a yacht is called the *sole*, the removable sections are *floorboards*, and the supporting structural members between the hull and sole are *floors*. What could be simpler?

The soles in most yachts are not as expansive and visually domineering as in land homes, partly because space is at a premium and partly because wide-open sections aren't terribly safe: In a rolling boat it becomes difficult for a person to negotiate a sole the size of a squash court without being thrown head over heels to the low side. For this reason it is good practice to keep traffic routes fairly narrow so

1

that solid handholds are within easy reach every step of the way forward, aft, or athwartship. This results in narrow sole spaces and diminishes their role in the overall design scheme to an understated one.

In the saloons of million-dollar megayachts, designers sometimes specify wild custom carpet art—for example, a spiral design that looks like the Yellow Brick Road or the interior of a chambered nautilus, drawing the visitor into and through the furniture. More often, however, the sole is carpeted with neutral colors (see Chapter 18, "Soft Coverings"). Functionality is key: The surface must be able to withstand heavy traffic in a confined area and resist the attacks of mildew, rot, and ultraviolet light.

CONSTRUCTION

Because the bilges of boats are seldom 100 percent dry, there is the ever-present danger of rot. If water doesn't find its way into the bilge through the hull, there are always deck leaks, condensation, and weeping hose connections to supply a dribbling source of moisture. Production fiberglass boatbuilders have dealt with the problem by covering wood or foam floor members with fiberglass. Some wooden boats are built with steel floors for added strength as well as to avoid rot (rust then becomes a concern). In a steel or aluminum boat it only makes sense to fabricate floors from the same material; fortunately, metal hulls tend to be dryer than either wood or fiberglass hulls, the latter proving over the years to be faintly water-permeable. Coating exposed wood with epoxy resin is one possible solution, though the best is probably just to avoid wood below the sole altogether.

The floors or sole bearers must be rigidly fixed to the hull and closely spaced to provide a solid base for the sole. Many builders of low- and intermediate-priced boats find it cheaper and less worrisome to mold fiberglass pans, which are then dropped into the hull before the deck goes on. These pans are then "tabbed" to the hull in strategic spots with pieces of resin-saturated fiberglass mat. The pan may then be left bare, carpeted, or covered with a hardwood such as teak. Unfinished fiberglass is slippery,

noisy, and cold, whereas wood, if left unvarnished, gives better traction and is a good insulator against cold and the racket of water slapping the hull outside.

Better-quality fiberglass boats may have fiberglass floors supporting a plywood sole (fiberglassed to the hull all around), over which teak and/or other hard or soft woods have been laid in strips about 1¼ to 2 inches wide and at least ⅝ inch thick. Teak is often alternated with strips of holly to create a lovely color contrast. The holly can be set on edge on the plywood underlay or fitted into rabbeted or dadoed grooves in planks of plywood. They may be slightly rounded and left slightly proud of the teak to provide sure footing if the sole is to be varnished. A poor man's substitute is commercially available plywood with teak and holly veneers already glued down; its biggest drawback is a shorter lifespan. Cork is another traditional sole surface that, while not glamorous, provides sure footing.

FLOORBOARDS

Floorboards should be large enough and properly placed to provide access to every part of the hull. Deep, narrow hulls require fewer floorboard openings than wide, shallow hulls. Of course it is often difficult to accomplish total, unrestricted access, but imagine for a moment grounding on a rock and holing the hull at a place you cannot reach. How does one then stem the proverbial tide?

Flush-mounted lift rings may be set in the floorboards for easy removal; these hardware items are available in several styles and are typically manufactured from stainless steel or chromed bronze.

VENTILATION

Alternatively, finger holes help to ventilate the bilge but at the same time permit dirt and debris to fall through; cleaning the bilge is never an easy or pleasant job. A better idea is to ventilate the bilge in places where the chance of dirt entering the openings is remote. Tube or box openings that are located under berths or cabinets and fitted with screens and that furthermore stand proud of the sole might make

1 *Cannonball*'s teak-and-holly sole is perhaps the most common treatment in contemporary sailboats; the holly may be left slightly proud of the teak to provide traction, which is especially important if the sole is varnished.

2 *Endeavour*'s dining area and main saloon are exceptionally well lit by the large hatch and the numerous opening ports through the deck. The paneling is cherry as are the chairs and cabinets, and the cabin sole is pine. America's Cup memorabilia serve as accents.

2

sense. In any case, the difficulties of ventilating wooden floors and soles make a good case for blowers and ductwork led to the decks even on diesel-powered boats, which don't have the same safety requirements as gasoline-powered boats due to the nonexplosive nature of oil fuels. Boats equipped with propane appliances have an additional reason to ventilate the bilge, since this gas is heavier than air and will sink to the lowest point on board.

MAINTENANCE

The task of keeping the sole clean merits forethought during the design and planning phase of your project. As mentioned earlier, unvarnished wood provides superior traction but may stain. Varnished wood is slippery but easy to wipe down. If you have carpeting, you should either carry a vacuum cleaner aboard or be able to beat the carpet in the cockpit like a chambermaid.

A trademark of the Henry R. Hinckley Company is a dust bin built into the saloon sole. A removable grate covers a plastic box so that dirt may be conveniently swept into this handy receptacle, then removed and emptied.

Inevitably, some dirt will lodge in the gap between the floorboards and the surrounding sole, and in turn can be expected to find its way into the bilge. Beach sand and hair are the nemeses of the cleaning crew. Perhaps if everyone is asked to take off shoes and step through a rinsing tub before going below. . . .

LEVELS AND LIGHTS

A multilevel cabin sole creates more interest in the layout below, but because walking the length of a boat underway can be tricky, small steps in sole levels are frowned upon. Some designs call for elevated wheelhouses and saloons to permit seating with a window view, and these by necessity call for cabin soles at a different level. One step, several steps, or even a ladder might be required. For safety's sake, the steps should be easy to see and negotiate.

Here and elsewhere around the cabin sole, discreet footlights are a blessing at night. A trendy alternative is micro-illumes, which are thin plastic strips with tiny lights embedded inside. These can be used high (overheads, curtain tracks) or low (bases of furniture). Both footlights and micro-illumes add an elegant, romantic touch, providing as they do a soft, indirect light that does not totally destroy night vision or upset the moods of the captain and crew.

1 The etched granite floors of *P'zazz*'s entry provide nonskid traction as well as elegance.

2 *Moondrift*'s oak cabin sole is light-colored, which helps prevent low areas from disappearing in darkness, especially in a traditional boat with small portlights.

3 The carpet in the 62-foot Pacemaker *Deluxe* is custom carved to display the motif (and corporate trademark) of the owner. The red-and-white inlays are cut from smaller pieces of the same material, and the carpet and backing are synthetic to prevent the mildew and odors often caused by the marine environment.

1

2

3

CHAPTER TWENTY

Going Aloft

I t is strange that on a sea so flat and essentially featureless, a man on a boat still desires to climb to the highest point just to see more of it. He has his reasons: weed lines, rips, and the telltale signs of fish; the gray outline of land where he has supposed it to be; the safe passage through treacherous reefs; or the body and character of a ship which from the deck appears merely as a smudge of smoke. Sometimes his reasons are no more complicated than those of the bear who went over the mountain—he just wants to see what he can see.

Readers of C.S. Forester's Horatio Hornblower adventures, Herman Melville's *Billy Budd,* or the lore of naval history are well acquainted with the crow's nest, that basketlike perch high on a mast where lookouts were stationed to watch for whales, pirates, and landfalls. While some objects of interest to yachtsmen have changed, many remain the same.

The crow's nest, or some metal cage that passes for one, still exists on some boats—the mast of an oceangoing trawler perhaps, or a bluewater schooner. More often, however, sailors today install ratlines in the shrouds and steps on the mast to gain an advantage in sight as well as to perform work on the rig. Powerboaters erect flybridges to sun themselves and to see the bow and quarters better when maneuvering in close; sportfishermen add several more steering stations in the form of tuna towers, where one feels as though one is riding on top of a crane doing 30 miles per hour on a bumpy road!

In the days of the tall ships, "learning the ropes" meant learning the names of hundreds of different lines as well as how to handle, belay, splice, seize, and serve them, and how to swarm up the rigging to set or hand acres of canvas. On sail training ships such as *Gloria,* cadets learn the same skills today.

RATLINES

This traditional means of scaling an old sailing ship's rigging uses short pieces of rope tied or seized to a pair of shrouds to form a ladder. Ratlines (pronounced "ratlins") are useful for lookouts, but as they are fitted to the lower shrouds of most boats they do not enable one to climb more than about two-thirds of the way up a mast; and because the journey begins at the rail, they aren't very helpful in working on the mast itself.

Beyond this limited utility, ratlines today are almost more an attempt to recapture a traditional appearance in the rig, encouraging one to imagine himself as a pirate in Blackbeard's bloodthirsty crew, saber in mouth, ready to swing from a halyard onto the deck of some plump treasure ship.

MAST STEPS

A wide variety of mast steps have been developed in recent decades, allowing a crewmember to climb quickly from deck to masthead. Some are fixed V-shapes of flat aluminum bar screwed or riveted to the mast; others are made of aluminum or stainless steel and fold flush against the mast when not in use, so as not to snag lines. (The climber must open and close the steps as he ascends and descends.) Mast steps obviate the need for a bosun's chair hoisted by a halyard, though for working on the rig the bosun's chair is superior, since it leaves both hands free and provides insurance against falling. Nevertheless, when an emergency occurs in the rigging, mast steps are the fastest, surest means to the top.

1

1 Ratlines are still used on traditionally rigged vessels, more for keeping lookout and keeping "the look" than for tending sails.

2 Mast steps are a quick way to the masthead if a new halyard must be reeved through the sheaves. While a bosun's chair is still standard equipment on most cruising sailboats, mast steps don't require crew below to man the winch.

3 Seemingly unaware of his precarious perch, a young deckhand works in the rigging of a sail training ship participating in the 1980 Tall Ships parade in Boston, Massachusetts.

296

2

3

LOOKOUT PLATFORMS

On large sailing vessels or trawlers with masts for steadying sails, it may be possible to build a crow's nest of sorts: a small, flat platform for the feet and a circular rail to retain the person above the waist. To justify the weight and trouble, one must anticipate spending a fair amount of time as a lookout in the rigging. In the reef-girdled islands of the South Pacific, such a perch is of great value, as the lookout can shout piloting directions down to the helm. And there is something to be said for just having a place to get away from the rest of the crew, a place where one can meditate upon the vastness of the sea and sky and the purpose of his own small journey through the cosmos. Answers are seldom found, but that matters little; simply asking the question elevates us to a higher spiritual plane, and that is an end in itself.

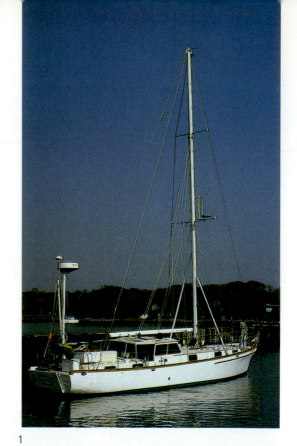

1

2

1 The lookout platform on this ketch berthed in Texas is an excellent vantage point from which to spot reefs while cruising South Pacific islands.

2 With the threat of squalls approaching, *Coffee Break,* a Bertram sportfisherman, sets out from Spanishtown Harbor of Virgin Gorda. The harbor channel is narrow and winds its way around a reef just yards from the entrance. If the skipper weren't familiar with the course, steering from the tuna tower would be a distinct advantage.

3 The swordfish tower on this sportfishing boat mounts a steering wheel, lights, and antennas.

4 Climbing the ladder to the top of the Ocean 63's tuna tower can be a daunting experience in heavy seas. But oh, the view!

FLYBRIDGES

A permanent steering station mounted on top of the cabin is a design arrangement born of function first, comfort second. Access is usually gained by means of a ladder from the cockpit or boat deck. From the flybridge the helmsman can better see all points of the boat when docking or maneuvering close to other boats, and can gauge distances more accurately because of the larger angle his line of sight makes with the water surface. Full engine controls as well as radio communication, radar, and instrument repeaters make the flybridge the preferred helm position in all but the worst weather, when driving rain and cold become too much for the protection offered by the windscreen, canvas bimini, and side curtains, and wild motion makes the position untenable.

Crew seats, lounges, and possibly even tables behind the helm offer airy locations for suntanning, entertaining, or just hanging out. Extended passages leave the crew staring vacantly for long periods into space, shedding their brains of worry about insignificant things such as jobs, futures, and relationships. Cruisers know that one reason they go to sea is to stare at it and wonder; they also know they can't stare at space from just anywhere on board. There must be an unobstructed communion with the elements that isn't possible below. And the flybridge serves this need admirably.

TOWERS

In south Florida, where sportfishing is king, so-called tuna towers are highly functional works of art, the styling of which is critical to the macho cool of the owner. The tower is to the offshore sportfisherman what fog lights and leather grill covers are to the sportscar-rally driver. The supporting structure must be polished stainless steel, with the aft tubes perpendicular (or nearly so) to the waterline and the forward tubes raked devilishly. Some towers have several levels, each with its own wheel and controls, the entire structure tapering at the top to a small platform with nothing more than a leaning post and a T-top. Armed with outriggers like a knight's lances, the sportfisherman guns his turbocharged diesels and barrels through 5-foot waves as easily as monster trucks crunching derelict cars. The higher he is above the deck and the crews of other boats, which skitter below like waterbugs, the more serious he is about fishing, and the cooler his unflappable air.

3

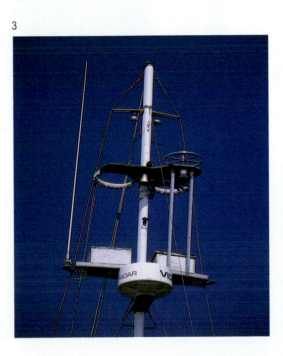

4

1 On *Hawkeye III*, stainless steel rails and triangular teak steps spiral upward through a heart-shaped opening in the deck above.

2 The stairs on *Numero Uno* are mounted on a single stainless steel column.

3 Wild design takes a backseat to utility on most sport-fishermen. This straightforward ladder provides security, and that is all that's asked of it.

4 Stairs between deck levels seem to offer designers and builders an opportunity for nearly limitless innovation. The teak steps from the swim platform to the afterdeck on *P'zazz* follow a curve to keep them inboard.

3

4

BIBLIOGRAPHY

This is a book of possibilities; a book of visions. The mechanics of translating these daydreams into the nuts-and-bolts reality of wood and canvas, fiberglass and bronze, Lexan and aluminum would require far more space than we have available. Fortunately, hand-holding literature abounds; though some of the following titles may be out-of-print and more difficult to find, we feel they are especially well done:

Best Boats to Build or Buy

Ferenc Maté

Vancouver: Albatross Publishing House, 1982. Over 30 of the best boats available in North America viewed through the discerning eye of a well-known boating author/photographer. Covers everything from rowboats through lightweight racers to trawler yachts.

The Best of the Best
The Yacht Designs of
Sparkman & Stephens

Francis S. Kinney & Russel Bourne

New York: W. W. Norton & Company, 1996. A stunning collection of 100 yacht designs from the legendary firm, including such all-time favorites as *Ranger*, *Dorade*, *Stormy Weather*, *Brilliant*, and *Bolero*. Descriptions include major specifications, a design commentary providing analysis and history, at least one photograph, and study plans.

Canvaswork & Sail Repair

Don Casey

Camden, Maine: International Marine, 1996. Find out step by step and picture by picture how to measure for, construct, modify, maintain, renew, and repair fabric aboard. The detailed text and illustrations render the techniques virtually foolproof.

Boatbuilder's International
Directory

Edited by Don Purdy

Benicia, California: International Association of Amateur Boat Builders, updated periodically. A source list of hundreds of boat plans and kits, from canoes to cruisers, both sail and power. Includes materials, hardware, tools, rigging, engines, magazines, books, and schools.

Boat Joinery &
Cabinetmaking Simplified

Fred P. Bingham

Camden, Maine: International Marine, 1993. A basic skills and projects book that can turn any left-thumbed dubber into a journeyman joiner. Learn how to choose and use tools, laminate beams, build lockers, berths, galleys, bulkheads, decks, rails, hatches, spars, and more.

Brightwork:
The Art of Finishing Wood

Rebecca Wittman

Camden, Maine: International Marine, 1990. The complete guide to keeping your brightwork in Bristol fashion. If you feel a yacht unembellished with beautifully joined, beautifully grained wood is no yacht at all; if you feel varnishing is a duty and a privilege, not a chore, then this book is for you.

Cruising in Comfort

Jim Skoog

Camden, Maine: International Marine, 1986. For those wishing to shed yachting's hair-shirt image, this book explains in detail how you can make your boat as comfortable as possible on the high seas or in a remote anchorage.

The Cruising Multihull

Chris White

Camden, Maine: International Marine, 1990, 1997. This is the complete guide to these spacious, stable, exciting boats—from one of America's most respected and innovative multihull designers.

The Finely Fitted Yacht, Volumes I, II, and III

Ferenc Maté

Vancouver: Albatross Publishing House, 1979. Well-illustrated series of project guides for fitting out, finishing, or remodeling cruising boats. Projects range from engine installations through book shelves to sewing wind scoops.

The Marlinspike Sailor

Hervey Garrett Smith

Camden, Maine: International Marine, 1993. Superb drawings cover knotting and splicing, whipping, serving, Turk's heads, end knots, matting, sennits, making a sea chest, stropped blocks, and all kinds of fancy ropework. Make your boat into a yacht with $10 worth of twine (and a lot of spare time).

Principles of Yacht Design

Lars Larsson & Rolf Eliasson

Camden, Maine: International Marine, 1994. Here is the volume critics praise as the replacement for the classic but obsolete *Skene's Elements of Yacht Design*. This comprehensive manual covers all the aspects of sailing yacht design, including structures, materials, and layout. It is truly the new bible of sailboat design.

Sailboat Refinishing

Don Casey

Camden, Maine: International Marine, 1996. Of all the improvements to a tired-looking boat, none will have a more dramatic impact than refinishing. Few boat tasks are easier—made even more so here by the step-by-step directions accompanied by detailed illustrations. Here's everything a motivated amateur needs to get professional results.

The Sailor's Sketchbook

Bruce Bingham

Camden, Maine: International Marine, 1983. Eighty-three projects for your boat, including navigation centers, cockpit tables, wood-shelled blocks, galley enhancements, portable showers, lamps, gimbaled tables, bunk boards, wooden hull ceilings, book racks, riding sails, boat lettering, bug screens, and more.

Sensible Cruising: The Thoreau Approach

Don Casey and Lew Hackler

Camden, Maine: International Marine, 1986. Practical cruising advice mixed with the prudent wisdom of Henry David Thoreau. The result: how to cruise more simply, cheaply, and with more satisfaction. Nuts-and-bolts advice on everything from sails, weather, power, sanitation, piloting, electronics, and cruising companions.

The Shipcarver's Handbook

Jay Hanna

Brooklin, Maine: WoodenBoat Publications, 1988. A complete guide to marine carving, from a simple star to an elegant eagle, from a single letter to a bannered nameboard, from a simple billethead to a complete figurehead.

Spurr's Boatbook: Upgrading the Cruising Sailboat

Daniel Spurr

Camden, Maine: International Marine, 1983, 1991. A stem-to-stern, project-by-project approach to beefing up any sailboat for offshore cruising, including strengthening major structural components, understanding seagoing interior design and construction, replacing an engine, and making a deck layout and rig more efficient.

Thirty Classic Boat Designs: The Best of the Good Boats

Roger C. Taylor

Camden, Maine: International Marine, 1991. Here are Roger Taylor's easygoing but insightful commentaries on what he and many readers of his *Good Boats* series consider the world's best boat designs. Accompanied by plans and photographs, descriptions include reports from owners and builders.

Voyaging Under Power, Third Edition

Robert P. Beebe, Revised by James F. Leishman

Camden, Maine: International Marine, 1994. Thoroughly updated to cover the advances of the past 20 years, this is the classic information source for those who wish to cross oceans with speed and comfort under power.

Yacht Design Details

Roger Marshall

New York: Hearst Marine Books, 1989. More than 50 projects to improve your boat, ranging from hatch covers and drop boards to drop-leaf tables and dinghies.

INDEX

P H O T O   C R E D I T S

Photos are listed first by page; the number following the decimal corresponds with the number of the photograph on each page:

Billy Black:
38.2, 39.3, 44, 60.2, 62.3, 86.1, 92.1, 94.1, 112.3, 128, 140.2, 154 lower left, 165, 173.4, 194.2, 197.3, 200.1, 206, 226.1, 233.3, 242, 245, 252, 267.3, 269.3, 275, 281.3.

James Boyd:
13 bottom.

Denise Briere:
234, 248.3, 260.2.

Robert Brown:
88.3, 268.2.

Sandy Brown:
Frontispiece, 4, 13 top, 14, 17.1, 24, 29.3, 33.2, 33.3, 35.2, 35.3, 36.1, 37.4, 38.1, 53.3, 53.5, 53.6, 58.1, 58.4, 58.5, 60.1, 66.1, 66.3, 69, 70.1, 70.2, 70.3, 73.3, 73.4, 78.3, 79.5, 79.6, 83.1, 85, 88.2, 89.6, 90.2, 90.3, 91.4, 91.5, 92.2, 92.3, 98.1, 98.2, 98.3, 99, 100, 101, 104.1, 106.1, 107.4, 109.2, 111.1, 111.2, 112.1, 112.2, 116.1, 118.1, 120.2, 125.3, 127, 130, 132, 133, 134.2, 134.3, 135, 142.1, 143.4, 146.1, 147.3, 149.1, 151.2, 152.2, 154 top, 155 top, 156.1, 156.3, 157.5, 161.2, 161.3, 162.1, 167, 169, 175, 176.2, 177, 178, 179.2, 180–182, 184, 186, 188.1, 189, 191, 192, 193, 196.2, 197.4, 202, 203.2, 203.3, 212, 217.5, 220.3, 222, 223.2, 227.4, 225.1, 225.5, 229.2, 229.3, 230.2, 236 bottom, 237 bottom, 239, 240, 241, 248.2, 249.5, 253.4, 255.3, 262, 266.1, 271.3, 280, 285.3, 285.4, 286, 287, 291, 293.3, 295, 296, 297, 298.2, 299.3.

Joe Devenney:
89.5, 114.2, 190.1, 208.1, 224.3, 235, 257.

Larry Dunmire:
204–205

Erich Eichhorn:
141.3, 141.4, 203.4, 278.1.

Charley Freiberg:
29.2, 78.4, 83.2, 86.2, 95.2, 95.3, 98.5, 107.2, 108, 126, 129, 134.1, 150.1, 157.4, 161.4, 163.4, 166, 177.3, 215.2, 217.6, 228, 247.3, 249.4, 266.2, 270.1, 277.

Rick Friese:
55 sidebar, 64.2, 71, 122, 137, 155 lower right, 170.

Danny Greene:
237 top.

Robert Hagan:
2, 3.1, 47, 78.2, 116.3, 121, 124, 142.2, 149.2, 154 lower right, 159, 172.1, 176.1, 179.1, 187.3, 207.2, 214, 215.4, 218.1, 221.6, 238, 263, 269.4.

Rick Klepfer:
54.1, 57.2, 58.2, 120.1, 209.

Little Harbor Yachts:
147.4.

Shaw McCutcheon:
66.2.

Charles Neville:
7.2.

Pacific Seacraft:
231.

Larry Pardey:
248.1.

Pearson Yachts:
80.1, 141.5, 233.2

Neil Rabinowitz:
1, 3.2, 3.3, 6, 8.2, 10, 31, 32, 33.1, 36.3, 37.5, 39.5, 40, 45.2, 46, 49, 51, 52.2, 54.2, 54.3, 55.4, 58.3, 59, 60.3, 60.5, 63, 65, 67.5, 67.6, 73.1, 78.1, 80.2, 87, 88.2, 90.2, 90.3, 93, 95.4, 95.5, 96, 98.4, 104.1, 106.1, 107.3, 109.2, 109.3, 115.3, 115.4, 115.5, 116.2, 117, 118.2, 119.3, 119.4, 123, 131, 150.3, 151.4, 152, 155 lower left, 163.3, 164, 168, 174, 188.2, 189, 190.2, 194.1, 195, 199.3, 201, 207.3, 207.4, 208.2, 211, 215.3, 216, 217.4, 218.3, 220.1, 221.5, 225.4, 227.3, 244, 246, 253.2, 254.1, 256.1, 259.2, 264, 265.4, 268.1, 270.2, 271.4, 272, 278.2, 279, 281.2, 282, 283.2, 283.3, 284, 292, 300, 301.4.

Daniel Spurr:
18, 29.1, 34, 53.4, 58.6, 60.4, 62.2, 62.4, 66.4, 73.2, 90.1, 91.6, 143.3, 146.2, 156.2, 160, 162.2, 173.3, 196.1, 198, 217.3, 221.4, 224.2, 226.2, 230.1, 230.3, 253.3, 259.3, 265.3, 274, 293.2, 298.1, 299.4, 301.3.

Onne Van Der Wal:
7.1, 8.1, 21, 35.4, 36.2, 39.4, 64.3, 68, 114.1, 139, 199.2, 218.2, 220.2, 223.3, 233.2, 247.4, 258, 260.1, 289.

Susan Thorpe Waterman:
17.2, 17.3, 22, 26, 52.3, 57.1, 62.1, 64.1, 105, 125.2, 172.2, 187.2, 236 top, 247.2, 251, 254.2, 255.4, 256.2, 265.2, 267.4.